A Monument to
Her Grief

The Sturtevant Murders of
Halifax, Massachusetts

John F. Gallagher

A Monument to Her Grief – The Sturtevant Murders of Halifax, Massachusetts is a historical work; all materials referenced may be found in the Bibliography and Notes sections at the end of this book. The author has taken some creative license based on the events in regard to dialogue.

Published in the United States by Riverhaven Books
www.Riverhavenbooks.com

ISBN: 978-1-937588-63-2

Printed in the United States of America
by Country Press, Lakeville, Massachusetts

Acknowledgements

This book would not have been possible without the invaluable assistance of many. I especially thank Susan Basile, Halifax Historical Commission, for sharing her vast knowledge of Halifax's history and for taking me on a tour of the highways and byways of the town. Susan spent many hours tracing records and digging up old photographs of the Sturtevant place, the Sturtevant family history, and newspaper accounts of the crime.

My thanks to Allan Clemons, Hanson Historical Society, who shared his extensive knowledge of Hanson's town history, as well as his great-grandfather's personal account of the Sturtevant murder; he also drew up a map of the murderer's trail and allowed me to use his personal "carte de visite" of William E. Sturtevant. Both Susan and Allan graciously reviewed my manuscript for historical accuracy.

Donna Brown, past president of the Hanson Historical Society and author of *Images of America: Hanson, Massachusetts*, first told me about the Sturtevant murders and provided pertinent archival newspaper articles and photographs; Donna also reviewed my manuscript and I am indebted to her. I thank John and Patty Norton, co-presidents of the Hanson Historical Society for permitting me to use photographs from their archives. I also extend my gratitude to William C. Morton for sharing the photograph of his great-great-grandfather, Stephen Lull, and for providing details of Lull's Civil War record.

I am grateful to Deputy Sheriff Liisa Budge-Johnson of the Plymouth County Sheriff's Department, for copies of century-old records in the department's archives; and to my friend, Mike Callahan, Supervisory Special Agent/Chief Division Counsel FBI (Ret.), for his perspective of legal aspects in the case.

In 1991, the late John Heller, an art professor at Bridgewater State College (now University), painstakingly restored the nearly 300-year-old house on Thompson Street where the murders occurred. Arnold and

Carol Klukas, the current owners, allowed me to see the interior of the house and to inspect the surrounding grounds. They also shared an 1874 crime scene photograph of the rear of the house. I thank them for their kindness.

Bob Neville of Abington, a friend and colleague from the Boston Police Department and a talented artist, generously provided his services as an illustrator for the book and I owe him a debt of gratitude.

Thanks to Annie Hartnett of Newton, Massachusetts, author of *Rabbit Cake*, for reviewing my manuscript and offering her perspective as a writer and developmental editor. To my brother, Jim Gallagher, who spent many hours reviewing and tweaking the text, I am very grateful.

Special thanks to Stephanie Blackman, Riverhaven Books, for her willingness to publish this, my third book, and for her continued guidance and support.

Lastly, but most importantly, I thank my wife, Jeanne, for her patience and encouragement.

Table of Contents

Illustrations

Foreword

Nearly 150 years ago, the Massachusetts state constabulary launched an investigation into the brutal murders of three elderly people at their farmhouse on Thompson Street in the rural town of Halifax. The story of the murders and their aftermath has been passed down through the generations and has become part of local lore. Many short summaries and news stories about the crime were written in later years but, until now, no comprehensive, definitive account has been published.

To fully disclose what happened, and why, required extensive research into the holdings of the Halifax Historical Society and Museum, contemporaneous news accounts, court and prison records, town histories, census returns, vital records, archival manuscripts, case law, and other documentary evidence. A genealogical study of the principal characters in the story helped in sorting out the intertwined relationships common to small communities of the era, giving shape to the characters' lives leading up to the murders, and lending context to the hard facts of the case.

The finest resource for knowing the people in this story cannot be recovered through research; that is, the conversation and dialogue that passed between them as the drama unfolded. Without it, much of the humanity of the story is lost. So, in an effort to honor that humanity and to bring the people involved to life, I've embraced a growing literary genre called *narrative nonfiction*, also known as *creative nonfiction*, and have taken the liberty of recreating some dialogue, based always on supporting facts, sometimes obvious within its context and, in the investigative aspects of the story, founded on my personal experience as a criminal investigator conducting countless interviews and interrogations.

Melanie McGrath, the author of *Silvertown*, a memoir of her grandmother's life, explained her reasons for using narrative nonfiction: the known facts of her story were "the canvas on to which I have embroidered," McGrath says. "Some of the facts have slipped through the holes – we no longer know them nor have any means of verifying them – and in these cases I have re-imagined scenes or reconstructed events in a way I believe reflects the essence of the scene or the event in the minds and hearts of the people who lived through it. To my mind, this literary tinkering does not alter the more profound truth of the story."

Noted author Erik Larson explained his approach to portraying his characters' thoughts in an interview published in the magazine *Creative Nonfiction*. "I will only propose what somebody is thinking or not thinking if I have something concrete in hand that makes that clear. But you absolutely cannot make that stuff up out of whole cloth because then you pass into another realm entirely." That realm is fiction, magazine editor Lee Gutkind observed.

Plymouth's *Old Colony Memorial* newspaper published, verbatim, the responses given by witnesses during trial. This transcript, the only known record of testimony at trial, has been incorporated into the text of the book. However, the newspaper chose not to publish the questions posed by the prosecution and defense teams and, therefore, these questions have been deduced based on the answers given. The opening statements and closing arguments of the prosecution and defense, as well as the judge's charge to the jury, have also been taken, in part, from the *Old Colony*'s coverage of the trial. Additional testimony was found in inquest records and in Massachusetts case law and has been presented as published.

Some may be satisfied to validate the oral accounts or to fill some holes in the story as they've heard it. Others will look for more; in historical accounts, the facts, so critical to the telling, are only the backbone of the story. The greater story is the people, the living, breathing human beings, like ourselves – we want to know them. I hope that taking this license enhances the telling while honoring the real people who survived this worst of human nightmares.

Chapter One: A Gruesome Discovery

Stephen Lull rose, half-awake, and sat on the edge of his bed. He picked up his spectacles from the night table, unfolded the wire bows, and curled them over his ears. Mary stirred beside him in bed when he rose to light a small lantern and carry it to the dry sink; dawn came late on this mid-winter morning of February 16, 1874.

He lifted the ewer from the washstand and poured some icy water into the basin. Removing his glasses and nightshirt, he bent low, cupped his hands, and braced himself before dousing his face. Now fully awake, he reached for a hand towel and patted himself dry, the water trickling through his whiskers. He reached hurriedly for his old flannel shirt, put his glasses back on, and did his best to neaten his hair with his rough fingers as he peered into the looking glass hanging on the wall.

"Where are you going?" Mary asked him from beneath a warm cocoon of bed covers.

"Dan Blake promised to sharpen my tools this morning if I came early," he replied as he dressed.

They'd been married some sixteen years now and conversations, like their day-to-day lives, required little embellishment. He pulled his trousers on over his long johns, tied his boots, and stepped to the chamber's fireplace to toss some cordwood onto the glowing embers.

Lull, a forty-one-year-old shoemaker, was born in the nearby town of Kingston. Seven of his eight siblings had either died or moved away before his father's death in 1850. Stephen's mother, Lucy, and his sister, Mary, were forced to seek assistance at the Kingston and Carver almshouses. Stephen boarded with Lemuel Bryant and his family in neighboring Plympton and honed his shoemaking skills under Bryant's tutelage. He supported his mother with his meager earnings until her death in 1857, one day after he married Mary.

They had moved into Mary's parents' house in Halifax, Massachusetts, after the wedding. Tragedy marked their marriage early on; their two-month-old son, Charles, was carried off by dysentery in 1859. They found a measure of consolation the following year when Mary gave birth to a daughter they named Lucy, in memory of Stephen's mother. The couple welcomed a second son in November 1869, but sadness filled their hearts once more when scarlet fever took him twenty-four days later.

Stephen, Mary, and Lucy continued to live in the Morton's two-story colonial on Plymouth Street after Mary's parents passed away. Despite the difficulties of their early years together, they were active in civic, social, and church affairs, and, like many others of the time who shared their challenging circumstances, the couple found happiness and fulfillment among their friends and family in Halifax.

First settled in 1669 as part of Plymouth Colony, the town was set off from parts of Middleboro, Pembroke, Bridgewater, and Plympton in 1734. Native Americans called Halifax and all the lands around it "Monponsett," meaning "at or near the deep pond." The geographic center of Plymouth County, it lies twenty-eight miles southeast of Boston and twelve miles northwest of Plymouth, and it contains more than eleven thousand acres of prime farmland, woodlands, and cedar swamp. By 1874, farming, lumbering, and shoemaking had become the chief sources of income for the town's 145 families. There were three churches, Congregational, Baptist, and Universalist, and five district schools. Nearly all of the 570 residents in this peaceful enclave either knew or were related to each other.

Lull left the bedroom with his lantern and descended the narrow stairway to warm the house. He lit a lamp and several candles in the keeping room and replenished the hearth's dying fire, then went into the kitchen, removed the lids on the kitchen stove, opened the firebox, and cleared the previous day's ashes before adjusting the damper. He placed several pieces of kindling across the grate and added a small amount of coal, then crumpled up some newspaper, laid it under the kindling, and lit it. When the coal began to glow, he added more, shut the firebox, and replaced the lids.

It had been an unusually mild winter. Snow had fallen the first week of February, but unseasonal temperatures and heavy rain over two days had melted the last traces, leaving the ground bare. He saw thickening clouds and felt a drastic change in temperature before he retired the evening before, so he was not surprised when he glanced out the kitchen window and saw that a light snow had accumulated overnight.

Mary and Lucy soon came down to the kitchen and greeted him with cheery dispositions.

Stephen Palmer Lull

"Awful cold this mornin'," he said, stating the obvious.

He finished his breakfast just before eight, rose from the table, and donned his hat and heavy overcoat. He bade his family good-bye as he gathered the leather pouch of dull awls, scrapers, and knives he had set aside the night before and departed.

He started out on foot for the one mile walk to Blake's, taking a shortcut through a wooded lot along a path to Tomson Cemetery. He heard the song of black-capped chickadees – *see-bee, see-bee* – as they flitted from tree to tree. Juncos flushed up from the forest floor here and there, the flash of white in their tails visible even in the dim light of the woods.

He descended onto Thompson Street from the crest of the burial ground, tramped southwest, and passed the humble Cape-style dwellings of Zebadiah Thompson on his right and John Holmes on his left. Tendrils of smoke curled from their chimneys in the crisp morning air. Next to Zebadiah's place was the Colonial-style residence of the Sturtevant brothers where, at the southwest corner, Lull turned right onto a well-worn path between the house and its adjacent woodshed. He walked within a few feet of the house, past the well-sweep and outbuildings, and into the woods toward Dan Blake's farm on Pine

3

Street.

About two hundred yards from the Sturtevant house, and maybe fifteen feet off the path, he noticed something out of place. Moving closer he realized it was a woman's body. Dusted with last night's snow, she was laying on her left side, stiff and motionless, her face embedded in the moist earth. She wore a heavy cloak fastened at the neck and a red and white head covering he had heard his wife refer to as a "cloud." Beneath the cloak she wore a plain gown gathered and pinned in several places at the hem, and rubber overshoes.

Lull was no stranger to violence, but he was repulsed by the severity of the wound on the right side of her head. He and Dan Blake had served with the 39th Massachusetts Infantry during the Civil War and he'd been detached for a time to the ambulance corps where he'd seen more mutilation than any person should. They'd both seen heavy action at the Wilderness, Spotsylvania Court House, Cold Harbor, and Petersburg. Except for several bouts of illness, he had survived the war physically unscathed.

Still, he was unnerved, never expecting to see anything like this so close to home. He dropped his leather pouch, knelt next to the body, and gently shifted the cloud to see if it was someone he knew, but caked dirt and blood obscured her features beyond recognition.

Sturtevant house, 1874

Lull stood and instinctively scanned the area for anything that

4

might explain this atrocity. The thin layer of snow gave the ground a smooth, consistent appearance. No disturbance was apparent on the trail or in the low pucker brush that surrounded it, save for where the body fell. He thought he might see tracks to indicate from which direction the woman had come, but none were obvious.

His eyes fell on a birch stake partially covered with snow lying about five feet from the body. Roughly four feet in length and two inches in diameter, it was tapered on one end and smeared with blood on the other. It was clearly a manufactured item, not windfall from the trees above, and looked similar to stakes he'd seen on local farm carts. He presumed it was the murder weapon.

The solitude was suddenly excruciating; Lull turned back on the path past the Sturtevant house and crossed the road to John Holmes's place. John's wife, Lucy, and her fourteen-year-old daughter, Edith, answered his urgent knocks.

"Is John here?" Lull asked, obviously agitated.

"He's not, Stephen," Lucy said. "He's gone to Plymouth on business. What's wrong?"

"There is a woman lying off the path behind the Sturtevant's house. She's dead. I don't know who she is."

Lucy was stunned.

"Give us a moment," she said and disappeared into the house.

She and Edith emerged moments later drawing their cloaks tightly about their shoulders, and followed Lull across the road to the house. Lull rapped loudly on the front door and received no response. Lucy tapped on the windows and tried to see inside but the drapes were gathered tightly and obstructed her view. She thought it odd that Thomas, at least, was not about at this hour of the day; Simeon's habits were less predictable of late.

They continued along the side of the house to the path. Lucy stopped abruptly when she caught sight of the body.

"Edith, perhaps you should wait here while Mr. Lull and I have a look," Lucy admonished her daughter.

5

Lucy steeled herself as she turned to approach the corpse with Lull. She instantly recognized the woman's clothes as those of Thomas and Simeon Sturtevant's live-in housekeeper.

"It's Mary Buckley," she gasped. "I know her cloak and cloud."

Lull knew that Mary Buckley was related to the Sturtevants in some way and that Dan Blake's wife, Margaret, was their niece. He needed to alert them. He conferred with Lucy and they agreed to send Edith to fetch the couple.

"Edith, I need your help. Will you continue on the path and tell Mr. Blake to come quickly?"

"I will, Mr. Lull," Edith answered with a frightened look in her eyes. Lucy shielded her daughter from Mary's corpse as she passed.

"Edith," Lull shouted after her, "ask Mr. Blake to send someone for Mr. Inglee, too."

"I will," said Edith as she disappeared into the woods.

Rear, Sturtevant house, looking northeast from entrance to path

Edwin Inglee ran a general store not far from Blake's on the road to the neighboring town of Hanson and was the chairman of Halifax's Board of Selectmen.

Within ten minutes, Edith returned with Dan and Margaret. Lull rushed to caution his friends before they encountered the grisly scene. Margaret, wringing her hands, sobbed as Lull explained the circumstances of his discovery.

"Did you send for Inglee?" Lull asked Blake as they approached the corpse.

"Yes, my son is on the way to the store," said Blake. "I expect he'll be here shortly."

Margaret caught sight of Mary's head wound and shrieked, then turned and buried her face in her husband's shoulder. Edith, seeing the traumatic wound for the first time, began weeping and rushed to her mother for consolation. Lucy comforted her in hushed tones.

"I'm sorry, Edith. I didn't want you to see that," Lucy whispered as she held her daughter in a tight embrace. "I want you to go home and wait for me. If your father returns in the meantime, send him to me."

As Edith departed, the four remaining followed her up the path to the Sturtevant house to try once more to raise the brothers. This time they'd try the back door of what the brothers referred to as a porch or el, an enclosed room attached to the rear of the house. They found the porch door unlocked. When they opened it, they started at the sight of Thomas Sturtevant, lifeless and battered, on the floor. He lay on his left side, his face covered in blood. Lull recoiled at the sight of a gaping wound on the back of Thomas's head. He crouched beside the body to check for signs of life but found none, and he noticed that the body was warm despite the chill in the room.

Lull saw an overturned pail containing what looked like a mash of meal and water and a toppled lantern, the candle inside extinguished, on the floor next to Thomas's body. Mary Buckley's parrot bobbed its head, flared its tail, and paced to and fro on its perch in a brass cage on a table near Thomas's head, squawking all the while, "Hello, hello Mary."

After discovering this second grotesque crime, all of them were considerably alarmed, so they retreated from the porch and closed the door. Lull and Blake, meanwhile, walked to the Sturtevant barn hoping they might find Simeon there. They found only hungry cows. They saw that someone had laid out fresh hay in front of the cattle. The animals had consumed what they could reach, but whoever had been feeding them evidently failed to finish the chore because the remaining fodder was largely undisturbed.

Edwin Inglee trundled up in his carriage just as Lull and Blake were leaving the barn. The fifty-five-year-old trader was one of Halifax's most respected citizens. Along with his position as selectman, he was the current town clerk and assessor and had previously served the town as a school committeeman and state representative. His counsel was highly valued and the agonized group of neighbors now looked to him for leadership and guidance.

Inglee met the two men and Lucy Holmes behind the house.

"Good morning," Inglee said. "Bill Crocker will be along soon. I told him to stay behind until he could find someone to cover the store counter. Blake, your son told me a body has been found and to come without delay. What has happened?"

"Something terrible, Edwin," Blake replied. "Mary Buckley and Thomas Sturtevant have been beaten to death."

Daniel Bosworth, passing by the Sturtevant place in his wagon, noticed the unusual activity and drew up to see what it was about. Blake filled the newcomers in on how Lull happened upon Buckley's body and about their subsequent discovery of Thomas's death in the porch. He and Lull led them along the path to the housekeeper's body. Inglee and Bosworth were appalled by the sight of the woman's wound. A chill ran up Inglee's spine.

"Where is Simeon Sturtevant?"

"We don't know," said Lull. "When we found Thomas in the porch, we came right back out. We knocked on the front door but no one answered. He wasn't in the barn either."

Fearing the worst, the group turned back toward the house. Inglee sent Bosworth ahead to notify Ephraim Thompson, a cousin of the Sturtevant brothers, who lived about a mile away.

Lull, Inglee, Blake, and Lucy Holmes entered the house through the porch and carefully stepped around Thomas's body. Margaret Blake, still shaken, remained outside. The parrot called out again – "Hello, Mary" – and Lucy shuddered.

An eerie stillness enveloped them as they crossed the threshold from the porch and into the keeping room. They proceeded with trepidation, unsure if the intruder was still inside. The door to the sitting room straight ahead was open and they could see that the room was in disarray. The wide, pine-planked floor creaked under foot as they continued through the room, past the fireplace, and into the front room on the west side of the house. They were taken aback by the hideous sight of Simeon lying motionless on his back in bed.

Lucy Holmes glimpsed into the room and, with a gasp, turned away in horror. Simeon's face was gruesomely disfigured and blood was spattered on the bed, the walls, and the ceiling. He was quite obviously dead. Nonetheless, Inglee, perhaps in response to his own disbelief, tried and failed to find a pulse. As with Thomas, Simeon's body was still warm though only embers smoldered in the room's small fireplace.

They couldn't help but notice that the door of a small closet opposite the foot of Simeon's bed was open, the interior disturbed, and coins strewn randomly about the floor.

Bosworth returned and a few moments later Ephraim Thompson pulled up in his wagon with his cousin, John T. Z. Thompson. Jabez Thompson, Ephraim's son, followed, and the three men joined the others inside the house.

The first and second floors were searched and no one was found. The rooms upstairs appeared undisturbed, but in the first floor sitting room they saw a piece of paper protruding from the top drawer of a bureau in the corner and a locked trunk, its leather straps unbuckled, moved away from the wall. Nickel pieces, copper coins, and an open, empty wallet were scattered on the floor. It was obvious a robbery had occurred.

"We can determine what's been taken later. For now, let's attend to the victims," Inglee said to the others.

No objection was offered, so all of the men went first to the porch, laid a sheet on the floor next to Thomas, and gently rolled him onto it. They gripped the sheet by its corners and sides and carried the body into the kitchen, where they laid it on the floor in a space Lucy had cleared. They went to the front bedroom and, again using a sheet as a stretcher, placed Simeon's body beside that of his brother.

Light snow had again begun to fall when the men left the house to recover Mary Buckley's body. As they reverently lowered Mary to the kitchen floor, Lull remembered the bloody stake and asked Ephraim Thompson to retrieve it. Thompson left with Bosworth and, before returning with the stake, he placed markers to pinpoint the locations of Buckley's body and the apparent murder weapon.

Lull found a pail and retrieved some water from the well in the backyard and, with a soft cloth, gently washed each victim's face and hands. Inglee led the somber gathering in a brief prayer when Lull finished, and a clean white sheet was placed over each body.

Sturtevant house, 1874 – Investigator at front door

William Crocker pulled up to the house in his carriage and saw a number of people milling about the front yard. Crocker, besides being a clerk in Inglee's store, was the town constable. He stepped down from his carriage and walked into the house where he met Inglee and the others.

He winced when he saw the bodies in the kitchen. Inglee brought him up to date on what had transpired since Lull had found Mary Buckley's body.

"Word has obviously spread," Crocker commented. "People are congregating out front and on the roadway."

"We'd better keep them away from the house," said Inglee.

"I'll move them back. I have some rope in my carriage that I can stretch across the yard."

Crocker coaxed the assembly onto the road and secured the front yard, tying the rope between two trees.

"What's going on, Bill?" a local farmer asked.

"I'm not at liberty to say," Crocker replied as he tightened the last knot. "I'd appreciate it if you'd all stay away from the house until we sort things out."

Inglee placed Crocker in charge of the house when he came back in and asked him to send a rider to alert the other Halifax selectmen, the county coroner, Deputy Sheriff Philip Kingman of Bridgewater, and East Bridgewater undertaker Judah Keene.

"I'm going to the Plymouth courthouse to notify the district attorney and have him telegraph the state constabulary," Inglee said to Crocker. "I'll be back as soon as I can."

***

Asa French, district attorney for Plymouth and Norfolk Counties, telegraphed Chief Constable George Boynton in Boston immediately after meeting with Edwin Inglee in his office at the Plymouth County Courthouse. Boynton contacted Deputy State Constable George Pratt, assigned to Plymouth County, and ordered him to the murder scene to investigate. The chief would dispatch two experienced detectives the same evening to assist Pratt with the probe.

Massachusetts established the state constabulary in 1865 to augment the efforts of local police and in response to the political pressure of temperance advocates and prohibition supporters. A legislative act authorized the governor's appointment of a chief constable and at least twenty deputies for Suffolk County (Boston) and

11

at least one for every other county. The legislation vested in the chief constable and his deputies the same powers exercised by local police and constables. They were charged with the enforcement of all the laws of the Commonwealth, especially the suppression of houses of prostitution, gambling places, and liquor shops. The governor appointed fifty-eight constables, including three specifically assigned to detective duty, who were paid three dollars a day plus expenses.

Legislation enacted in 1871 replaced the chief constable with three police commissioners appointed by the governor and increased the force to seventy men, then one hundred. Three years later the legislature abolished the board of commissioners and reinstated the office of chief constable.

Forty-three-year-old Pratt was a shoemaker by trade and had worked as a clerk at Culver's dry goods store in North Abington before Governor John Andrew appointed him to the newly organized state force in 1866. Unlike most of the men on the force, Pratt was not a veteran of the late war and had relied on political connections to secure his position. He displayed the constabulary's silver, eight-pointed, Maltese cross badge, engraved "Deputy Constable of the Commonwealth," with great pride.

State Constable George Pratt

Pratt hastened by carriage to Halifax from his home in North Abington as soon as he received Boynton's telegraph. It was two o'clock, the intermittent snow had ceased, and the skies had cleared.

He encountered the growing throng of curious onlookers at the edges of the yard and on the roadway in front of the house when he arrived at the Sturtevant house. A dozen carriages were lined up on the shoulder of the muddy road. He ducked beneath the rope that Crocker had tied off and, as he approached the old, weather-beaten house,

Crocker emerged from the front doorway and greeted him.

Crocker briefed Pratt on the facts as he knew them and identified the victims, all residents of the house, as Thomas Sturtevant, seventy-four years of age, his brother, Simeon Sturtevant, age seventy, and Mary Buckley, sixty-eight-years-old, a live-in housekeeper who was a first cousin to the two men. Thomas had been widowed almost ten years since the death of his wife, Mary. Neither Simeon nor Mary Buckley had ever been married.

"Where are the bodies?" Pratt asked.

"They're on the floor in the kitchen."

Crocker escorted Pratt to the back of the house and led him into the porch. The parrot, now calm and quiet, looked on as Pratt surveyed the room, noting the bloodstains on the floor, the upended lantern, and the spilled pail. He also saw several chairs and a hand lamp, unlit, with a little oil in it on a table.

The two policemen proceeded into the main house where eight people, including Edwin Inglee, who had returned from Plymouth after his meeting with the district attorney, were present. Pratt followed Crocker from the keeping room into the kitchen where the bodies lay. When Crocker removed the shrouds to expose the battered features of the dead, Pratt could only stare in stunned silence.

He had seen such cruelty only once before, six years prior, when he investigated the bludgeoning death of Cornelius Holmes in Kingston. For that murder he had arrested Deacon Samuel Andrews, who was convicted and sentenced to twenty years at the state prison in Charlestown. Pratt recalled how sickened he was by the sight of Holmes's fragmented skull and the scattered blood and brain tissue. It was unsettling to see the same ghastly atrocity – this time inflicted upon not one victim, but three – in this humble, old farmhouse in the quiet community of Halifax. He feared he had one or more madmen on his hands.

Pratt was astounded by the alarming frequency of multiple-victim homicides of late. Only last December, George Kimball killed his wife and stepdaughter in Charlestown, Massachusetts. Then, in the presence of an investigating policeman, Kimball slit his own throat with a straight razor. Two other highly-publicized murders had occurred in rural Maine. Boston newspapers had reported the arrest of Louis Wagner for the March 1873 murders of his sister and sister-in-law on Smutty Nose Island and, three months later, of John Gordon for the axe murders of his brother, his brother's wife, and their one-year-old daughter at Thorndike. Pratt would never underestimate, nor understand, the human potential for violence.

Pratt took a moment to look about the house and collect his thoughts. The house he surveyed was ancient, even in 1874. Pratt learned later that Thomas Thompson had built it in 1715 as a wedding gift for his wife. The two-story, post-and-beam structure must have seemed grand by early eighteenth century standards. It featured a center chimney, a side-gabled roof with ends facing east and west, and cedar shingle siding. Pratt also noted the care that had been taken to ensure that the front of the house, with its many large windows, faced south to allow more light and warmth in the winter when the sun is low and less in the heat of summer when the sun is high.

Pratt also learned that Thompson had originally installed casement windows of diamond-shaped glass held in place by diagonal lead muntins and that each of the windows were hinged on the side and swung out like shutters. The casement windows were later replaced with sash windows, double-hung, twelve panes for each sash, or "twelve over twelve," on the first floor, and double-hung, "eight over twelve" windows on the second floor. Pratt noted that wood muntins, rather than lead, secured the window panes.

The front entryway had a paneled door with a hand-made latch and a simple pediment with a five-paned rectangular transom through which daylight could stream to illuminate a foyer and a set of spiral stairs leading to the second floor of the house. Interior doors were of the batten type with wooden buttons as knobs. Off the foyer were entryways leading to Simeon's front bedroom and the front sitting room, each with small fireplaces and wainscoting halfway up the walls. A massive hearth, five-feet-high and topped with a mantel, warmed the back of the house, and included a five-foot-deep brick oven. The kitchen was in a wing on the west side of the house and the enclosed porch, or ell, was on the east side of the house in the rear.

Many within the town knew that Thomas died in 1742 and bequeathed the homestead farm of one hundred-and-seventy acres, including six acres of meadow, two acres of cedar swamp, and all personal property, to his son, Amasa Thompson. Amasa married Lydia Cobb, a Mayflower descendant, in 1744, and they had three daughters to whom he left the estate, in equal shares, upon his death in 1807. Daughter Ruth, who married Simeon Sturtevant, Sr. in 1764, ultimately acquired the shares of her sisters, Lydia Holmes and Molly Tomson, and ownership of the estate remained in the Sturtevant family, unbroken to the day of the murders.

***

Edwin Inglee stepped forward in the kitchen of that house and introduced himself to Pratt. He then introduced the others – Daniel and Margaret Blake, Ephraim, John, and Jabez Thompson, Daniel Bosworth, and Judah Keene. Stephen Lull and Lucy Holmes had been there earlier but had left for home at noon, Inglee told Pratt.

Inglee offered Pratt his account of the discoveries of the victims, the ensuing search of the house, and then produced the cart stake Lull had found near Mary Buckley's body. Pratt listened dutifully to Inglee's telling of the story, but he had learned to take such narratives with a grain of salt; each witness had his own perspective and biases. The stake, on the other hand, was strong physical evidence, so he inspected it carefully, making note of the reddish-brown stains and white powder residue in the splinters at the thicker end of the club.

Inglee guided Pratt back to the porch and described in detail the position in which they had found Thomas's body. Pratt noticed several gouges in the ceiling and an indentation on the door casing leading into the keeping room, noting that he would need to remove a portion of the casing as evidence.

The two men proceeded next to Simeon's room. Pratt saw the blood-soaked blankets on the bed, the blood spatters on the floral wallpaper above the headboard, on the ceiling, and over the fireplace mantel opposite the bed. There were several gouges in the plastered ceiling consistent in size and shape to those he had seen in the porch and on the end of the club. A ladder-back chair with a rush bottom seat stood

Scene of Simeon Sturtevant's murder

next to the bed, spattered with blood. He noted the plundered closet at the foot of the bed and the papers and coins scattered on the floor.

Pratt was curious about the quilts and bedsheets.

"Is this what the bed looked like when you first came in?" Pratt asked Inglee.

"No, the quilts and sheets were covering Simeon from the neck down," Inglee explained. "We turned them aside before we lifted Simeon from the bed and carried him to the kitchen."

"Well, then, it looks like he may have been attacked while he slept...or was surprised and had no time to defend himself," Pratt theorized.

Pratt was struck by what he found in the sitting room. It was clear the murderer or murderers, in haste and excitement, had overlooked a significant amount of legal tender, bills, coins, and Civil War scrip.

"I haven't seen this old scrip in quite a while," Pratt said as he sorted through the bills.

"Nor have I," Inglee replied. "Appears it was issued in '63, but the bills are still crisp. I doubt they were ever in circulation."

Pratt recalled his investigation into the theft of two hundred dollars in stock and twenty dollars in "old-fashioned coppers" from a store in North Abington a few years back. He solved the case when one of the two men responsible for the break-in bought train tickets at the East Abington depot with the unusual coins.

"Well, it's likely that some of it has been taken. If it's circulated now, it should attract some notice," Pratt conjectured.

Pratt wanted to see the place where Lull found Buckley's body. As they exited the house, Ephraim Thompson drew Pratt's attention to several footprints leading from the porch to the path. Pratt crouched for a closer inspection but was unable to discern any distinctive patterns amid the jumble of prints created by those who'd traveled on the route since the time of the murders.

Blake, Inglee, Thompson, and Pratt proceeded along the path to the scene of Mary Buckley's slaying. Pratt noted that the path was particularly hard and compacted from long and frequent use and was devoid of footprints.

Inglee pointed to the spot off the path where Mary had fallen. Pratt could see the outline of the housekeeper's facial features still visible in the mud. Surrounding the impression Pratt saw many overlaid and trampled footprints, obviously left by Lull and others. He sighed in resignation; any tracks left here by the killer had been obliterated.

"Where did Lull find the cart stake?" Pratt asked Inglee.

"Right over there, by the marker."

"Was anything else found near the body?" Pratt inquired, now addressing the group.

"No," they replied in unison.

"Any ideas as to why she was out here?" asked Pratt.

"Maybe she was lured away on a pretext. Or she might have been sent on an errand to the Blake house," Inglee suggested.

Pratt conceded this was possible, but seemed unlikely; no one had found a lantern the woman might have used to light her way in the darkness.

"The pail of meal and the lantern next to Thomas's body – what do you make of that?" Pratt asked.

The farmers in the group assumed that Thomas was on his way to the barn, probably for the late feeding; the mash was a supplement often given to cows that were producing milk.

"Do you suppose that Miss Buckley went to the barn ahead of Thomas?"

The unfinished hay set out for the cows seemed to support that theory.

"That's quite possible," Blake said. "She often helps with the livestock, especially since Simeon's health has failed."

"Any idea when she might have gone out to the barn?" Pratt asked.

"The brothers normally went out for the last feeding at about nine o'clock, then retired for the night," said Blake.

Pratt was formulating a theory that Mary had gone out to the barn at about nine expecting Thomas to join her. The robber, concealed somewhere in the yard, watched her leave the house and, for some reason, thought it advantageous to enter while she was engaged in the barn. Did he know that Simeon was infirm and think he'd encounter only Thomas?

It seemed likely that Buckley was prompted to leave the barn and return to the house when Thomas was delayed, or perhaps a noise from the house had caused her to investigate. Of one thing Pratt was fairly certain: the housekeeper was the last to be murdered. She'd run a good distance from the house before she was caught. Pratt suspected she'd come face to face with the killer as he exited the house or after she discovered Thomas's body on the porch. She fled down the path toward Blake's for help, her access to nearer neighbors blocked by her assailant. Her pursuer caught up with her, struck her with the stake, and thoughtlessly discarded it near her body.

"It's likely the crime occurred after nine o'clock," Pratt said to

Blake. "As for who or how many committed these crimes, it's too early to say, but I suspect it was someone who was known to the victims. The only way to keep from being identified was to kill everyone."

Chapter Two: The Investigation

Plymouth County Coroner Philip Kingman arrived at the crime scene late that Monday afternoon; he spoke with Pratt, Crocker, and the other witnesses, and then viewed the bodies. He wasted no time presenting Crocker with a warrant convening an inquest at the Sturtevant house at ten o'clock the following morning and directing him to summon six men to serve as jurors.

Crocker served notice that evening on Halifax residents Edwin Inglee, Ephraim Thompson, Charles Paine, John T. Z. Thompson, Martin Howland, and Charles Lyon. His selection of men who knew the deceased or who were witnesses to the crime or its aftermath was deliberate; coroners relied upon local constables to select such jurors. It was common for jurors empowered to indict to also provide testimony in the same inquest and later, if necessary, at the trial of the accused.

Crocker knew from experience that the coroner would turn to a local physician to perform an autopsy and render a medical opinion as to the cause of death. He also knew that in many instances the district attorney for the county in which the death occurred would assist the coroner during the inquest. Such practices were the norm until 1877, when Massachusetts enacted legislation to revise its system of death investigation. The state abolished the coroner's authority and turned to trained medical examiners, "discreet [men], learned in the science of medicine" to conduct on-site investigations of sudden, unexplained, or suspicious deaths and determine cause of death independent of the influence or direction of the prosecutor. The change rendered that the medical examiner would not conduct an inquest but would perform autopsies duly authorized by law enforcement officials. If an autopsy confirmed a death by violence, the medical examiner would report his finding to the district attorney and a justice of the district, police, or municipal court, or a trial justice. The court or trial justice would then assume the duty of holding an inquest.

***

James Collingwood reined in his horse and secured his carriage behind Kingman's in the yard of the Sturtevant house. The forty-four-year-old deputy sheriff made the twelve-mile trip from Plymouth, where he operated a furniture store with his sons, James and Joseph.

State Constable Pratt briefed Collingwood as he ushered him to the rear of the house and into the porch. The parrot, named "Captain Kidd" by Mary Buckley, greeted the two policemen with a screech.

"Too bad the bird can't tell us who did this," Collingwood cracked in an uneasy attempt to prepare himself for the horrific scene he was about to encounter.

"It would make our job a damn sight easier," Pratt countered.

Inside the house, Collingwood briefly viewed the bodies in the kitchen and could not stifle his revulsion. Like Pratt, Collingwood was disturbed by the degree of savagery inflicted on the victims, particularly in the case of Simeon Sturtevant. These were acts of a cold, calculated, and personal nature.

He followed Pratt into the adjoining rooms to search for clues. Collingwood saw that only two rooms in the house had been disturbed. Coins and scrip were strewn about, closets and bureaus ransacked, and the straps of a locked trunk unbuckled. He also noticed two other trunks – one marked "S. S.," the other "T. S." – in a northeast room. Both were locked and apparently untouched.

Collingwood remained on the premises to continue searching and Pratt left to interview Lucy Holmes, who had returned to her house across the road hours before. In the meantime, Constable Crocker followed the path from the house to see where Lull had found Mary Buckley's body and to search for clues which had possibly been missed by others. He spent a few moments there then continued on the path toward Dan Blake's. At a gap in the fence at the end of the path he found Cyrus Wood, a shoemaker who lived near Inglee's store.

"Morning, Cyrus," Crocker said. "What brings you here?"

"I was at the store and heard about the murders. Everyone's talking about it," replied Wood.

"It didn't take long for word to get out."

"I found some coins here, Bill," said Wood, and he handed Crocker two five-cent pieces and a one-cent piece.

"These must have come from the house," said the constable, fingering the coins in his palm.

The two men continued to search and Crocker noticed some deep footprints in the mud just beyond the fence near the roadway. They were pointing away from the murder scene. He recognized their importance at once.

"Did you make these tracks?" asked Crocker.

"No, I came straight into the path from the road. Those are facing the other way," Wood answered.

Crocker found some fallen branches in the woods and placed them around the tracks to keep them from being inadvertently trampled. He left Wood and hurried back to the house.

Back at the Holmes's house, Pratt questioned Lucy and found her statements to be consistent with the account given by Stephen Lull.

"When did you last see the brothers?" Pratt asked.

"Thomas came by on Sunday morning," said Lucy, still visibly shaken. "I didn't see Simeon at all that day."

"And the housekeeper, Miss Buckley?"

"No, I didn't see Mary yesterday, either. I do remember looking out just before I went to bed on Sunday night and seeing a light on in the house. That was around nine o'clock, I'm sure."

"Have you noticed anything out of the ordinary or suspicious lately? Any strangers about the place?"

"I haven't," Lucy replied. "Nor has anyone mentioned it to me. We try to look out for each other."

She verified Lull's arrival at her door at about eight-fifteen on

Monday morning, recounted her walk with Lull and her daughter Edith to the body, and confirmed her recognition of Mary Buckley. She had returned then to the Sturtevant house with Lull after the Blakes arrived. She described the conditions she had witnessed when they and Mr. Inglee had entered the porch, sitting room, and Simeon's bedroom. She was horrified by what she had seen.

"Who would possibly want to rob those simple, hard-working people? What would possess someone to harm them so brutally?"

Pratt consoled Lucy as best he could and assured her that he would do everything possible to find the person or persons responsible. With that, he crossed back to the Sturtevant property to interview Daniel Blake, who was standing with his wife and others in the backyard.

Daniel Blake

At the outset of their conversation, Pratt detected a slight impediment in Blake's speech. Blake couldn't help but notice Pratt's reaction and explained that his tongue had been partially severed by a bullet at the siege of Petersburg.

"I understand, Mr. Blake," Pratt offered respectfully. "When did you first become aware of what's happened here?"

Edith Holmes had knocked on his door at half-past eight, Blake recalled, informed him in great agitation that someone had been killed, and relayed Lull's urgent request that he and Mr. Inglee come right away. He had sent his son to notify Inglee, and he and Mrs. Blake followed Edith along the path between his house and the Sturtevants' farm. They met Stephen Lull and Lucy Holmes standing near a body that he soon realized was Mary Buckley. A stake with blood on one end was lying next to Mary's lifeless form.

"Lull and I left the body and went to the house," Blake relayed. "We went in through the back door and found Thomas lying on the floor of the porch in a pool of blood. He was quite obviously dead. The back of his head was crushed."

"What did you do?" Pratt asked.

"Nothing. We backed out and closed the door to wait for Inglee. He arrived soon after."

"What happened when Inglee arrived?"

"We went to the porch, stepped around Thomas's body, and entered the main house through the doorway that opens into the great room. The kitchen door was on our right; it was closed. We glanced inside the sitting room and saw that it had been disturbed. We went on to the front bedroom and found Simeon in bed. His head was pulverized; I barely recognized him. The sheets and pillows

Margaret (Sturtevant) Blake

were soaked with blood and blood was all over the walls and the ceiling."

"You seem to know the house…can you be specific about what was out of place?"

"Both front rooms were a mess," answered Blake. "I saw a watch hanging in a closet and some coins and scrip were scattered on the floor in the bedroom and, in the sitting room, more coins and scrip were on the floor in front of a bureau. The bureau's top drawer was slightly ajar. Inside the drawer we saw a pocket book (wallet), twenty dollars in bills, a ten and two fives, I think, and some scrip."

"I gather you're somehow related to the Sturtevants?" Pratt prompted.

Blake explained that his wife was a niece to the murdered brothers. Her uncles had become reclusive and withdrawn since Simeon, the younger of the two, began showing signs of confusion.

"Did they have much money?" asked Pratt.

"You wouldn't think it, seeing how they live, but some would say they were wealthy," Blake responded. He offered that they possessed a significant amount of property in Halifax and Plympton. He further confided that the brothers distrusted banks and kept their money hidden in the house.

Pratt was intrigued.

"Was that widely known?" he asked.

"A few relatives knew, and some close friends," said Blake.

"Who, specifically?"

"Well, my wife and I, obviously. Edwin Inglee, Charles Paine, Ephraim Thompson. They all know; Thomas and Simeon considered them trusted friends. My brother-in-law, Joseph Dow, and his wife, Angeline, are also aware. Angeline and my wife are sisters."

"Anyone else?"

"Let's see...my wife's nephew, Willie Sturtevant, Thomas and Simeon's grandnephew. He also knew there was money in the house."

"Do you mean William Sturtevant?" Pratt asked.

"Yes," replied Blake. "Sometimes he's called Bill Everett."

"Is he missing the tips of two fingers on his left hand?"

"Yes, he lost them in the war."

Blake's last comment sent Pratt on a tangent. Several months before, he had investigated the theft of two hundred dollars in gold coins from the home of Joel White in South Hanson. White's nearest neighbor was Joseph Dow, whose name Blake had just mentioned.

Pratt recalled White being certain of William Sturtevant's culpability.

"What makes you so sure it was him?" Pratt remembered asking the indignant White.

"I suspected him right away," White had responded angrily. "The day I noticed the coins were missing was the same day I saw the wretch visiting his uncle, Joe Dow. I confronted Sturtevant on several occasions, and when I asked him if he had stolen the gold, he didn't deny it."

"Did you see him anywhere near your house on the day of the theft?" Pratt had asked.

"No, but he's a shiftless character and has a bad reputation in these parts. I live alone and keep to myself. I don't know anyone else who would want to steal from me."

Pratt had spent considerable time in that investigation canvassing local businesses and stores but the merchants had noticed nothing unusual in their transactions with customers, nor had they remembered anyone passing an inordinate amount of gold coins.

He had questioned Sturtevant about the theft, hoping for an admission or confession, and was met with steadfast denials. Pratt's instinct, based on what he knew about Sturtevant's demeanor, was that Sturtevant was responsible, but he was unable to uncover concrete evidence sufficient to warrant an arrest.

Pratt remembered, too, that he had briefed his superior, Chief Constable George Boynton, on his investigation into the theft from White and Boynton was not surprised to hear Sturtevant's name.

"Is he a shoemaker from Halifax?" Boynton had asked Pratt.

"Yes," said Pratt. "Do you know him?"

"I arrested him a few years ago. It was '66, I think, on Friend Street in Boston at the National Horse and Carriage Mart. He was desperately trying to sell a horse and wagon, saying he'd take just $150 for both when they were easily worth twice that. I never figured out why he was so anxious to unload them so cheaply. Sturtevant claimed he bought the hitched pair in Abington for $325 from a man named William Perkins. I asked him how he happened to come by the $325 he'd used to purchase the rig and he told me it was bounty money, for war service. (The Enrollment Act of 1863 authorized a bounty payment of $325 for men enlisting in the military service for three years, and $100 to men enlisting in the naval and marine service for the same period.)

"Anyway, his story didn't add up so I held him and later confirmed that no one by the name of William Perkins resided in Abington and that a horse and hitch had been stolen from a stable in the same town.

"I visited the Adjutant General's office at the state house and learned that Sturtevant had, indeed, been in the navy, but deserted two months after he enlisted.

"I took him before Judge Rufus Thatcher in North Bridgewater (now Brockton) and the judge found him guilty and sentenced him to serve a year in the Plymouth House of Correction."

Pratt returned from this reverie and continued his interview with Blake.

"Have you seen anyone acting suspiciously in the area lately?"

"No, I haven't," Blake replied.

"When was the last time you saw your nephew?"

"My wife's mother, Lucinda Sturtevant, died several weeks ago. We held the funeral here at the house and Willie, who is Lucinda's grandson, came and paid his respects."

"Was Joseph Dow there as well?"

"Yes, he and Angeline were there," Blake confirmed, noting Pratt's sudden shift to Dow.

Pratt quickly shifted back.

"Tell me what you know about William's past."

Blake's expression turned dark and he began, with a sigh, to recite a bleak history.

"Willie must be going on twenty-six, I'd say. Yes, I'm sure he was born in '48. His parents, Caleb and Mary, lived in East Bridgewater then. They had two other children already, Mary and George. Just a year after Willie was born, they had a fourth child, Willie's brother, James. When Willie was about two, I think, Caleb moved his family into his father's house in Halifax; that's the house Margaret and I live in now.

"Hold on," Pratt interjected. "William Sturtevant used to live in the house you live in now?"

"That's right. They weren't there long before they had a fifth child. Benjamin was born in 1851, I think.

"Things went badly after that. In the summer of 1852, James, who was just two years old, died of dysentery. Mary gave birth to another child a year or so later; they named him James as well.

"The second James was just two when Mary fell ill with typhoid fever and died. She was only twenty-nine-years of age.

27

"Caleb wouldn't stay in the house and went back to East Bridgewater with his five children. That was '55 I think. He was only there about a year when his eleven-year-old daughter, Mary, died. Shortly after, Caleb abandoned Willie and his three brothers. Just up and left. Can't say I approve but a man has his limits."

"Where did he go?" Pratt asked.

"Last I heard he was in Lewiston, Maine."

"We took custody of Willie's brother George," Blake continued, "and Willie went to live with Joseph and Angeline in East Bridgewater. The two other boys were placed with friends."

Willie soon expressed deep resentment and became hostile to the Dows, according to Blake. Despite their efforts to provide a stable environment for the boy, he remained defiant and rebellious. His behavior left the Dows with no alternative but to seek court intervention.

Blake recalled that a constable arrived at their home to take Willie into custody and transport him to the court for disposition. While in transit to the courthouse, the twelve-year-old boy feigned thirst and convinced the constable to stop at a house. Willie was tied to the wagon with a rope while the constable went inside for water. When the constable came out, Willie was gone.

"He returned to the Dows but they wouldn't take him back," Blake said. "Margaret and I were living in East Bridgewater at the time. We agreed to give him a second chance, but nothing had changed; he continued his errant ways. In 1862, when he was fourteen, he was caught stealing and the police arrested him. The judge in Plymouth found him guilty and sent him to the nautical school."

The Nautical Branch of the State Reform School, later known as the Massachusetts Nautical School, was established by legislation in October 1859. Governor Nathaniel Banks had proposed the statute to address a shortage of qualified merchant marines and sailors by training delinquents in seamanship and navigation. His stated aim was "to turn some of the excess of vicious youth to pursuits so congenial to many of them and tending to the enlargement and security of our commerce, the extension of American liberty, and the honor of our national flag."

Willie remained under the jurisdiction of the school until February 1864, when, as Blake told it, he was discharged and enlisted for a three-year term in the navy. A few months later, Willie deserted. Willie later claimed he had enlisted in the army after deserting the navy and had served in the west, where he lost parts of two fingers on his left hand fighting guerillas.

Blake admitted his nephew had served a year in the Plymouth House of Correction in 1866 for stealing a horse. When Willie was released, Blake said, he took him in and put him to work in his shoe shop.

"Willie met a girl over in Hanson by the name of Abbie Standish. He married her in the fall of 1871. The following year they had their first child, George. For a while they lived in South Hanson with Abbie's mother, Lucy Parris. They stayed with her this past November, I believe, then took rooms in the old Ebenezer Keene place at Keene's Corner, not far from the Parris place in South Hanson. That's where they live now."

"Is Sturtevant still working with you?" Pratt asked Blake.

"No," answered Blake. "He's been working in South Abington (present-day Whitman) at a shoe factory owned by Henry Blake."

"Henry Blake, you say…is he related to you or your family?"

"No, he's not," Blake replied.

Constable Crocker came up from the path and excitedly interrupted Pratt's interview with Blake.

"You might want to have a look at this, Mr. Pratt. We've found some coins along the path and a single set of footprints in the mud."

Pratt signaled to Collingwood to follow and Crocker led the two men to a spot just outside a gap in the fence opposite Blake's house. The tracks pointed north toward Stump Brook and Inglee's store.

The heavy stress placed on the heels and toes and the length of the stride suggested to Pratt that whoever left the tracks had been in full sprint. The imprint of the left foot was slightly different; it revealed a clear impression that Pratt, putting his knowledge of shoes and boots to good use, found consistent with a patch on the sole at the toe.

While the others stood by, Pratt hurried back to his carriage and removed from his valise an old, folding, shoemaker's size-stick. He returned to the tracks and measured the length and width of the impression, gauging the footwear that left it to be a size seven. Pratt surmised from this that he was looking for a man of less-than-average height. He asked Crocker to retrieve some planks from a pile of drying lumber he'd seen behind the Sturtevant house. When Crocker returned, Pratt carefully covered the tracks in an effort to preserve them.

The policemen returned to the house and checked the shoes and boots of everyone who had been on the path, but none matched the track found near the gap in the fence. They rechecked any distinguishable tracks leading to and from the house, comparing them to the unique prints they'd found; none were similar.

"I'm fairly certain now that we're looking for a lone suspect," Pratt said to Collingwood, "but I can't discount the indistinguishable footprints Ephraim Thompson pointed out near the house. If someone else was involved, he may have fled in a different direction."

Pratt later learned through interviews that Sturtevant's relationship with his granduncles was strained. Blake had earlier confirmed Sturtevant's attendance at his grandmother's funeral in the Thompson Street house. A source later told Pratt that he had overheard William, after the funeral, grumbling that he had not felt welcome at the house, that Thomas and Simeon "did not talk much, nor appear at all sociable."

***

"At last the most dreaded of all visitors upon society has been reached," the *Middleboro Gazette* would declare a week after the murders, "and the town of Halifax has a monument to her greatest grief and affliction in the old Sturtevant homestead…"

Fear and speculation spread throughout the town and beyond. Windows and doors ordinarily left unlocked were bolted. Residents in the tight-knit communities cast a suspicious eye on strangers and passersby while police set about identifying those responsible for the atrocity perpetrated on the Sturtevant brothers and Mary Buckley.

"...It is still difficult to realize," an anonymous Halifax resident wrote to the *Old Colony Memorial* newspaper a month after the murders, "that this old puritan soil has been made the scene of such a murder – one of the foulest in the annals of crime – a murder where not the innocent person was beaten to death in cold blood, but three, and with the evident and express purpose of robbery; a most fearful illustration of the truth of the apostolic declaration that 'the love of money is the root of all evil.' Truly we are led to think that the traditional calm which is said to precede the earthquake in countries subject to their visitations, might bear a resemblance to the former peace and good order which had generally prevailed within our borders,

State constable's badge, ca. 1866

making the 'shock' all so much the more sudden when it came. This had been a quiet old town so long, with 'no lawyer' and 'none needed,' that the belief seemed to be rooted in the minds of some people that it could never be any other way. But there is no argument so convincing as the 'stern logic of events.'"

***

State Detective Chase Philbrick, delayed by investigative duties elsewhere, boarded the last Plymouth-bound train in Boston and arrived in South Hanson at about six o'clock on Monday evening. Halifax Constable Crocker, alerted beforehand, was at the depot waiting in his carriage to convey the policeman to Edwin Inglee's house. Philbrick dined there and spent several hours speaking with Inglee and Crocker about the case.

"You're welcome to stay here tonight, Officer Philbrick," Inglee said.

31

"Thank you, Mr. Inglee. I didn't have time to arrange for accommodations," said Philbrick and turned to Crocker.

"Is it too late for me to take a look at the crime scene?"

"Not at all, Philbrick," Crocker said. "Judah Keene, the local undertaker, is keeping watch at the house throughout the night."

The two policemen arrived at the Sturtevant place at nine o'clock. Keene met them at the front door with a lantern and led them through the dark, empty house to the kitchen, where Philbrick viewed the bodies. After a cursory inspection of the other rooms, Philbrick returned with Crocker to Inglee's place and retired for the evening.

On Tuesday morning, February 17, Philbrick borrowed a carriage from Inglee and met his colleague, State Detective Hollis Pinkham, as he disembarked from the train at South Hanson. It had been a busy week for the two policemen. On Friday last they had raided an afternoon faro game in Boston and, later that evening, Pinkham had arrested a burglar for a jewelry theft at the Beacon Hill home of a prominent physician.

Philbrick, fifty-two, hailed from Sanbornton, New Hampshire, but by 1850 he was living in Massachusetts and working as a stone cutter in the quarries at Quincy. He mustered in as a captain with the 15th Massachusetts Volunteer Infantry in 1861 and, a year later, sustained a gunshot wound to his right ankle at the Battle of Fredericksburg, Virginia. After being honorably discharged from the same regiment as a lieutenant colonel in 1863, he became city marshal in Lawrence, Massachusetts, a position he held until 1871, when Massachusetts Governor William Claflin appointed him to the state constabulary.

Pinkham, age thirty-nine, was also a New Hampshire native and Civil War veteran. He, too, enlisted in 1861, but with the Massachusetts First Cavalry Regiment. He was mustered out in 1865 as a first lieutenant and quartermaster of the Second Cavalry Regiment. Governor William Washburn appointed him to the state constabulary in 1872.

The two men rode hastily to the Sturtevant house; they wanted to

32

speak with Pratt before the inquest began. They found Pratt among the dozen or so witnesses and jurors engaged in animated conversation outside the house, waiting for the coroner to call the inquest to order. The detectives acknowledged Constable Crocker as he raised the rope that was still strung across the front yard. Increasing numbers of people had congregated since dawn along the roadway huddling in garrulous groups, gawking at the house.

Pratt briefed them on the progress of his investigation and related his past experiences with, and growing suspicion of, one William E. Sturtevant.

"There is still much to be done," Pratt said to his colleagues. "In the absence of an eyewitness any hope for conviction will depend upon strong circumstantial evidence.

"I don't believe we can rule out the possibility that some passing drifter had somehow learned about the money being kept by the brothers in the house, but it seems apparent to me that whoever had committed the robbery had a prior apprehension of where the money might be.

"More than a few friends and relatives were aware of the Sturtevant brothers' bias against banks. In my experience, that means many more knew…people talk. I'm reasonably confident about the integrity of Margaret Blake, the brothers' niece, and her husband, Daniel. As for Charles Paine, Edwin Inglee, and Ephraim Thompson, it appears they were trusted by the brothers and are highly respected here in Halifax. The only others who had knowledge of the brothers' habit of hoarding money was Joseph Dow and his wife, Angeline, another niece of the Sturtevants. I haven't spoken with them as yet."

Pinkham asked Pratt if the housekeeper, too, kept money in the house.

"I don't know for certain. There are several trunks that still need to be inspected," Pratt said. "There were notes of credit in the drawers and on the floor of the house. Perhaps a payment was due and the debtor was unable or unwilling to pay."

Just then, a buggy rattling up to the house drew their attention. A middle-aged man alighted and after some brief words with Crocker, he entered the yard and introduced himself to the officers as Martin Howland, a neighbor of Daniel Blake's and a Halifax selectman. He had been summoned as a juror for the inquest.

Rear of Sturtevant house and entryway to porch (Note the two policemen wearing dark uniforms and custodian helmets)

Unbidden, Howland related that he was at John Drayton's grocery store in South Hanson that morning and Drayton showed him some rare scrip that a patron had given him the previous night.

"Neither of us had seen this type of scrip for quite some time. It occurred to us that it might have something to do with the Sturtevant robbery and murders."

Philbrick and Pinkham exchanged glances with Pratt who asked Howland to describe the scrip.

34

"It was Civil War scrip – two ten-cent pieces. It looked like it had never been used before."

"Did Drayton know the person who passed this tender?"

"Yes," Howland answered. "He said Willie Sturtevant came into his store on Sunday and asked to buy a few items on credit, which Drayton granted him. Sturtevant returned to the store on Monday and settled his debt with scrip."

"Does Drayton still have the scrip?"

"Yes, I told him to set it aside until I had an opportunity to speak with you."

"Where is Drayton's store located?"

"It's on Main Street next to the South Hanson depot."

"Thank you, Mr. Howland," said Pratt. "We'll call on Drayton today."

Howland entered the house and Pratt said to his colleagues, "You can see now why I'm focusing on Sturtevant but let's see where things take us. Kingman intends to reconvene the second session of the inquest on February 23. He won't call me to testify this morning, so I'm off to South Abington. Sturtevant works in Henry Blake's shoe factory there. I hope to speak with the stationmaster at South Hanson on the way. I'll stop at Drayton's store, too, and ask him to hold the scrip until you come for it."

"Alright, Pratt," said Philbrick. "We'll do what we can here. We'll take a ride to Sturtevant's house in South Hanson and stop by Drayton's when we're finished. Where exactly does Sturtevant live?"

"He lives in Keene's Corner, about four miles north of here. Crocker can tell you how to get there."

Knowing it might take some time, Pratt had earlier sent for a photographer to capture the scene. Since its inception in 1839, photography had vastly improved and, despite its limitations, had become an important tool for criminal investigators and prosecutors. For this purpose, Pratt relied on Albert Chamberlain of North Abington, a boot and shoe manufacturer who was also a part-time photographer.

Pratt had known Chamberlain for years and had worked as a clerk in his shoe factory before entering the state constabulary. When Chamberlain arrived on Tuesday, Pratt directed him to record, with photographs and sketches, the interior and exterior of the house, the grounds, and the footprints found outside the fence near Blake's house.

Chapter Three: The Inquest

On Monday night, Judah Keene had cracked several windows in the kitchen and sealed the room off from the rest of the house in the hope that the cold February air would help to delay the decomposition of the bodies. He kept fires bright in the keeping room's fireplace and in the two small hearths in the front rooms to warm the rest of the house overnight.

Early on Tuesday morning, Keene and several others had fashioned three makeshift biers overlaid with cedar planks and arranged them in the kitchen. Keene spread blankets over the planks and the corpses were lifted from the floor and placed on the biers. Keene had procured blocks of ice from an ice house at nearby Silver Lake, placed them in wooden tubs, and positioned the tubs beneath the biers to further slow

Dr. Asa Millet

decomposition. He then measured the bodies for coffins and covered each with a sheet.

Drs. Asa Millet, James Brewster, and Warren Pillsbury gathered at the house with the coroner, jurors, and witnesses. The three physicians would autopsy the bodies as the inquest proceeded.

Dr. Millet conducted a cursory examination of the victims before the inquest was called to order. The sixty-year-old physician, balding and wearing a full beard, had lost the sight in his right eye at the age of nine after a neighborhood boy struck him with an arrow in a game of "Indians." His disability had not deterred him from securing a medical degree from Bowdoin College of Medicine in 1842, nor had it prevented him from contributing to the Union effort during the Civil War as a contract surgeon under General George

McLellan.

Millet's preliminary opinion was limited to the conclusion that all of the victims had been murdered at about the same time and with the same weapon. He estimated that at least eight hours had transpired between the time of death and the discovery of the bodies.

The housekeeper's body had chilled rapidly overnight due to exposure, but the other two bodies were warm to the touch when found. Millet knew that the temperature in the porch and Simeon's bedroom, where live embers were still present in the fireplaces, had slowed the cooling process. Thomas's thick clothing and Simeon's heavy bed coverings had insulated the bodies, and each man's strapping physique had also contributed to a delay of the cooling. Millet also subscribed to the theory that body temperature continues to rise for up to an hour after death in cases of violent death, and that it drops more slowly when there has been a severe head injury.

Millet and his colleagues decided to perform the full autopsies in the room where Simeon's body had been found. After Simeon's bed was removed, Millet set up a portable embalming table and laid out his instruments. Pillsbury separated the window drapes to let some light in and cracked the room's two windows for ventilation. Once the bodies had been viewed by the jury, each would be moved so that the men could perform their task.

Coroner Kingman called the inquest to order at ten o'clock in the sitting room. Constable Crocker returned the warrant to Kingman and advised him that everyone he had summoned was present.

"Stand and raise your right hands," Kingman instructed the six jurors. "Do you solemnly swear, that you will diligently inquire and true presentment make, on behalf of this Commonwealth, when, how, and by what means, the people whose bodies lie here dead came to their death; and return a true inquest thereof, according to your knowledge and such evidence as shall be laid before you; so help you, God?"

"I do," said each of the men in unison.

Kingman gave a brief summary of the facts gathered up to that time and, when he finished, he escorted the jurors to the kitchen where Judah Keene uncovered the faces of each of the victims. Kingman then led the men through the other rooms in the house and outside along the path to the scene of Mary Buckley's death. When they returned to the house, Stephen Lull testified at length about his discovery of the bodies.

Zebadiah Thompson, who lived in the house next to and east of the Sturtevants, told jurors he was with Simeon Sturtevant and Mary Buckley at half past six on Sunday evening in the porch of their house. In Thompson's presence, Simeon carried in an armful of wood for Buckley to build a fire in his bedroom. Thompson testified that it was customary for the Sturtevant lights to be on as late as ten o'clock in the evening.

Daniel Blake once again recounted his observations about the conditions he had found inside and outside the house after being summoned to the murder scene by Lull. He acknowledged his relationship, by marriage, to the victims and stated he had last visited them at four o'clock on Sunday afternoon, returning to his house along the same path where Buckley's body was later discovered. He described the path between his house and the Sturtevants' as being a little less than a quarter of a mile. When asked if it was unusual for Mary Buckley to be on the path at night, he said that she had come over to his house as late as eleven o'clock on occasion. He hadn't seen anyone suspicious on the path or around the Sturtevant house recently.

Margaret Blake testified as to her familial relationship with the victims and corroborated, in part, the testimony of the previous witnesses.

Millet, Brewster, and Pillsbury went to the kitchen after the jurors had viewed the corpses, lifted Mary Buckley's shrouded body from the bier and carried it to the bedroom, placing it on the portable table.

Rigor mortis was at its peak, causing her arms to be stiffly flexed at a grotesque angle. This was significant because the doctors knew that rigor mortis generally began between eight and twenty hours after death, often sooner if conditions were right. They knew by training and experience that rigidity begins in the lower jaw and back of the neck then proceeds to the face, neck, thorax, arms, and lower extremities. The condition disappears in roughly the same order and can continue from one to nine days.

Brewster and Pillsbury disrobed the body after massaging and stretching the limbs. The sixty-eight-year-old woman appeared healthy but for the wounds about her head. There was no evidence of disease. They noted contusions on the right eye and the nose and similar bruising on several areas of Mary's scalp. There was a severe fracture on the back of the skull, the meninges (the membranes beneath the skull) were torn, and the cerebellum was crushed. The three physicians concurred that a single blow to Buckley's head with a blunt instrument had caused her death.

The physicians returned Mary's body to the kitchen, carried Simeon to the examination table, and undressed him. His body, too, was in an advanced stage of rigor mortis but otherwise showed characteristics consistent with general good health for a person of his age. A thorough visual inspection revealed no contusions, abrasions or lacerations below the neck. On his head, however, the lower lip was lacerated and fractures were appreciated in the mandible (lower jaw), nose, and maxilla (upper jaw bone), a portion of which was completely detached from the skull.

"Gentlemen, this man sustained three or four blows to the head. I believe they were delivered with a blunt instrument. For the record, do you agree?" Millet asked his colleagues.

Brewster and Pillsbury nodded.

"I would also suggest, given the angle of the wounds and the spatter on the walls in the room, that the injuries were inflicted from the right side of the victim's body," Brewster added.

"Would you also agree the assailant wielded the weapon in his right hand?" asked Millet.

"Yes," his two colleagues replied.

Doctor Brewster was born in Plymouth, Massachusetts, in 1842 and was a direct descendant of Elder William Brewster of the *Mayflower*. He left his studies at Tufts College, Boston, to serve nine months with the 44th Massachusetts Regiment during the Civil War. He continued his studies when he returned home and received his undergraduate degree from Tufts in 1863. He reenlisted as acting Assistant Surgeon of the 2nd Division, 9th Army Corps.

Brewster attended Bellevue Hospital Medical College, New York, after the war and graduated with his medical degree in 1866, then traveled abroad to study at the University of Vienna, where he received a Master of Arts degree in obstetrics in 1868. Brewster later became Surgeon-General of the Department of Massachusetts, Grand Army of the Republic. He was appointed a physician at the Plymouth County Jail and House of Correction in 1869.

Pillsbury had graduated only a year before from Millet's alma mater, Bowdoin Medical College. He lived in Bryantville (Pembroke) and practiced in Hanson.

Coroner Kingman interrupted Dr. Millet to have him testify about his preliminary examination of the victims. When Millet concluded his testimony, Kingman adjourned the session and continued the inquest until Monday morning, February 23, at nine o'clock. Millet returned to his colleagues and commenced the autopsy of Thomas Sturtevant.

Thomas's limbs were also inflexible with post-mortem rigor. After they had relaxed the limbs, the physicians removed Thomas's clothing. They observed a slight laceration on the left shoulder blade and a contused wound over the right ear extending to the back of the head. Dr. Millet removed the scalp and beneath it found profuse ecchymosis (bruising) on the right side. One blow fractured the back of the skull from ear to ear; another had fractured the top of the skull. The doctors agreed Thomas's injuries were also caused by a blunt instrument and were consistent with those received by Simeon and Mary.

The skulls of Mary Buckley and Simeon Sturtevant were not preserved as evidence; it was deemed that both had been damaged in such a way as to render them useless as evidence. However, a portion

41

of Thomas's skull, fractured but intact, would be helpful in illustrating at criminal proceedings the force of the blow he had sustained and the direction from which the blow had come. Millet used a saw to free the fractured section of the skull and laid it aside for chemical cleaning and drying.

Thomas's body was returned to the kitchen and placed in Judah Keene's care. Keene later collaborated with Inglee, Ephraim Thompson, Crocker, and family members to procure coffins and suitable clothing for each of the deceased and to finalize visitation, funeral, and burial arrangements.

***

As the autopsies progressed, Inglee and Charles Paine assisted the coroner in accounting for all the cash, promissory notes, and jewelry in the house. Inglee located the keys for the two trunks in the northeast room and unlocked them. In the trunk marked "S. S." they found about $650 in gold and silver. Thomas's trunk, marked "T. S.," contained $200 in silver and $800 in bills.

Judah Keene had earlier found a key in Mary Buckley's gown. Paine fit the key into the lock of the unstrapped trunk in the sitting room and found $900 in bills, gold, silver, copper, and nickels, bank books, and a gold watch.

Paine and Inglee pored over the papers and ledger books meticulously maintained by the Sturtevants and compared the records with the assets they had found in the house. They concluded that they had accounted for all but $650.

Chapter Four: A Suspect

Pratt left Philbrick and Pinkham and boarded his carriage for the trip to South Abington. He reached Drayton's store on Main Street in South Hanson and secured his rig to a post. When he entered the store he found the grocer stocking his shelves.

"Good morning, Mr. Drayton. My name is Pratt and I'm a state constable investigating the murders on Thompson Street. You may have heard..."

Collamore's store (formerly store of John Drayton), ca. 1880

"Good morning, officer," Drayton replied as he stepped down from his stool. "Yes, I know about the Sturtevants. I was sad to hear it."

"I spoke with Mr. Howland this morning," Pratt said as he looked around the store. "He tells me you received some unusual scrip from William Sturtevant yesterday."

"Yes, I have it here," Drayton replied as he opened a cash drawer beneath his counter. Pratt took it from him and saw that it was similar to the scrip found inside the murder house.

"Two of my colleagues will be here to see you later in the day," Pratt said as he handed the scrip back to Drayton. "Do you have a safe place to keep these until the officers come by to collect them?"

"Yes, I'll keep them under lock and key," Drayton assured him.

Pratt left his rig at the store and walked over to the railroad depot to engage stationmaster Cyrus Bates. Bates at first seemed reluctant when asked if he'd answer a few questions. Pratt inquired if he knew William Sturtevant.

"Yes," said Bates. "I see him some mornings when he takes the train for work in South Abington and from time to time in the evening when he returns."

"When did you last see him?"

"He was here yesterday. He boarded the train for South Abington in the morning."

"Was he here today?"

"No, he must have walked," said Bates. "He does that often."

Bates was still uneasy about Pratt's visit; he didn't want any trouble. Sturtevant had been in the depot on the previous Saturday and Bates advanced him two tickets on credit. Yesterday, he came in for two more tickets and paid for all four with a crisp, fifty-cent scrip note. Bates hadn't seen scrip like it in years and was suspicious, but he took it from Sturtevant anyway. He no longer had the note; he had deposited it in the bank with the rest of the fares he had collected that day. Pratt hadn't asked him how Sturtevant had paid his fare and Bates wasn't about to volunteer the information. He wished now he had set the scrip aside.

Pratt returned to Drayton's and climbed into his carriage. He headed northeast toward South Abington (Whitman) and Blake's shoe shop at South Avenue near Broad Street, arriving at about ten-thirty. He pulled his carriage up the expansive drive, through the carriage-house arch, and stepped down to tether his horse on a post. He found the shop

44

behind Blake's impressive residence and stepped inside. Henry Blake was seated at his office desk.

Pratt introduced himself and asked Blake if Sturtevant was working there.

"He is," said Blake.

"Can you excuse him for a few minutes? I'd like to ask him some questions."

"Of course," Blake replied with a puzzled look on his face.

He nodded to a clerk in his office. The clerk went to fetch Sturtevant and returned with him several minutes later. Sturtevant was dressed in a white long-sleeve shirt with a paper collar, a gray vest, and black trousers. A shadow crossed Sturtevant's face when he saw the badge and recognized Pratt.

"Is there someplace I can speak with Sturtevant privately?" Pratt asked.

"Yes," Blake said and escorted them to his counting room.

After Blake left the room and closed the door, Pratt pointed to a chair. Sturtevant shrugged and sat down.

Henry Blake house and shoe shop, South Abington (Whitman)

"Are you here to speak with me about White's gold again?"

Sturtevant snarled.

"Only if you're ready to admit you stole it. Otherwise, I'd like to ask you about the murders in Halifax. You have heard about them?" Pratt asked coolly.

"Yes, I've heard," said Sturtevant. "Two of the men killed were my uncles."

"Before I ask you any more questions, I want you to know that you are not obligated to speak with me. If you do speak with me, I can use your statements against you. Do you understand?"

Sturtevant stepped back and straightened himself.

"Do you think I killed my own people?" Sturtevant asked incredulously.

"I didn't say that," Pratt snapped. "Right now I'm trying to sort out what happened. I intend to question everyone I think may have information bearing on this case. Will you cooperate with me, Sturtevant?"

Sturtevant's shoulder relaxed.

"Yes," he replied calmly, "I have no problem answering your questions."

"Were your uncles considered wealthy?"

"They were farmers and had money, but they had to use nearly all of it to pay property taxes."

"Did you know them to keep money in the house?" Pratt asked.

"Not to my knowledge."

Pratt observed Sturtevant closely as he spoke, inspecting his clothing and assessing his demeanor. He noticed a small, dark spot on Sturtevant's shirt collar.

"Where were you last Sunday?"

"I was in East Bridgewater. I left my wife and son at home and spent the day with a friend, Daniel Blanchard." (Sturtevant's wife, Abbie, was a half-sister to Blanchard's wife, Lydia Parris Blanchard.)

"When did you return home?"

"It was about five o'clock."

"Was your wife there?"

"Yes, she was entertaining two friends of ours, Ella Drayton and Mercy Bonney. They had stopped by for a visit."

"How long did they stay?"

"They stayed until nine o'clock. I saw them to the door and Abbie and I went to bed."

"Did you leave the house at any time after that?"

"Not until the next morning when I left for work."

"Alright," Pratt said. "I'm going to your granduncles' place and I'd like you to come along with me. Get your coat and hat."

William E. Sturtevant (Note partial fingers on left hand)

"Am I under arrest?" Sturtevant demanded.

"No, but I have more questions and I think some of them would be better answered at the house in Halifax."

Sturtevant left the counting room and spoke briefly with Blake, retrieved his undercoat and hat upstairs, and returned to Pratt. Pratt thought it odd, given the chilly temperature outside, that Sturtevant didn't have a heavier coat.

"Mr. Pratt," said Sturtevant as he donned his coat and hat, "I hope you find those who were responsible for these horrible murders. I'll do whatever I can to help you."

"Where is your overcoat, Sturtevant?"

"I thought it was upstairs, but I can't find it. I may have left it at home. I wear it occasionally to and from work, but it's old and ragged."

Pratt noticed another dark spot on Sturtevant's black felt hat. He removed it from Sturtevant's head and examined it closely.

"Is this a bloodstain on your hat?"

"It looks like blood."

"How did it get there?"

"I have no idea," Sturtevant replied indifferently.

Pratt met Sturtevant's eyes and held them. Sturtevant never blinked, nor did he turn away. Pratt immediately sensed deception, but was not prepared to jump to any conclusions just yet.

Pratt tossed the hat on a nearby desk.

"What size is your shoe?"

"I wear size seven or eight," Sturtevant said.

This answer was not lost on Pratt. Here's a shoemaker who's not sure of his shoe size. Was he being purposely evasive?

From his pocket Pratt removed the size-stick he had used to measure the footprint at the crime scene and placed it on the floor alongside Sturtevant's left shoe. The shoe was a size eight; the footprint was a size seven. Pratt sighed.

"Do you own another pair of shoes?" Pratt asked.

"I have a pair of congress boots at home, but I haven't worn them in two months," replied Sturtevant.

Pratt took possession of Sturtevant's hat and undercoat, left the counting room, and asked Henry Blake if he had an extra hat and overcoat. Before Blake returned with both, Pratt searched Sturtevant's undercoat and found a small wallet containing scrip issued in 1863, nine postage stamps, and some nickels, which he seized.

"Where did you get this money, Sturtevant?" asked Pratt.

"My uncle, Joe Dow, sent that to me while I was visiting in Maine. I left before it arrived and the postmaster in Lisbon sent it back to me along with the postage stamps. Why are you taking them, Mr. Pratt?" Sturtevant demanded.

"I'll give them back to you when I've substantiated what you've told me. Until then, I'll keep them," Pratt replied.

Blake returned with a coat and hat and Sturtevant put them on.

"I'll need to take Sturtevant with me to Dr. Copeland's office," Pratt said to Blake. "It's a short walk and I'd like to leave my horse and carriage here."

Dr. Horatio Copeland

"I understand, Mr. Pratt," Blake replied. "You're welcome to leave your team for as long as you like."

"Sturtevant, let's take a walk over to Dr. Copeland's. He'll be able to tell us whether those stains on your collar and hat are blood or not," Pratt suggested.

Sturtevant voiced no objection and donned the borrowed hat and overcoat. The two men exited Blake's shop and walked up South Avenue, past the high school, to Washington Street and turned left. They reached Dr. Horatio Copeland's office a block south of the Baptist church.

Pratt had met the physician on several occasions and knew something of his background. Copeland was a Harvard Medical School graduate and had established an extensive practice in South Abington after his discharge from the army in 1865. He had served the Union as an assistant surgeon and hospital administrator in Bermuda Hundred, Virginia, during the war.

They stepped inside and Pratt motioned for Sturtevant to take a seat in the waiting room. Pratt spoke privately with the physician in his office and emerged a few moments later.

"Come in here with me, Sturtevant," Pratt directed, "and unbutton your paper collar."

Sturtevant removed the collar and gave it to Pratt. Dr. Copeland handed Pratt a magnifying glass and the two men inspected the spots. Both agreed they were consistent in appearance with bloodstains. Pratt then handed the glass to Sturtevant.

"What do you think those spots are on the collar, Sturtevant?"

Sturtevant hesitated and studied the spots. Pratt waited patiently.

"It looks like blood. If it is, I must have picked up the spots from a beef shin I bought last Saturday night from Mr. Drayton in South Hanson. I've worn the same collar since but never noticed the stains."

Pratt and Copeland examined the spot on Sturtevant's hat and were certain that it, too, was a bloodstain.

"I'll need to see your overcoat, Sturtevant."

Pratt turned to Copeland. He wasn't keen on taking Sturtevant to South Hanson alone.

"Doctor, Sturtevant here tells me he left his overcoat at home in South Hanson. Would you mind taking us there in your carriage?"

"I don't mind at all, Pratt, but let me check my schedule."

Copeland crossed the room and scanned the appointment book on his desk.

"I'm not expecting any other patients today. Drs. Dudley and Hastings are nearby and can handle any emergency that might occur."

Copeland retrieved his hat and coat and the three men left the office and boarded his carriage. Pratt returned to the subject of Sturtevant's visit with Daniel Blanchard on Sunday and asked Sturtevant where Blanchard lived. Sturtevant told Pratt that if Copeland continued south on Washington Street toward East Bridgewater, Blanchard's house would be on the left, near Oak Street, just past the South Abington town line. When they came to the house, Copeland pulled his carriage over and, at Pratt's direction, stayed with Sturtevant while Pratt went inside.

Sturtevant couldn't believe what was happening. He didn't need this trouble, especially now. He and his wife, Abbie, were expecting their second child in April.

They had lived with Abbie's mother for a time after their marriage in 1871, but four months ago they had found a place to board at Keene's Corner in South Hanson. He had struggled to provide for his family, occasionally making shoes or chopping wood. Only recently had he found permanent work in Henry Blake's shoe shop, but the meager wages were inadequate and his debts continued to mount. He was sometimes forced, for lack of train fare, to plod eight miles roundtrip to work. With few other prospects, and despite his best efforts, his growing family's security was precarious at best, perhaps even desperate. There would be little he could do for them behind bars.

Sturtevant pleaded his innocence to Copeland once more.

"If Pratt arrests me and I have to face trial, I'll be found not guilty. Those blood spots on my clothes came from the beef shin and nowhere else."

In the house, Blanchard confirmed Sturtevant's visit on the previous Sunday. Blanchard told Pratt that Sturtevant had been at his house from three o'clock until half past four in the afternoon.

"Do you recall if Sturtevant was wearing an overcoat when he came to visit?" Pratt asked Blanchard.

"No, I don't believe so. He was wearing a black suit," Blanchard replied.

Pratt left the house, saying nothing as he climbed back into Copeland's carriage. Copeland slapped the reins and the team lurched forward.

***

Copeland, Pratt, and Sturtevant pulled up to Sturtevant's house in South Hanson at about 2:00 p.m. Abbie was cradling young George in her arms when she answered Pratt's knock at the door. When she saw her husband standing behind Pratt, she blanched.

Sturtevant house, O High Street, South Hanson, ca. 1900

"What is going on, Willie?"

"Don't worry, Abbie. Mr. Pratt seems to think I might have had something to do with my uncles' murders, but he is mistaken. You and I both know I was here throughout the night on Sunday."

When the three men stepped inside, Pratt explained the purpose of his visit and left Abbie and the child with Copeland and Sturtevant to begin his search for the overcoat.

Abbie looked to her husband with doleful, pleading eyes.

"There, there, Abbie," he said as he embraced her. "There's no cause for worry. Everything will turn out right."

Sturtevant turned to Copeland.

"This is a waste of Mr. Pratt's time. I had nothing to do with the murder. Pratt should be looking at Frye's, on the Pete Hagan place in Bridgewater. There are plenty of bad characters there who are capable of such a thing." (Hagan, an Irish immigrant and iron worker, ran a notorious saloon on his property on Oak Street in Bridgewater).

Copeland later related Sturtevant's comment to Pratt, adding that Sturtevant had taken his wife aside and spoken with her privately in an adjoining room while Pratt searched the bedroom.

In the bedroom, Pratt opened a trunk and found a black sack suit. He used Copeland's magnifying glass to uncover potential bloodstains but found none. He examined other clothing in the room and met the same results.

Pratt couldn't find Sturtevant's overcoat, but he did notice a pair of congress boots in the bedroom closet. The boots were damp and looked as though they had been recently washed. He measured them and concluded they were size seven.

The policeman inspected the sole on the left boot and noticed a patch at the toe. He was certain it would match the impression found yesterday at the end of the path, but he didn't want to confront Sturtevant just yet. He left the boots in the bedroom, knowing that Pinkham and Philbrick would be along soon to confiscate them.

Pratt continued to search the rest of the house. Satisfied the coat was not there, he returned to the kitchen. Sturtevant breathed a sigh of relief when Pratt emerged empty-handed.

Pratt was perturbed.

"The coat's not here, Sturtevant. Where is it?" he demanded.

"I don't know," said Sturtevant, shrugging his shoulders. "I'm sure I wore it to work last Friday. Maybe one of my co-workers has borrowed or stolen it."

Pratt was growing increasingly impatient with his suspect; Sturtevant seemed to have an answer for everything.

"I won't be satisfied until I've seen your coat, Sturtevant," Pratt said. "We'll be returning to South Abington to look again."

Sturtevant didn't object.

Abbie rushed to her husband, fear in her eyes. Sturtevant assured her he'd return home as soon as he had convinced Pratt he was not involved in the murders. He kissed his wife lightly on the forehead and hugged little George. Pratt then led him out of the house and back to Copeland's carriage. Abbie sobbed quietly as she gently closed the door and lifted George from the floor. She clutched him tightly to her bosom and, sensing her angst, the toddler began to cry.

Copeland exited the house a few moments later, took the reins, and headed southeast toward Halifax. Pratt was anxious to see Sturtevant's reaction when he saw the bodies of his relatives in the kitchen.

***

At the murder scene, Philbrick and Pinkham re-examined the entire house for any evidence that might have been overlooked. Philbrick noticed a shard of wood on the floor behind the door in Simeon's room and picked it up. He retrieved the cart stake to inspect it more closely and discerned a small void near one end. When he inserted the splinter into the empty space it fit perfectly.

Philbrick stood next to the bed and raised and lowered the stake to simulate the killer's actions.

"Pinkham, I think the murderer was standing about here," Philbrick

53

said. "Watch me as I raise the stake. The arc of my arm brings the end of the stake to the exact point at which the gouges were made in the ceiling."

"It makes sense," Pinkham replied. "And given the castoff pattern of bloodstains on the ceiling and the wall above the fireplace mantel, I suspect that the attacker was right-handed."

Pinkham removed three pieces of bloodstained wallpaper from the wall above Simeon's headboard and the fireplace mantel. He also clipped a piece of the bloody pillowcase lying on the bed and secured all of the items for later analysis.

The constables left the house and walked toward the path to trace the suspect's escape route. Near the gap in the fence at the end of the path they removed the planks Pratt had laid down the day before and studied the footprints.

It was about two-thirty when Philbrick and Pinkham completed their investigation. They placed all of the physical evidence they had collected in a satchel and placed it in the back of their rented carriage. They proceeded west and just beyond Lucas Brook, turned right. They passed Blake's house on Pine Street, crossed the Plymouth road, and clattered across the wood-planked bridge at Stump Brook toward Inglee's store and the one-room schoolhouse on Elm Street.

On the rutted roadway ahead, their attention was drawn to an approaching carriage and, as it neared, they recognized Pratt. Pratt signaled and Philbrick reined in his horse.

"This is Dr. Copeland. The other man is William Sturtevant," said Pratt after Copeland's carriage had pulled alongside. The four men nodded to one another.

Pinkham and Pratt stepped down and walked several yards out of Sturtevant's earshot.

"I noticed some spots on Sturtevant's clothing when I interviewed him at Henry Blake's. I'm certain they're bloodstains," Pratt related. "We just left Sturtevant's house. Sturtevant told me his overcoat was there, but I couldn't find it. I did notice a damp pair of congress boots

54

in his bedroom. They're size seven, the same size as the footprint we found near Dan Blake's and… there was a patch on the toe of one of the boots. I'm sure it's a match."

"What did he say about the boots?"

"I didn't confront him with them. They're still in the bedroom."

"Is anyone at the house, now?"

"Sturtevant's wife is there with a toddler."

"We'll be sure to stop by for the boots. Hopefully, she'll let us in."

"I also dropped in on Drayton and saw the scrip Howland told us about," Pratt said. "I told him you'd be by to collect it."

"We'll take care of it. Have you arrested Sturtevant?" Pinkham asked.

"No, although at this point I think I have enough evidence to do so. I'm taking him by the crime scene. I want to see how he reacts when he sees the bodies. Then I'm taking him back to the shoe factory to look again for his overcoat."

"Has Sturtevant admitted anything?"

"No," Pratt replied.

"Did you ask him where he was at the time of the murders?" asked Pinkham.

"Yes," said Pratt. "And he insisted that he was at home from five o'clock Sunday evening until the next morning when he left his house for work. We'll need to follow up on this alibi."

"Alright, Pratt," said Pinkham. "We'll meet you at Inglee's later this evening."

Pinkham and Philbrick continued northeast over Brown Bread Hill, so-called by locals because of its loaf-like shape, and through the thickly forested stretch of Sodom Woods. They slowed as they passed the houses along the way, scouting for a cart with stakes similar to the murder weapon. The area was sparsely settled; they counted no more than sixteen houses by the time they reached South Hanson.

Philbrick turned southeast on Main Street and passed Drayton's store and the railroad depot. Several hundred yards beyond he abruptly reined in his horse.

"Look there, Pinkham, in that yard," Philbrick exclaimed. "I think we may have found the cart we've been looking for."

The two investigators stepped down and walked into the yard. A hay cart stood not far from the road. The racks that comprised the sides rose up like ribs from the wagon's base. Upon closer inspection, they saw that the stakes in the rack were similar in size and shape to the murder weapon and that a stake was missing from one of the twelve slots in the cart bed. Philbrick returned to the carriage, retrieved the bloodied stake, and effortlessly inserted the tapered end into the vacant slot. It was a perfect match.

Luther Keene house and barn, South Hanson, ca. 1880

Containing their excitement at this good fortune, they walked up to the door of the house and knocked. Pinkham identified himself and his colleague to the middle-aged woman who answered the door. She introduced herself as Sophronia Josselyn and cordially invited the two policemen into her home, gesturing to seats at her kitchen table. She offered them refreshment, but they politely declined.

"We'd like to ask you a few questions about the hay cart in your yard. Does it belong to you?" asked Pinkham.

"No, it belongs to my father, Luther Keene. This is his house. I've been living with him since my husband died four years ago."

"Is your father home, now?

"No, he's gone out. I don't know when to expect him."

Josselyn's eyes widened.

"Is something wrong?" she asked.

"No, ma'am," Pinkham said. "There's no cause for alarm. We can't discuss why we're interested in the cart but, I promise you, our investigation has nothing to do with you or your father. We noticed that a stake is missing from the cart rack. How long has it been like that?"

"I didn't realize there was one missing," Josselyn remarked.

"Have you noticed anyone acting suspiciously near the cart recently?"

"No, but I rarely go out in cold weather, and I avoid the windows for the draft," she explained.

"Some of the stakes seem fairly new," said Pinkham. "Did your father add them?"

"No, Bill Jefferson, a sawyer just up the road, borrowed the cart last January. A few of the stakes were split and broken so he replaced them."

"So the cart was whole when Jefferson brought it back?"

"Yes, as far as I know."

"Has anyone other than Jefferson borrowed it since January?"

"No, I don't think so."

Both officers thanked Josselyn, apologized for intruding on her time, and left for Sturtevant's house.

Chapter Five: An Arrest

Pinkham and Philbrick returned to their carriage and drove three hundred yards southeast to the house at Main and High Street where Sturtevant boarded.

"Not far from Luther Keene's cart, is it?" Pinkham remarked to his partner.

"No, it isn't, but we need to be cautious," Philbrick replied. "It's more likely than not that Sturtevant took the stake, but that cart is accessible to anyone walking by."

The old Cape-style home, originally built by Ebenezer Keene in 1821, was divided into two separate residences. Sturtevant and his family occupied one side, while a widower, Daniel Daland, and his live-in housekeeper, Lydia Reed, inhabited the other.

A young woman heavy with child answered their knock on the front door when they arrived at about four o'clock. A small boy was clutching her leg.

"Are you Mrs. Sturtevant?" Philbrick asked.

"Yes, I am," Abbie nervously answered.

"I'm State Detective Philbrick. This is Detective Pinkham. May we come in?"

Abbie widened the door and allowed the two policemen into the house.

"We're investigating the Halifax murders, Mrs. Sturtevant. May we have a look around?"

Abbie picked up her son and broke into tears. She told the officers that Officer Pratt had just left and had already searched the house.

"Do you think my Willie has something to do with the murders?" she sobbed.

"We can't discuss the case, ma'am, but at this stage of the

investigation, we're not going to rule out anyone as a suspect," Philbrick answered.

"Shouldn't my husband be here while you search?"

"It's not necessary. You live here with him. If you cooperate and consent to the search it might help him," said Pinkham.

"Was your husband home last Sunday evening?" Pinkham asked.

"Yes, he was."

"Was he here the whole night?"

Abbie averted her eyes.

"No, he wasn't," she said softly. "He left the house sometime after seven-thirty and didn't return until a late hour."

This incriminating statement stunned the two policemen; it clearly contradicted Sturtevant's statement to Pratt that he had remained at home throughout the evening of the murders, but they knew the court could not compel Abbie to give testimony against her husband under the rule of spousal privilege. She could voluntarily agree to testify, but both officers knew this was unlikely. If Abbie refused to appear as a witness, neither officer could testify as to her statement because it was legally inadmissible as hearsay evidence.

"Did he tell you where he went?"

"No," Abbie murmured.

The officers weren't sure if Abbie had let slip that her husband had gone out or if she had purposely informed them, but she refused to answer any other questions.

Pinkham and Philbrick went into the bedroom and closed the door. Hanging on a nail behind the door was a gray, double-breasted overcoat. Pratt had either missed it or Sturtevant's wife had hung it there after Pratt left.

Pinkham unhooked the coat from the nail and laid it flat on the bed. He noticed numerous reddish-brown spots on the breast of the coat and near the lower button hole.

"I think these are bloodstains, Philbrick. Have a look."

Philbrick studied the spots and agreed.

Abbie Standish Sturtevant crooned to her child as she paced back and forth in the kitchen. The gentle song belied the turmoil of her thoughts as she struggled to comprehend how she and her family might survive still more misfortune.

Her maternal grandfather, Albert Edson, a stone mason, had been killed in a rock explosion in East Bridgewater in June 1852. Five months later, Abbie's father, John Standish, a fifth generation descendant of Captain Myles Standish, had succumbed to the ravages of consumption, leaving her mother, Lucy, widowed and destitute. They found refuge with her mother's brother, Albert Edson, Jr., and stayed with him until 1854, when her mother married Orrin Parris, a widowed local farmer nearly forty years her mother's senior.

Abbie's step-sister, Lydia, was born the next year, followed by Emma, in 1858, and Edith, in 1860. The joy of a growing family was quickly and brutally tempered when Emma, emaciated by consumption, died in the summer of 1859, and extinguished when Edith died of croup in the winter of 1862. Two step-brothers, Charles and William, followed, but William died in infancy.

Orrin moved his new family to South Hanson after he married Lucy Standish. Abbie met Willie Sturtevant there. Willie was working in a shoe shop and boarded on the Harding farm just over the Hanson town line in East Bridgewater. She knew that Willie had little money, that he had worked sporadically, and that his prospects for the future looked bleak. He also had a knack for finding trouble, but she loved him anyway. She was only eighteen when Reverend Joseph Horton married them at the South Hanson Baptist Church three years prior.

Just short of a year later, Abbie gave birth to George. Now she was in a delicate condition again, expecting a second child soon. How would she manage if Willie was sent to prison for murdering his uncles and the Buckley woman? Her shoulders slumped and her eyes filled with tears as an overwhelming wave of fear and hopelessness swept over her.

In the bedroom closet, Pinkham found the congress boots Pratt had seen earlier. He picked them up and, like Pratt, noticed they were uniformly damp, as if someone had recently washed them. He also noted the patch on the sole of the left boot that Pratt had mentioned.

"Seems likely he washed these. To remove bloodstains, maybe?" Pinkham posited.

Congress boots similar to Sturtevant's

"Likely, but I wonder why he didn't do the same with the overcoat," Philbrick mused.

The officers searched the other rooms in the house and inspected the attic. The only other evidence they found was a bloodstained piece of brown wrapping paper from the floor of a closet in the kitchen.

Both investigators were certain Abbie Sturtevant knew more than she had revealed. Did her husband tell her where he was going when he left on Sunday night and what he intended to do? Did she wait for him to return? If she had not known his intentions, did she help him, when he returned, to clean his boots to remove any visible bloodstains? The answers, if she were willing to provide them, would be invaluable yet inadmissible. Even if they had sufficient evidence to show her complicity, they knew it to be highly unlikely, given her expectant condition, that the district attorney would consider prosecuting her for murder, conspiracy to commit murder, or as an accessory before or after the fact.

The two officers didn't want Abbie to know what they had found so, while Pinkham distracted her in conversation, Philbrick quietly gathered the evidence, took it outside, and stowed it in his carriage.

"We're finished, Mrs. Sturtevant. We apologize for any inconvenience," said Pinkham. "Good day to you."

The two policemen emerged from Sturtevant's house and found a woman standing in the yard. She approached and identified herself as Lydia Reed, the live-in housekeeper who shared the house with the Sturtevants. Philbrick asked about Willie Sturtevant's movements in the last few days.

"I saw him today when he came out of the house and got into a carriage with two other men. Before that, I saw him here, at the house, on Sunday afternoon. I left after that and didn't return until late the same night."

In response to Philbrick's questioning, Reed said she did not know if the Sturtevants were up when she returned. She did state, however, that sometime during the night she had heard what she thought to be the rattle of stove covers on two occasions.

"Did you see the Sturtevants the next morning?"

"No, but I heard activity in their part of the house at about five o'clock, which seemed unusual to me because I've never heard them up so early. The husband came to me at about that time and asked to borrow my scraper to clean out his stove."

The investigators thanked the housekeeper and, after boarding their carriage, reversed their direction and headed back toward the depot and Drayton's grocery store, a quarter-mile away.

"Mr. Drayton?" Pinkham asked as he entered the store. "We're State Detectives Pinkham and Philbrick. We're told you have some scrip here for us."

"Yes," Drayton replied. "Officer Pratt was here earlier and told me you'd be by."

Drayton repeated to the officers that Sturtevant had stopped in the store on Sunday, February 15, and had purchased several articles on credit. Sturtevant returned the next day and paid his debt with two, crisp pieces of scrip in ten-cent denominations. Drayton produced the scrip at Pinkham's request and Pinkham could see that the money was similar to the scrip he had seen at the Sturtevant farm. It was solid circumstantial evidence.

"I'll have to take this scrip with me, Mr. Drayton," Pinkham said.

"The district attorney may call you as a witness in the event of an arrest. I'd like you to initial each of these bills in my presence. If the prosecutor decides to use the scrip as evidence, there will be no confusion as to how I came into its possession."

***

Pratt, Sturtevant, and Copeland proceeded out of Sodom Woods, over Brown Bread Hill, and past the district school and Inglee's store. They crossed Plymouth Street and continued along Pine Street in the direction of Thompson Street.

Sturtevant bristled as they passed Daniel Blake's house on the right. He had spent his early years with his parents and siblings in this house that had once belonged to his grandfather. He was six years old when his mother died there in 1854 and his father took him and his siblings to East Bridgewater. His Aunt Margaret and her husband, Dan Blake, moved into his grandfather's house. He remembered how his sister, Mary, had died when he was eight years old and how the next year his father had abandoned his four sons and fled to Maine. He'd never forgive him for deserting them.

Copeland turned left on Thompson Street and rattled up to the Sturtevant farmhouse shortly after three. He stopped the carriage about twenty feet from the barn and the three men climbed out.

While Copeland tethered his horses on a fence and covered them with blankets, William Sturtevant, without waiting for direction from Pratt, strode intently toward the barn.

"Where are you going, Sturtevant?" Pratt asked, trying to keep up.

Sturtevant ignored him, opened the barn door, and stepped inside. The moment Pratt entered, Sturtevant turned suddenly with an awkward motion and exited. Pratt got the sense that Sturtevant had discarded something before he went out. Taking a closer look near the threshold, Pratt found a tight roll of bills on the floor by the haymow. He picked it up and put it in his pocket.

Pratt said nothing when he came out of the barn to rejoin Sturtevant and Copeland. The trio walked from the barn to the house and knocked on the porch door, but no one answered. Pratt tried the door, found it unlocked, and stepped inside. Someone had removed the parrot and its cage. He called out for Judah Keene and was met with silence. Pratt motioned to the others and together they made their way to the kitchen where the three shrouded bodies were still laid out on the biers. Flickering candlelight cast sinister shadows upon the macabre spectacle.

Sturtevant showed no emotion when Pratt exposed the bodies. Pratt replaced the coverings, left Sturtevant with Copeland at the house, and returned to the barn. He removed the roll from his pocket and counted two hundred and eight dollars. The bills were identical to the 1863 scrip he had seen at the murder house the day before. One of the bills was smeared with what appeared to be a bloodstain. He searched the rest of the barn to see if Sturtevant had discarded anything else but he found nothing.

Pratt returned to the house and asked Copeland to take them back to Blake's shoe shop.

They arrived in South Abington at about twilight and found Henry Blake still in his office. Pratt accompanied Sturtevant through the building to search for his coat but it wasn't there. Pratt took Copeland aside.

"I'll be taking Sturtevant back to Halifax, Doctor," Pratt said to Copeland. "Thank you for your help today."

"It was a modest contribution to solving this awful crime, Pratt. Safe journey," Copeland replied and departed for home.

Pratt retrieved his horse and carriage from Blake's carriage house and headed for Halifax with Sturtevant in tow.

***

Pinkham and Philbrick found twenty-six-year-old William Jefferson at his home in South Hanson. Philbrick showed Jefferson the stake and he identified it immediately as one of several stakes he had cut for Mrs. Josselyn's cart the previous January. Philbrick, looking at the plain wooden dowel, wondered how he could be so certain it was his work. Jefferson pointed out some distinctive marks left by the dull hatchet he had used to trim it.

"I can show you where I cut it," Jefferson offered.

The sawyer led the two investigators to a wooded area nearby.

"What's this about?" he asked them.

"We can't say, but the stake is very important to our investigation."

"Right over there," Jefferson said as he pointed to a birch stump in a clearing.

"That stump is evidence now. What would it take to dig it up?"

"Let me get a shovel and ax. I'll be back in a few minutes."

When Jefferson returned, he dug around the stump and hacked away until it was uprooted. Philbrick shook it free of debris and tossed it in his carriage.

"You may be needed as a witness at trial in the event of an arrest," Philbrick said. "The court will send you a summons to appear. Thank you for your help."

***

Pratt left Henry Blake's carriage house with Sturtevant at six-thirty. Little was said between the two men during the eight-mile trip in the darkness. They arrived at Edwin Inglee's house in Halifax at about eight o'clock. Pratt found Inglee, Constable Crocker, Charles Paine, and several women he did not know inside Crocker's quarters. Pinkham and Philbrick were also present, having arrived about an hour before. Pratt enlisted Crocker to keep a watchful eye on Sturtevant and went into an adjoining room with Pinkham and Philbrick.

Pratt was surprised but pleased when Pinkham showed him the overcoat they found in Sturtevant's South Hanson home. Pinkham also showed him the congress boots they recovered from the bedroom closet.

The three lawmen discussed the case at length and agreed they had probable cause to place Sturtevant under arrest for the murders. They emerged from the room and confronted Sturtevant to whom Pratt pronounced, "William Sturtevant, I now formally arrest you for the murders of your uncles and Mary Buckley. You are not obliged to answer questions."

"I am not guilty," Sturtevant blurted, clenching his fists. "Ask any questions you want. I can tell where I was."

"Then maybe you'd better explain," said Pratt.

"I told you I was at Blanchard's in East Bridgewater on Sunday. I left his house and arrived home at about five o'clock. I didn't go out the rest of the night. I went to bed at about ten o'clock and got up again at midnight and fixed the fire. I got up on Monday morning at five and went to work."

"Did you spend any money on Monday?"

"No, but on Saturday night I bought a shin at Drayton's and paid fifty cents for it and at the same time I bought a fish, which I got on credit."

Philbrick produced the overcoat he and Pinkham had found in Sturtevant's bedroom. Sturtevant stirred uncomfortably as he sat on the living room sofa.

"Do you recognize this coat, Sturtevant?" Philbrick asked.

"Yes, it's mine," he admitted, stone-faced.

"We think these are bloodstains," said Pratt, pointing at the front of the coat. "Do you have anything to say now?"

"So what? I told you about the beef shin."

"These aren't stains from the shin, Sturtevant. You killed those poor people."

"No. I told you I had nothing to do with the murders."

Pratt felt he had Sturtevant in a vulnerable position and took advantage in an attempt to resolve the White robbery. If he could get the scoundrel to admit to the theft, maybe he'd break down and confess to the murders.

"What about Joel White's gold, Sturtevant? Are you ready to admit you stole it?"

"I've told you before, Mr. Pratt. I had nothing to do with that, either."

Pratt asked the ladies to step into another room and, after they had withdrawn, he closed the door and ordered Sturtevant to remove his pants. Sturtevant rolled his eyes in exasperation and sighed. He lowered his pants and sat down on a sofa, then reached down to raise his pant leg and slip off his left shoe. Using his hands as cover, he furtively removed something from his sock and slipped it under the sofa. Philbrick advanced.

"Slide over, Sturtevant," Philbrick growled and reached under the seat to find two pieces of scrip – one in the amount of one hundred dollars, the other twenty dollars. The bills were of the same 1863 issue he had seen at the murder house and the floor of the barn.

"What's this, Sturtevant?" Pratt demanded.

Sturtevant offered the same explanation he had given to Constable George Boynton when he was arrested in 1866 with the stolen horse.

"It's bounty money from the war."

"Take off both shoes and give me your socks."

Sturtevant removed his shoes and socks and handed them to Pratt. He was wearing two pairs of socks on each foot. Pratt turned the socks inside out, checked the shoes, and satisfied himself that there was no additional money or evidence in either.

"Let me have your pants, Sturtevant."

Pratt searched the pants and discovered two holes in one of the pockets. He knew right away that Sturtevant had worn the pants on the night of the murders. How else could he explain the coins found along the path between the house and Blake's? Pratt carefully examined the pants for bloodstains, found none, and tossed them back to the prisoner.

Pratt turned to Crocker while Sturtevant dressed.

"Will you ride with me to Plymouth jail in the morning? Pinkham and Philbrick will be staying behind to continue their investigation."

"Of course," replied Crocker.

Pratt turned to Edwin Inglee and asked if he could accommodate them overnight.

"Certainly," said Inglee. He led Pratt, his two colleagues, and

Sturtevant up a flight of stairs to two bedrooms in another part of the house.

"Philbrick, why don't you and Pinkham take the bedroom on the left? I'll take the one on the right with Sturtevant. I suggest we guard the prisoner in shifts. I'll take the first shift and wake one of you in three hours."

Philbrick and Pinkham agreed and all bid each other good-night.

Chapter Six: The Funeral

At six o'clock on Wednesday morning, February 18, Constable Crocker harnessed his horse and carriage and, with State Constable Pratt, ushered Sturtevant from the house. Several people were outside Inglee's store and had heard about Sturtevant's arrest.

"Did you murder those people?" one of the men dared ask.

Sturtevant shot him an ugly, defiant look and answered, "I'm not guilty of anything."

"Who do you think did it?" the man taunted.

"How do you suppose I know?" Sturtevant snorted as Pratt tightened his grip on his prisoner's arm and steered him toward the carriage.

As Pratt, Crocker, and Sturtevant set off on the Plymouth road toward the courthouse, Pinkham and Philbrick finished a hearty breakfast at Inglee's and left for Blake's house on Pine Street with the congress boots. At the gap in the fence opposite Blake's house, Pinkham removed the boards covering the muddy tracks. Philbrick placed the sole of the left congress boot they had found in Sturtevant's house alongside one of the imprints and saw that it was a mirror image. He particularly noted the line of leather on the sole and the patch made by re-lapping the boot.

***

Alpheus Harmon, the warden of Plymouth County Jail and House of Correction, greeted Pratt, Crocker, and their prisoner at the main gate. Harmon managed Plymouth County's two-building compound for the detention of prisoners and convicts on Court Street in Plymouth, just behind the county courthouse. The original building, constructed in 1820, had functioned as both jail and house of correction until 1853, when the county transferred long-term inmates convicted of serious offenses to a new, separate house of correction on the same site. Inmates serving time for lesser offenses, or awaiting trial, remained at the jail.

Designed by architect Jonathan Preston, the new, two-story, red brick house of correction measured nineteen hundred square feet and contained thirty-two cells, each one measuring four-and-a-half-feet by eight feet with an eight-foot high ceiling. The second floor of the building served as a workshop.

In 1870, Sheriff James Bates again combined the two populations when he transferred prisoners held in the jail to a segregated section of the house of correction and converted the old jail into a storehouse. Sturtevant entered the new house of correction to be held pending arraignment.

Inside the small guardroom, a clerk entered Sturtevant's place of residence, age, and physical description into the jail ledger. A turnkey then led the prisoner to a cell on the main floor where he was stripped, searched, and supplied with prison garb to replace his personal clothes, which Pratt seized as evidence. A loud clang resounded through the corridor of the jail when the turnkey slammed the cell door to lock it.

Warden Harmon, described by a *Boston Globe* reporter as "a tall, stout, strong figure" with a "big, full beard and straightforward face," was well acquainted with Sturtevant. He had served as a turnkey at the jail during Sturtevant's one-year commitment for horse stealing in 1866. In his brief period of incarceration, Sturtevant had proven, as Harmon had put it to an *Old Colony Memorial* correspondent, to be a man of "dissimulation and cunning contrivance" and deserving of "a jealous eye." Harmon warned his officers to be especially vigilant, as Sturtevant would make every effort to escape if given the chance.

Pratt and Crocker left Sturtevant in Harmon's custody and proceeded to the courthouse where Pratt found District Attorney Asa French in his office. French was a formidable prosecutor whose reputation was burnished when he prosecuted John Moran for the murder of Constable Charles Packard in Stoughton three years earlier.

Moran was found guilty of second-degree murder and received a life sentence.

The forty-four-year-old French, a Braintree, Massachusetts, native, had graduated from Yale in 1851 and had received a bachelor of law degree from Harvard Law School in 1853. He was admitted to practice law in the Supreme Court of New York that same year but soon returned to Boston for further study and was admitted to the Massachusetts bar in 1854. Massachusetts Governor William Claflin appointed him as southeastern district attorney for Norfolk and Plymouth counties in 1870.

Pratt summarized for French the events of the previous day and the circumstances of Sturtevant's arrest. French documented the list of items Pratt, Philbrick, and Pinkham had seized as evidence, as well as the names of witnesses they had interviewed, and informed Pratt that he would be in the courtroom for Sturtevant's arraignment later that afternoon.

At about 1:45 p.m., a turnkey removed Sturtevant from his cell. Two deputy sheriffs shackled him and placed a heavy woolen blanket over his shoulders before leading him out of the jail for the brief march to the courthouse. They entered a rear door and passed the blanket to another deputy, then ascended the steps to the second floor courtroom and placed Sturtevant in the dock.

The old courthouse, built in 1820 and renovated in 1857, was then, as it is today, a two-story Georgian-style structure of red brick standing in Plymouth's Court Square. Beneath a copper-domed cupola, the brick façade at the front of the building was painted to imitate brownstone, a popular style of the era. It was adorned with stately, rectangular windows in arched recesses and a statue of the goddess of justice

Plymouth County Courthouse, 1880

high in a central niche. Beneath Lady Justice was a marble tablet bearing the seal of Plymouth County, inherited from its predecessor, Plymouth Colony.

Twin entrances, north and south, on the front of the courthouse were trimmed with white columns supporting ornate porticos. They provided access to corridors that ran east and west through the building. The south entrance opened to the first-floor offices of the clerk of courts, the register of deeds, probate and chancery, the district attorney, and the county treasurer. A stairway at the north entrance ascended to the spacious courtroom, the court law library, two jury rooms, and two other rooms for the judges. Gas lighting softly illuminated the interior, and coal fed the furnaces that provided heat.

The judges' bench and the rail surrounding the bar in the courtroom were of mahogany, as were the jury box and witness stand. Tables and chairs for the defense team and the prosecutors stood within the bar. At one end of the jury box was a station for the sheriff and the prisoner's dock. The court crier sat in a similar station on the opposite side of the room. Pine wainscoting along the perimeter of the courtroom, doors, window casings, and bookshelves behind the judge's bench were stained a dark reddish-brown to resemble mahogany. Above the wainscoting, plastered walls were painted in neutral tones. Two chandeliers hung suspended from the plastered ceiling, and sconces were affixed to the wall behind the judges' bench.

***

"All rise," barked the court crier as Judge William Osborne emerged from his chambers at 2:00 p.m. and stepped briskly to the bench. Osborne was a short man with a receding hairline and a drooping moustache whose unassuming appearance belied his underlying character; he had received the Congressional Medal of Honor for heroic actions in the Civil War Battle of Malvern Hill.

"Hear ye! Hear ye! All persons having anything to do before the Supreme Judicial Court now sitting in Plymouth, give your attention and you shall be heard. God save the Commonwealth and this honorable court," the crier pronounced. "Be seated."

Judge Osborne glanced briefly at the prisoner in the dock then motioned for the clerk of court, William Whitman, to call the case.

"William Everett Sturtevant, rise," Whitman directed.

William E. Sturtevant

"William E. Sturtevant, you are charged with the most heinous crime known to our laws," declared Osborne. "I deem it proper to say that if you desire the aid and advice of counsel in this matter that an opportunity to do so should be afforded you."

Sturtevant declined the court's offer of counsel so Judge Osborne proceeded to the formal citation of the complaint against him.

"William E. Sturtevant, what say you to this complaint – are you guilty or not guilty?" asked the clerk when Osborne finished.

"Not guilty," the prisoner declared.

"Are you ready for your trial?" Osborne asked.

"Yes," Sturtevant replied. "I am."

A *Boston Globe* correspondent seated in the courtroom conveyed his impressions of Sturtevant's demeanor in an article published the next day: "Sturtevant seemed singularly cool and unconcerned. He appears perfectly indifferent to the whole proceeding, and professes a confidence in being able to free himself from the accusation."

District Attorney French addressed the court with a brief synopsis of the murders and the subsequent investigation, then called Constable Pratt to the witness stand to describe the events leading up to the prisoner's arrest.

"I arrested William Sturtevant on Tuesday night in Halifax. He expressed no surprise at the arrest but said that he was not guilty. I found a coat belonging to him at his house," Pratt testified, hedging somewhat on the facts, "the front and sleeves of which were literally covered with fresh blood. The prisoner admitted this was his coat and one which he usually wore. I found blood stains upon his hat and numerous spots of blood upon his collar and vest. He made no explanation of how these stains came upon his clothing, though requested to do so."

Sturtevant glared at Pratt. He had told him about the beef shin, yet Pratt never mentioned it.

"We then searched him. He wore two pairs of stockings. On one of his feet between the stockings I found a $100 bill and a $20 dollar bill. In his vest pocket I found a $5 bill, and about his clothes several pieces of twenty-five and ten cent fractional currency, nearly new of the issue of 1863. This currency corresponded exactly with currency found in and about the room and bureau where Simeon Sturtevant, one of the murdered men, was found; there were also some pieces of coin similar to those found in the house.

"The prisoner made no explanation of how he came by this money. The prisoner admitted to me that he was the nephew of the deceased and one of the heirs to his property."

Sturtevant frowned. He had told Pratt about the bounty money and he had never mentioned anything to the constable about an inheritance.

"I am satisfied," Judge Osborne said, "that the prisoner ought to be held for trial. Although the evidence fell far short of that which would warrant his conviction, it raises such strong suspicions of his connection with the bloody deed that I feel it my duty to commit him, and thus afford the government an opportunity of pursuing the investigation unhindered."

Osborne then ordered Sturtevant held without bail until the June term of the Supreme Judicial Court.

Pratt and Crocker headed back to Halifax after the arraignment to continue their investigation. French had given Pratt specific instructions to interview Henry Blake and any other employees who might have associated with Sturtevant at the South Abington shoe factory. French wanted to know more about Sturtevant's financial condition.

***

As the arraignment proceeded in Plymouth, Margaret Blake, Angeline Dow, and other women of the Sturtevant and Buckley families, prepared the Sturtevant house, as was the custom, for visitation and a funeral on Thursday. The women solemnly removed the sheets covering the bodies and dutifully groomed each of the deceased before clothing them in their finest apparel. Curtains were drawn and all the furniture, with the exception of two small tables, was removed from the sitting room to accommodate the three wooden coffins that had arrived earlier in the morning. The women adorned the fireplace mantel, the doorways, and window frames with black crepe, and draped white veils over mirrors and picture glass. They arrayed candles on the mantelpiece and on the tables and tacked a black crepe wreath with ribbons to the outside of the front door.

On Wednesday evening the bodies were laid out – Mary reposed in a rosewood coffin adorned with a decorative metal plate bearing the inscription, *Mary Buckley – Died February 15, 1874 – Aged 68 years.* The Sturtevant brothers lay in coffins of black walnut lined with white cassimere. Plain metal plates inscribed with their respective names and ages were fastened to the coffin lids.

The coffins were left open for viewing despite the severity of the victims' wounds; apart from some residual bruising, the serene faces of Mary and Thomas showed little evidence of the violence inflicted upon them. In contrast, the shattered facial bones of Simeon's face grossly distorted his features.

Mary was dressed in a black robe with a white linen collar about her neck and shoulders. An archaic lace handkerchief was folded neatly upon her bosom. Simeon and Thomas were attired in black robes, white vests, and neckcloths.

On the frigid morning of Thursday, February 19, more than two thousand mourners, sympathizers, curiosity seekers, and newspapermen filed through the candlelit sitting room to pay their final respects and to console family members. Many openly wept; some stifled gasps, others remained thin-lipped and silent as they gazed upon the ghastly corpses, a vision indelibly imprinted in their minds.

Men wearing black crepe armbands on their overcoats and women in bonnets that matched the dark shawls and cloaks they wore over black mourning dresses, clustered about the yard after passing through the house, many fondly recalling the lives of the Sturtevants and their devoted housekeeper. The brothers had held a prominent place in the community, especially during the war, building upon their land holdings throughout town with the steady procurement of additional woodland, arable pasture, and meadow. They kept to themselves, for the most part, but enjoyed the goodwill of friends, neighbors, and acquaintances far and near.

Much of the family's notoriety drew from the Sturtevant legacy which began in America about 1641, when Samuel Sturtevant emigrated from England to Plymouth. He married Ann Lee of Plymouth three years after his arrival, and together they had nine children. Their son, Samuel, Jr., married Mercy Cornish about 1676. Samuel and Mercy had nine children. Their fifth child, William, married Fear Cushman in 1707 at Plymouth, and they produced a son, Isaac, who married Sarah Fuller at Plympton in 1731. Among the issue of Isaac and Sarah Sturtevant was Simeon, who married Ruth Tomson at Halifax in 1764 and who came to own the house built in 1715 by Ruth's grandfather.

Simeon and Ruth's first born son, Simeon, Jr., married Margaret Johnson in Kingston in 1790. At his death in 1851, he left portions of his homestead, barn, buttery, and cellar, as well as fourteen acres of land, a piece of woodland, and a section of Cedar Swamp to his now deceased sons, Simeon and Thomas.

Mary Buckley was highly regarded by her friends and neighbors as a kind and generous woman who never hesitated to help those in need. She had spent most of her life in Bridgewater, boarding with her widowed mother in various homes. Mary supported her mother as a dressmaker, but her earnings were meager and they fell into debt. Her mother became gravely ill in 1856 and remained under a doctor's care until her death in 1858, at the age of eighty-five. After the settlement of her mother's personal estate, Mary was able to meet the financial obligations she and her mother had amassed.

Mary, no longer supporting two, sustained herself with the proceeds of her tailoring skills while boarding at the Perkins and Edson homes in Bridgewater. She was thrifty and enterprising but charitable, often sharing a portion of her savings with the sick and needy.

Mary's mother, Deborah (Johnson) Buckley, was the sister of Thomas Sturtevant's mother, Margaret (Johnson) Sturtevant. Cousin Thomas had pleaded with her since the death of his wife Mary, in the summer of 1865, to move in with him to keep house and care for Simeon. By 1870, Mary had relented.

Shortly before the murders, she had confided to a Bridgewater friend that she was unhappy in Halifax. A sense of foreboding had enveloped her at the old farmhouse. Breaking into tears, she explained to her friend that she wasn't unhappy with her cousins; it was the ancient house itself that bothered her.

"A gloom seems settled about the place," Mary remarked, "and I can't tell why I feel so." She had considered moving back to Bridgewater and had even sent some of her things back to the boarding house where she had lived but had misgivings adding, "...but then I don't know but that it is my duty to stay; Thomas is getting old, and poor Simeon is so weak in his mind he is a great care, and if I don't stay things won't go on right."

Reverend Horace Walker, pastor of the Bridgewater Congregational Church, arrived at the Sturtevant home at noon to conduct the funeral services. After brief remarks and a blessing by the minister, the coffin lids were nailed shut. Black palls were placed over the coffins before they were borne outside to three horse-drawn hearses. Ten pallbearers ceremoniously attended each of the coffins. Family and friends followed the hearses on foot and in carriages in a solemn, one-mile procession past Tomson Cemetery to the Halifax Congregational Church.

At the church, the pallbearers somberly lowered the coffins from the hearses, carried them inside, and placed them on biers in front of the chancel. Pews on the main floor and the gallery of the church were filled to overflowing. Hundreds of mourners spilled into the vestry beneath the sanctuary and outside onto the front lawn.

Reverend Courtland DeNormandie of Kingston assisted Reverend Walker in the service, which began at one o'clock with a hymn sung by a choir of seven townspeople, accompanied by the plaintive sounds of a reedy seraphine organ. Reverend Walker ascended the pulpit and opened with Psalm 20.

> "The Lord hear thee in the day of trouble; the name of the God of Jacob defend thee; send thee help from the sanctuary, and strengthen thee out of Zion; Remember all thy offerings, and accept thy burnt sacrifice; Selah. Grant thee according to thine own heart, and fulfill all thy counsel. We will rejoice in thy salvation, and in the name of our God we will set up our banners: the Lord fulfill all thy petitions; now know I that the Lord saveth his anointed; he will hear him from his holy heaven with the saving strength of his right hand. Some trust in chariots, and some in horses: but we will remember the name of the Lord our God. They are brought down and fallen: but we are risen, and stand upright. Save, Lord: let the king hear us when we call."

Reverend DeNormandie took the pulpit at the conclusion of several hymns and addressed the congregation.

"We meet here as never before," he began. "God grant no such occasion may ever again call us together. Neighbors, friends, and kindred have often gathered in this quiet town in tenderest [*sic*] sympathy with hearts most deeply moved. There have before been times when from a wide circuit the steps of all the dwellers have been turned sadly and slowly to a desolate home. But the bell never sounded as it has this day. Never did this people so look into each other's faces, every eye dimmed with tears, every heart saddened, overwhelmed with awe; never did the shadow of death rest down so deep, so dark, shrouding in its terrible gloom all things, bringing the black pall over the brightness of the midday sun. Were there ever such sights in the hours of our recollection as those since the sight of that day? These lessons, shall they be sealed to our hearts? How should our estimate of the value of the sacredness of life be heightened as we feel now what a mystery life is?"

Several ladies seated at the front of the church wept quietly and dabbed their eyes with frilly, white handkerchiefs embroidered in black.

"They were lovely in their lives, and in their death they were not divided. Being a stranger somewhat to the old gentlemen it is not fitting that I should speak to neighbors, friends, and kinsmen, among whom they were born, lived, and died. But she who died with them had a home in the hearts that are all around. I came from a place where her memory is blessed and I walked the streets that the feet have trod on errands of mercy. I entered homes into which she often came a ministering angel; I met hearts that throb with the love of children; brothers, sisters to her – hearts that call her more than friend, mother, kindred – in gratitude and affection, if not in blood. Her life was laid a sacrifice to her sense of duty, her longing to benefit and bless."

DeNormandie paused and looked out over the congregation, then solemnly stepped down from the pulpit and joined Reverend Walker in front of the chancel. As the choir began to sing, the pallbearers rose from their pews in the nave and took their places along each of the coffins. Women sobbed to the sounds of the seraphine's mournful dirge as the pallbearers proceeded up the center aisle and out of the church to the hearses.

79

Reverend Walker and a small group of friends and family followed the hearse containing Mary Buckley's remains to a small cemetery in North Plympton where she was laid to rest in the family plot of her parents, Henry and Deborah, and her sister, Angeline.

Many others accompanied the bodies of Simeon and Thomas back to Tomson Cemetery, where friends had opened graves atop a small hill overlooking the burial place of the brothers' forebears. The wind whispered through the pines and leafless limbs clattered under leaden skies as Rev.  DeNormandie offered a final prayer. Family members lowered the coffins and, shovelful by shovelful, covered the remains for eternity.

Slate markers etched with each man's name were later erected. Inscribed in bold letters beneath the names, reproachful and accusatory, is the simple epitaph, "MURDERED."

Chapter Seven: The Investigation Continued

Pratt returned to Henry Blake's shoe shop on the day of the funeral and interviewed Blake and his employees.

"Has Sturtevant worked here long?" Pratt asked Blake.

"I hired him in mid-January," Blake responded.

"How much is he paid?"

"I paid him ten dollars on February second. I still owe him twenty-one dollars for work he did after that."

Blake escorted Pratt through a door to the shop. They were met by the distinctive smell of leather and dye and the din of commerce as workers cut and assembled shoes and boots at rows of tables. Blake interrupted Frank Osborne, who was working at a sewing machine, and introduced him to Pratt.

"How long have you known William Sturtevant?" asked Pratt.

"I've known him for some time, although he's only been here for four or five weeks," Osborne answered. "He and I frequently work alongside each other. Sturtevant would tack soles to the shoe vamps and pass them to me for sewing."

"Did you see him last Monday?"

"Yes, he came in that morning, and he was here the next morning."

"Was there anything unusual about his demeanor on either day?"

"No, he acted as he always did, but…" Osborne stammered.

"But what?" Pratt pressed.

"Well, I had loaned him seventy-five cents a short time ago. Honestly, I didn't expect to get it back, but he made good on the debt on Monday morning. He paid me with three twenty-five cent pieces of scrip. It seemed odd that he had scrip – you don't see much of that these days."

"What became of the scrip?" Pratt inquired.

"I still have it," said Osborne. He reached into his pocket, pulled out the three bills, and handed them to Pratt, who instantly recognized them.

"Mr. Osborne, this scrip may have a connection to the recent Halifax murders. I know it will create an inconvenience for you, but I'd like to keep it."

"By all means, Mr. Pratt. I read about Sturtevant's arrest in the newspaper. I probably should have contacted you about the scrip before this," Osborne said sheepishly, "but I never put it together."

Blake walked down a few work stations and introduced Pratt to another of Sturtevant's co-workers, twenty-two-year-old William Hill of South Hanson. Hill said he had taken the train with Sturtevant on Monday morning from South Hanson depot. They walked the two-thirds of a mile to Blake's shop from the South Abington station and, in conversation, Sturtevant mentioned that he was tired because he had walked to and from the East Bridgewater house of his brother-in-law, Daniel Blanchard, the day before.

"Did you ever have occasion to loan money to Sturtevant?" Pratt asked.

"Yes," Hill replied, "he borrowed seventy-five or eighty cents from me at the end of January or beginning of February."

"Did he pay you back?"

"Yes, he paid me back a few days after I loaned the money to him."

That exchange was well before the murders. Pratt surmised that Sturtevant likely paid the debt with a portion of the ten dollars in wages he had received from Henry Blake on the second of February.

***

On Friday, February 20, Pratt, Philbrick, and Pinkham returned to the murder scene. Judah Keene, still present as caretaker, met them at the door and led them to the sitting room.

"I found more scrip in the bureau on Tuesday and Wednesday. I put it inside this small box," Keene said as he lifted the box from the bureau drawer and handed it to Pratt.

Pratt looked inside and saw twenty-five and fifty-cent pieces, all issued in 1863.

"I'll keep this as evidence, Judah," Pratt said. "Was there anything else in the house?"

"No, I believe that's all of it."

"Alright, let's see if there is any more on the path," Pratt said.

Keene accompanied the investigators as they painstakingly searched for additional evidence along the path leading to Blake's. They found several more coins near the gap in the fence on Pine Street. Along with the coins found by Ephraim Thompson and Dan Blake, this brought the total found in that area to seven.

Pratt, Pinkham, and Philbrick met again on Saturday, February 21, and, at the direction of District Attorney French, gathered all of the bloodstained evidence they had seized during the course of their investigation and submitted it to Dr. Edward Wood of Harvard Medical School. Wood was a professor of chemistry and a specialist in blood analysis. The evidence included the felt hat, paper collar, overcoat, and congress boots seized from Sturtevant, the sample cut from Simeon Sturtevant's pillowcase, and the several pieces of wallpaper stripped from the wall above his bed and over the fireplace. They also delivered the brown wrapping paper found in Sturtevant's kitchen closet. Pinkham and Philbrick delivered the cart stake to Wood two days later.

***

Pratt, Pinkham, and Philbrick likely considered other potential suspects during their investigation, but the evidence had continued to lead them in the direction of William Everett Sturtevant as the prime and sole suspect in the murders. In their minds, this evidence, although circumstantial, was wholly consistent and supportive of a theory they had conceivably formed as to how and why the crime occurred.

All three were by this point well aware of Sturtevant's unstable past, his artful dodge as a twelve-year-old in escaping from his jailer on the way to the courthouse, his previous conviction for horse theft, his desertion from military service, and his likely involvement in the theft of gold from his uncle's neighbor.

The investigators also knew that Sturtevant was penniless, borrowing regularly from various sources, buying small items on credit, walking to work for lack of train fare, and expecting shortly to have another mouth to feed. Sturtevant knew, or reasonably should have known, that his granduncles were men of some financial standing; many in the small town went to them for loans. Though he had no specific evidence of it, Pratt likely suspected that Sturtevant himself had borrowed money from the old gentlemen and had been unable to meet his obligation of repayment. Perhaps, Pratt conjectured, Sturtevant had asked for another loan (an advance on his inheritance?) and been turned down. Maybe he had asked for that loan during his grandmother's funeral when, according to witnesses, Sturtevant had later complained about his uncles being unsociable and uncommunicative.

Was it possible that, driven by desperation, Sturtevant determined to go back to the old farmhouse to pressure, or perhaps force, Thomas and Simeon Sturtevant to help him? Sturtevant was aware of the difference in physicality between himself and the two men; he was small compared to both his uncles who, though of advanced age, were toughened by years of persistent labor. It was hard to know Sturtevant's initial intent in procuring the stake from Luther Keene's cart; had he planned to take it at the outset or had his fears of his uncles' physical advantage prompted him to consider its value as he passed by Keene's yard?

Pratt and his colleagues may have further speculated that after Sturtevant had armed himself with the stake, he had walked without detection in the dark February night. Sturtevant had lied about the time his visitors left on the Sunday night of the murders. Abbie Sturtevant's statement to Pinkham and Philbrick confirmed it. They would have calculated the timeline. An average person walking at a purposeful pace of, say, four miles per hour over a familiar route, unobstructed by traffic or weather, might cover the four-and-one-half miles from South Hanson to Halifax in an hour-and-a-half. If Sturtevant left the house in darkness shortly after his visitors departed at seven-thirty, he could have arrived well within the range of time in which the physicians estimated the deaths occurred.

The policemen may have additionally envisioned a scenario in which Sturtevant had arrived at the farm to find Mary Buckley in the barn. The parrot foiled his quiet entry into the house, resulting in a confrontation with Thomas in the porch. He issued his demands; Thomas refused him and ordered him out. When he ignored Thomas's order to leave, Thomas prepared to force him out by bending over to put the lantern and the meal pail on the floor. He would have avoided placing the items where they would impede his advance toward his grandnephew, so he turned to his side to put them down. Sturtevant saw an advantage and struck a blow that, with Thomas turned sideways, landed over the base of the older man's skull. Thomas fell and was unable to rise but protested in some way, so Sturtevant hit him again, this time from a position over and behind Thomas, who made no further noise.

Sturtevant then entered the house, focused on getting the money he'd come for. Perhaps Simeon was disturbed by the noise from the porch and called out for quiet or for Mary Buckley; perhaps not. Either way, he was still in bed when Sturtevant entered the room. Did he speak with Simeon who, though confused, knew him? Did he demand money from Simeon? Had Simeon dismissed him in some contemptuous way that inspired resentment and agitation? Simeon was the head of the household; it was, after all, his house. Did Sturtevant somehow consider Simeon to be the decision maker or the keeper of the household money? Something particular had compelled Sturtevant to kill Simeon with a telling first blow to the face and to continue striking him in the face with apparent rage. This was an act with a strong emotional component, something not typically found in killings where robbery was the primary motive.

Sturtevant had likely rummaged for the money, searching the bedroom and sitting room as quickly as he could, looking in the obvious

85

places, filling his pockets blindly with whatever he could find. He then sought the locked chests knowing they contained valuables. He was interrupted as he moved the chest in the sitting room and unbuckled the straps encasing it; Mary Buckley must have, at that point, returned to the house.

Perhaps her parrot's screeching summoned her as she knew the bird's complaining might disturb Simeon. Or maybe she was concerned when Thomas failed to come out to the barn as she expected. Something brought her back in and, when she entered the porch, she found Thomas incapacitated and bleeding on the floor. The summation was that Sturtevant responded, determined to leave no witnesses. Mary bolted for the nearest neighbor; he blocked her way. She turned toward the path to Blake's; he pursued her. She veered off the path in desperation and exhaustion. He swung the club and caught her with a stiff blow. He'd had no time to return to the house since Mary's shouts may have alerted the neighbors. He threw the club in frustrated disgust and ran down the path toward Blake's, coins spilling from the holes in his trouser pocket along the way.

Did it happen this way? Unless Sturtevant confessed and filled in the investigators with the details, it would be impossible to know. For now, the investigators had to satisfy themselves with the assumption that Sturtevant's motive was robbery and that something between him and his uncles had sparked his rage, resulting in their murders.

Whether he had decided at the moment he seized the cart stake in Keene's yard to kill them, or had taken the stake to defend himself and decided to kill them within moments of the assault made no difference. Sturtevant's deliberation, premeditation, malice, and extreme atrocity, they reasoned, would lead to a conviction of first-degree murder.

***

Applicable law mandated a continuation of the inquest into the deaths of the Sturtevant brothers and Mary Buckley, Sturtevant's arrest notwithstanding. At nine o'clock on Monday morning, February 23, the inquest reconvened in Halifax Town Hall. Originally the Old First

Church in Halifax, the town hall was donated to the town in 1854 and converted to government service.

The late arrival of key witnesses and participants delayed the inquest for nearly three hours. A large crowd of townspeople, anxious to hear the testimony, took advantage of the unseasonably mild and pleasant weather and bided their time on the town hall's vast lawn by discussing what they knew or had heard about the murders.

ASA FRENCH.

Just before noon, Constable Crocker emerged from the hall and announced that the inquest was about to begin. Seats were filled quickly; many stood in the back or along the aisles of the old building. After a signal from Crocker, Kingman called the proceedings to order and polled the jurors. When all were accounted for, the examination of witnesses began, this time under the direction of District Attorney Asa French. The first witness was Jabez Thompson, who testified that he lived an eighth of a mile from the Sturtevant house and was notified of the murders at about nine o'clock on the morning of February 16. He immediately went to the house and found several men standing outside.

"Did you enter the house?" French asked the witness.

"Yes, I went in through the rear porch and saw the body of Thomas Sturtevant lying dead in a pool of blood. I then went into Simeon's room and saw him lying on his bed, also dead, covered in blood, his head and face crushed and disfigured."

"What else did you observe inside the rooms?"

"The sitting room was ransacked. I saw a bureau with an open drawer containing several nickel pieces and an open pocket book.

There was a five-cent piece and a two-cent piece on the floor, but no bills or scrip."

"Did you see the body of Mary Buckley?"

"Yes. I went out on the path where several men were standing about her body. She was lying face down just off the path. The back of her head was battered and bloody."

"What happened after you saw the body?"

"I helped my father, Ephraim Thompson, and others carry the body into the house. There was a pool of blood beneath her."

"Did you notice anything else near the path?"

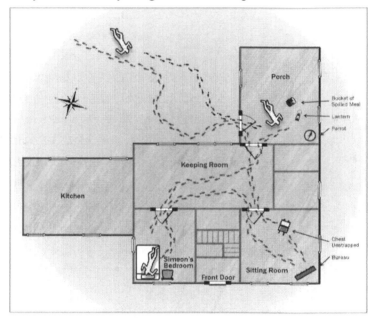

"Yes, I saw a stake, about two inches in diameter, lying in the field near Miss Buckley's body. One foot of the stake was covered with clotted blood."

"How long did you remain at the house?"

"I stayed for about seven hours."

"Thank you, Mr. Thompson. I call Ephraim Thompson as the next witness," French said.

Thompson, one of the inquest jurors, stepped forward and took a seat in the middle of the room.

"Mr. Thompson, please identify yourself for the record," French requested.

"My name is Ephraim Thompson. I am sixty years old and live one and one-eighth miles west of the Sturtevant place on the road leading to Bridgewater."

"How long have you lived in Halifax?"

"I have always lived in the town of Halifax."

"Did you know the murder victims?" asked French.

"I have known Thomas Sturtevant, Simeon Sturtevant, and Mary Buckley from my earliest years. I went to school with them."

"Please describe how you came to learn of the murders."

"On Monday morning, February 16, at about nine o'clock, Daniel Bosworth came to my place and told me that Thomas Sturtevant and Miss Buckley were murdered and that Simeon Sturtevant was missing. Bosworth said that Mr. Inglee wanted me to come as soon as possible."

"What did you do as a result of Inglee's request?"

"I immediately got in my wagon and, on the way, took in John T. Z. Thompson, my next neighbor towards the Sturtevant place."

"Who was at the Sturtevant house when you arrived?" French inquired.

"Edwin Inglee, Stephen Lull, and Daniel Blake were there. They informed us that Simeon had died in his bed."

"Did you go inside the house?"

"Yes. Just before we did so, Jabez Thompson arrived. The six of us first went into the porch where Thomas was laying. By him on the floor was a large pool of blood and near the stove where the floor was worn down. I should judge the blood was three-quarters of an inch deep. There was an old-fashioned tin lantern lying on the floor on the right side of Thomas. In the west front room we found Simeon in his bed with his face and head most fearfully bruised and mangled.

"We then all went into the field where Miss Buckley was laying.

89

There we found a birch stake, the large end of which was covered with blood."

"What happened next?"

"I then went into the house and assisted in moving Thomas into the kitchen. I then went with John and Jabez Thompson and Mrs. Daniel Blake into the east front room and saw several pieces of money on the floor near the bureau standing in the southeast corner of the room. I opened the upper large drawer and there was loose change lying in the drawer, also a pocket book which had been opened was there. When I examined the pocket book I saw there was no money inside but several notes. There were also loose papers in the drawer. From their appearance I should judge they had been overhauled as some of them were shut partly out of the drawer. Afterwards, I discovered blood on the plastering overhead near the bureau."

"What was the next thing you did?"

"At the suggestion of Mr. Lull, I went out to the field and brought back the stake to the house. Daniel Bosworth went with me. I put up stakes where the body of Miss Buckley was found, also where the stake was taken from."

Stephen Lull followed Ephraim Thompson in the witness chair and repeated the story he had given to Officer Pratt on the day he discovered the bodies.

DA French recalled Jabez Thompson to clarify the exact location of Mary Buckley's body in relation to the path. Thompson said he had calculated the distance as twelve feet.

Dr. Millet described for the jury the results of the autopsy he had performed on the afternoon of February 17 with Drs. Brewster and Pillsbury. He went into meticulous detail about the wounds on each body. Millet presented the portion of Thomas Sturtevant's skull he had preserved to show the fractures Thomas had sustained during the attack.

"In your medical opinion, Doctor, what was the cause of death?" French inquired.

"All of the victims died as a result of blunt force trauma to the head."

Millet then testified that he believed all of the victims were murdered within a relatively short period of time and that their deaths had occurred sometime between 9:00 p.m. and midnight on Sunday, February 15.

Kingman called a one-hour recess during which he transported the district attorney in his carriage to the Sturtevant house. He guided the prosecutor through the premises, familiarizing him with the interior layout, then took him outside to the path leading to Dan Blake's, indicating the site of Mary Buckley's death and the location of the footprints at the gap in the fence.

At 2:00 p.m. the inquest reconvened and deputy state constable George Pratt revealed the details of his investigation, the evidence he had recovered, and the circumstances surrounding his arrest of William Sturtevant. At the conclusion of Pratt's testimony, Kingman dismissed the jury to deliberate. An hour later the jurors returned their verdict:

> The Jurors upon their oaths do say that the said Thomas and Simeon Sturtevant and Mary Buckley came to their deaths between the hours of 9 and 12 o'clock in the night time of the 15 day of February last, in Halifax, in the County of Plymouth, by death blows inflicted upon the heads of each of them, with a cart stake in the hands of William E. Sturtevant, of Hanson.

The day after the inquest, Pinkham and Philbrick returned to the Sturtevant house in South Hanson. Pinkham knocked several times at the door but received no answer. Lydia Reed emerged from the opposite side of the house and informed them that Abbie Sturtevant had left with her son for her mother's home in East Bridgewater.

Reed provided access to Sturtevant's quarters at Pinkham's request. Once inside, the officers searched for additional evidence and found three watches hidden in one of the rooms. One was still in its case and bore the mark of "J. Goding, 1801." The other two were marked "Abner Pitts and Charles Babbitts," one bearing the date "1817," the other "1830."

Satisfied there was nothing of further evidentiary value in the house, the officers thanked Reed and departed with the watches. They returned to Halifax and stopped at Daniel Blake's house. Neither Daniel nor his wife, Margaret, could identify the watches. They showed the watches to neighbors and friends of the murder victims, as well as Constable Crocker, but no one had ever seen them in the possession of the brothers and their housekeeper.

The two investigators alerted officials in neighboring towns and received word almost immediately about a recent theft in East Bridgewater. On Friday evening, January 2, someone had broken into the watchmaker shop of J. Henry Potter on Central Avenue and had stolen assorted jewelry and timepieces.

Pinkham and Philbrick went to Potter's shop with the watches and Potter positively identified all four as among the items taken from his shop. Pinkham notified District Attorney French of the recovery and identification of the stolen items but French deferred filing charges against Sturtevant pending the outcome of his upcoming indictment and trial.

***

On Wednesday, April 22, Warden Harmon visited Sturtevant in his narrow eight by four-and-one-half-foot cell. Sturtevant was laying on his iron bed reading the Bible when the warden came to his cell door, unlocked it, and stepped inside. The two men conversed briefly while Harmon made a cursory inspection of Sturtevant's effects. Harmon noticed that the tin dipper was missing from Sturtevant's water container. He scanned the room and saw part of the dipper's handle protruding from beneath two books on a shelf secured to the wall. The warden immediately suspected subterfuge. He had never considered Sturtevant an educated man, but he knew him to be clever. Rather than examining the dipper or challenging Sturtevant, he opted to keep him under surveillance.

"I want everyone to keep a close eye on Sturtevant," Harmon said to his clerk when he returned to his office. "I suspect he may be using the dipper in his cell for something other than quenching his thirst, but I don't want anyone to confront him right away. Let's see what he's up to. Make sure all the guards are notified."

Several weeks later, a turnkey watched Sturtevant from a covert position and saw him extend his hand between the cell bars and insert something into the lock of the door.

"That's as far as you're going," the turnkey said as Sturtevant opened the door and stepped outside the cell. "I think the warden will be very interested in knowing about your intentions."

The turnkey took Sturtevant by the arm and led him to the warden's office. Another guard was dispatched to notify the warden, who was in the prison yard, of the escape attempt.

"Well, Sturtevant. I suspected you might have had plans to escape from here," Harmon said when he arrived at his office ten minutes later.

The warden reached into Sturtevant's trousers and removed two crude keys from one of the pockets. He looked at the keys and then into Sturtevant's expressionless eyes. Sturtevant said nothing.

"I'll be back," Harmon said to the turnkey. "I'm going to try these keys in the locks." Harmon inserted one of the keys in Sturtevant's cell door lock and found that it released the locking mechanism. The other key unlocked the adjoining cell of William Dean, an inmate serving a three-year sentence for assault with an axe. Dean had tried to escape once before.

Inside Sturtevant's cell he found the remnants of the scorched dipper handle. Sturtevant had somehow gained access to the gas burner in the jail's kitchen to fashion the keys. Other keys hidden throughout the cell had been carved from pine wood and fragments of a comb, faced with tin, and bound and riveted with wire from a broom. These, Harmon determined, opened the locks on doors in the corridors of the jail. Sturtevant had ingeniously fabricated these keys with nothing more than his authorized knife and fork.

Sheriff Bates, upon learning of the attempted escape, ordered Harmon to confine Sturtevant and Dean in the dungeon of the old jail for several days "…where they will have plenty of time to reflect upon the mutability of human affairs as exemplified in their experience."

Chapter Eight: Indictment

After hearing testimony and weighing the evidence, a Plymouth County Grand Jury returned indictments on May 8, 1874, charging William E. Sturtevant with the murders of Simeon Sturtevant, Thomas Sturtevant, and Mary Buckley. Deputies brought Sturtevant before the Supreme Judicial Court at Plymouth on the same day. At the request of the district attorney, the presiding justice arraigned him solely on the indictment charging him with the murder of Simeon Sturtevant. The court determined that Sturtevant was indigent and appointed attorneys Jacob Harris of Rockland and Jesse Keith of Bridgewater to represent him at the state's expense. A trial date of Monday, June 29, was scheduled.

Harris and Keith spoke briefly with their client before deputies whisked him back to the jail. They later questioned him at length outside his cell and advised him not to speak with anyone about the case.

***

On Wednesday morning, May 13, Sturtevant had an unexpected visitor at the jail. James Costley, manager of the Howard House, a hotel in Hanover and a popular stopover between Boston and Plymouth, had taken great interest in newspaper accounts of Sturtevant's case.

Costley signed in at the warden's office and a guard escorted him to Sturtevant's cell. It is not known what, if anything, the two men discussed. However, it was later established that Costley left the jail after his visit and met a friend, Simeon Chandler, for lunch at a restaurant overlooking Plymouth harbor. After the meal, the two men boarded a Boston-bound train at Plymouth depot and, during the trip, Costley told Chandler of his call on Sturtevant.

"Sturtevant made a bad piece of work," Costley remarked. "He made some foolish moves in trying to cover his tracks. I could cover up tracks better myself."

At the Quincy depot, Chandler prepared to disembark and asked Costley if he wanted to come along. Costley declined and said he had business in Boston.

"I guess your engagement is with a woman," Chandler jested as he rose from his seat, and Costley smiled.

The same evening, Costley rented a horse and carriage at Riedell's Livery near Boston Common and headed for a boarding house in Boston's South End. There, he met his fiancée, Julia Hawkes, and asked her to accompany him to nearby Weymouth. Before they reached their destination, Costley shot Hawkes in the head with a .22-caliber revolver, tied a rope around her neck, attached a heavy tailor's goose to the other end, and covered her head with a carriage robe secured with a second rope. He hid her body in the back of the carriage, hurried to Whitmarsh's Bridge near Weymouth Landing, and heaved her body into the Monaticquot River.

Eleven days later, two men crossing the bridge saw a pair of legs protruding above the water line, swaying in the current. Bystanders rowed out, secured the body with a boat hook, and hauled it back to shore. It was the bloated body of a woman, clad in a black-and-brown-striped dress. Her left foot was shoeless, but on her right foot she wore a low-cut shoe. A heavy weight had been tied around her neck and had kept her upper torso and head submerged. As her body decomposed, the lower part of her body had risen to the surface.

A curious crowd had gathered but no one recognized the woman when the carriage robe was removed from her head. A Boston newspaper printed a description of her clothing and she was eventually identified as Julia Hawkes, a former housekeeper at the Howard House in Hanover. The state constabulary launched an immediate investigation and on May 26, they arrested James Costley for her murder. Hollis Pinkham and Chase Philbrick were the arresting officers.

Later that afternoon, Costley found himself confined at the

Plymouth jail in the same cellblock occupied by William Sturtevant – the man who had, in Costley's own arrogant words – "made a bad piece of work." Costley thought he had planned the perfect crime, but he, too, had "made a bad piece of work" by failing to weigh down the victim's legs and leaving Julia's matching left shoe in the back of the carriage he had rented from Reidell's.

On January 2, 1875, a jury found Costley guilty of first-degree murder. Six months later, he was hanged.

***

Jesse Edson Keith

Attorneys Harris and Keith did not delay in preparing a defense for their client. They had less than two months to ready themselves for trial. They interviewed Sturtevant repeatedly and sought out as many witnesses as possible to counter what they knew was a compelling circumstantial case. They also filed discovery motions with the court to obtain as much information as they could about the government's case.

They knew that the blood found on Sturtevant's clothing would be the most damaging evidence from the government, and they expected Dr. Wood of Harvard to be a powerful witness. They would need a medical expert of their own to contradict Wood's testimony.

"Where do we begin?" Harris asked Keith as the two men sat in Keith's office in Bridgewater.

"Let's start with improbabilities. The government alleges that Sturtevant acted alone and confronted all three people with a cart stake. Sturtevant is a slight man and, from what I understand, both of his uncles were strong, agile men. The woman, well, we don't know much about her. But if they argue that Sturtevant's primary intention was robbery, we can counter that he might easily have done so without

97

killing them."

"I have to wonder about the origin of this stake and how the government intends to put it in Sturtevant's hands. There is no witness who actually saw our client with the stake in his possession," Keith said.

"Arguably, anyone could have taken that stake from the cart in South Hanson; it was out in plain sight," said Harris.

"I believe that it is possible to create doubt about the blood evidence, as well," Harris remarked. "The government's depiction of the brutality of the crime supports an argument that the clothing of the murderer would be covered with blood. Yet, Sturtevant tells us that Pratt found small spots of blood on his hat and collar and Pinkham and Philbrick confronted him with limited staining of his overcoat on the night of his arrest."

"Doctor Wood's testimony will carry great weight with a jury. We'll have to discredit his analysis," said Keith. "When Wood showed us the stained evidence submitted at Harvard by the police he insisted that most of the stains were human blood. We can challenge that assertion; there is still much doubt about the scientific accuracy of techniques identifying the biological differences between human and animal blood. I've spoken with Drs. Chase and Treadwell. They have agreed to testify for the defense and have assured me that there is no way to positively differentiate between humans and animals by analyzing a dried bloodstain."

"Sturtevant maintains that the blood came from a beef shin he bought at John Drayton's store. I think a jury would find it reasonable to assume that blood from the shin might transfer onto his clothing as he carried it home," Harris said. "He tells me that he suffered a nose bleed after a horse kicked him in the head a few days before the murders and that some of the blood had dripped on his clothes. I've also spoken to a witness who tells me that Sturtevant killed a hen hawk with an axe back in December. Any of these incidents may have caused the blood to come into contact with Sturtevant's clothing and shoes. In any case, we can hold these incidents in reserve as the testimony of Chase and Treadwell will render them moot."

"Let's talk about the money taken from the premises. The government intends to show that Sturtevant was in debt on Sunday but possessed of means on Monday. We can contend that Sturtevant had been steadily employed for more than two years before the murders and had earned funds equivalent to that stolen from the house. We have a list here somewhere…here it is – Bourne, Nash, Gurney, Reed, and Beal. They have all agreed to testify that Sturtevant was in their employ and that he had been paid, collectively, about five hundred dollars."

"What about the uncirculated scrip?" Harris asked. "How do we explain that?"

"We may have a problem with this. Sturtevant insists the scrip was part of the bounty he had received during the war. It's my understanding that Sturtevant enlisted in the navy in 1864 but deserted three months later. He claims that he re-enlisted in the army but there is no record of service in his name credited to Massachusetts after his desertion. Besides, even if he did receive a bounty, can we convince a jury that a man in his circumstances still had some of it nearly ten years later?" Keith posed.

"I think we should stay away from the subject of Sturtevant's service and focus on the state's contention that the scrip is rare. Something like fifty million dollars in scrip was authorized during the war. Certainly it is much more common than the prosecution alleges. I wouldn't be surprised if many people kept scrip as a souvenir of the war." Harris added.

"Sturtevant tells us that he walked to East Bridgewater to visit his friend, Daniel Blanchard, on the Sunday of the murders," said Keith. "I've spoken to Blanchard and his wife, as well as two others who saw our client that day. All insist that he was cheerful and talkative."

"That doesn't sound like someone with murder on his mind," Harris observed.

"It certainly doesn't. I've asked all four to testify about his demeanor."

"Sturtevant made it clear to us during our last visit at the jail that he does not want his wife involved as a witness. Calling her would be unwise, anyway. I recently spoke with her and she admitted that she had made a statement damaging to Sturtevant's alibi when the police visited her in South Hanson after the murders. She assured me that she will not testify against her husband. She has just given birth; I think that timely development excuses her as neither physically nor emotionally fit to endure the stress of a trial," said Harris.

"The government can't compel her to testify," Keith noted, "nor can the police testify about the statement she made to them."

"We have other potential witnesses to interview," Keith told his colleague, "and we don't have much time. I've asked Arthur Lord to assist us with the case and he's agreed to do so. He's a very good attorney. Let's reconvene with him tomorrow."

***

Sturtevant was confined in the middle cell of three cells on the main floor of the jail. His stint in the dungeon of the old jail had apparently done him some good because he had become, to some extent, a model prisoner since his failed escape in April.

"He [Sturtevant] has never been a whining or grumbling prisoner, and has given little trouble to his keepers, aside from the active watchfulness which his known traits and energetic ingenuity made necessary," an *Old Colony Memorial* newspaper correspondent wrote on June 29, the first day of trial. "He has been neither sullen nor morose; nor, on the contrary, has he shown habitual levity or barbarous recklessness. Always lively, ready to converse or be occupied, employing his mind and body to the full extent allowed under his circumstances, he has shown little of that dreamy pre-occupation or absent wandering of mind and thought, popularly supposed to be the peculiarity of those annoyed by remorseful feelings or haunted by terrible memories. If he is utterly hardened, he exhibits none of that coarseness in it which makes such a state so fearfully repulsive and he

100

certainly has never satisfied the ideal which a visitor might have formed of the personal appearance of a bloody murderer.

"Since his incarceration he has shown a fondness and aptitude for mechanical employments, and has often turned his attention to the making of models and such drawings and sketches as an uninstructed hand might be supposed to undertake, and has displayed considerable ability in these directions. He has read a considerable portion of his time, such works as are allowed in the prison, including the Bible and works of history. His ingenuity has at times been naturally turned to schemes for effecting his release, and as will be remembered he once was partially successful in the construction of instruments for this purpose. Knowing the capabilities of the prisoner, the officials have been especially vigilant, and though rumors have often been extensively circulated regarding operations of this kind, with the exception of the above instance, none of them have had serious foundation. He has uniformly eaten and slept well, has been in sound health and, with the exception perhaps of one case, has never shown strong vindictive or revengeful feeling. He could never forgive Officer Pratt for the services he rendered in the case against him, and seems to have visited upon that person the blame for all the consequences to himself of his own acts."

Chapter Nine: The Trial

Day One – Monday, June 29, 1874 – Morning Session

"It is rare," a *Boston Globe* correspondent noted when the special session of the Supreme Judicial Court convened in Plymouth on Monday, June 29, 1874, "that an occasion of so general interest as the trial of a man for his life occurs in this quiet section of the Commonwealth, sacred to memories of the Puritan pioneers and imbued by their sturdy integrity and virtue. Therefore, it is not strange that today there has been a great gathering in and about the spacious and noble courthouse, and that only one topic of conversation has been in everybody's mouth – the trial of William Edward [*sic*] Sturtevant..."

Sheriff James Bates had supplemented his force with a contingent of local police and deputies from neighboring counties for security and crowd control. Scores of hopeful spectators, the majority of which were women, formed a line outside the courthouse waiting for one of the few seats in the courtroom. A festive atmosphere prevailed as people chatted and laughed. Ladies fluttered paper and lace fans beneath fashionable parasols and men fanned themselves with their hats in the sultry heat.

Bates posted deputies at the north and south porticos of the courthouse to prevent unauthorized entry. All other entrances and exits were securely locked. Court and police officials, members of the jury pool, and witnesses accessed the building through the south entrance. Newspapermen gained admission through the north entrance after showing proper credentials. Spectators also entered through the north entrance and were allowed access on a first-come, first-served basis until all available seats in the gallery were filled. If a spectator relinquished his or her seat and left the building, the next person in line would be admitted to fill the vacancy.

Each of the eleven rows of benches in the courtroom gallery accommodated ten people. Bates reserved six rows for the jury pool on one side of the courtroom and one row on the opposite side for members of the press. The forty remaining seats were set off for the general public. By nine o'clock, the courtroom had reached its capacity.

At 11:00 a.m. deputy sheriffs clad in blue frock coats and top hats escorted Sturtevant from the jail into the courtroom and, after removing his handcuffs, placed him in the iron, open-top cage of the prisoner's dock. Sheriff Bates settled himself in his box to the left of the dock and surveyed the audience. Sturtevant, dressed in a black sack suit and a white shirt with no collar, "appeared cheerful and unembarrassed," according to an *Old Colony Memorial* reporter in the gallery.

All in the courtroom craned their necks to get a better view of the accused murderer as he sat in the cage. A *Boston Post* correspondent commented that the prisoner "...manifested some curiosity in the spectators...but otherwise seemed utterly indifferent and unmoved."

By noon, temperatures outside had soared to ninety-seven degrees. Court officers raised the windows on either side of the courtroom to improve ventilation. A gentle, salty breeze from Plymouth Bay wafted into the room but provided little relief. Glasses and pitchers of water were placed at each of the tables inside the bar and at the judges' bench. Water and folding fans for spectators were also set on a table in the back of the room. A local gardener had arrayed the room with freshly cut flowers in clear glass vases, "an unusually pleasant feature of such occasions, attended as they are with much that is painful and repulsive, and all that is devoid of sentiment," a *Boston Journal* reporter noted.

Massachusetts Attorney General Charles Train and District Attorney for the Southeastern District (Norfolk and Plymouth Counties) Asa French represented the government. Attorneys Jesse Keith of Abington, Jacob Harris of Rockland, and Arthur Lord of Plymouth, made up the defense team.

Train and French were aware that their case was entirely circumstantial but were confident they could secure a conviction without an eyewitness to the murders. The physical evidence was overwhelming and, in their estimation, would leave no doubt that Sturtevant was guilty as charged.

The two prosecutors had met on numerous occasions with police investigators at the district attorney's office in the Plymouth courthouse and at Attorney General Train's office in Boston to prepare for trial. French had devoted hours upon hours reviewing evidence and interviewing potential witnesses before and after the grand jury indictment was handed down.

CHARLES R. TRAIN

The government's case would focus on five critical areas: the bloodstains found on Sturtevant's clothing; the murder weapon and its connection to the cart near Sturtevant's house; the bloodstained scrip he had tried to hide from investigators and his sudden ability to pay past debts; the distinctive footprint found at the gap in the fence opposite Blake's house that matched the boot seized by police inside Sturtevant's home; and the inconsistent statements Sturtevant had made to the police to establish an alibi.

"Sturtevant told Pratt he retired at nine o'clock on the night of the murders and never left the house until the following morning," French said. "He also stated that several visitors had been at the house the same evening and had left just before he and his wife went to bed. When Pratt interviewed the two visitors they both insisted they had left at half after seven. Given the time it would take Sturtevant to walk the four-and-a-half miles to his uncle's home, he would have had to leave the house shortly after that time to have committed the murders within the time of death established by Dr. Millet. The only person who can refute Sturtevant's assertion that he never left his house that evening is his wife."

"And she can't be compelled to testify against her husband," Train said. "The statement she made to Pinkham and Philbrick that her husband left the house at seven-thirty and did not return until a late hour would condemn him."

"The defense has to know she made that statement; they'd be fools to call her as a witness," said French, "and they certainly don't want to subject her to cross-examination. I expect they'll come up with an excuse as to why she can't testify. It goes without saying that the court will not allow Pinkham and Philbrick to repeat her statement because it's hearsay."

"Disappointing," grumbled Train, "but not without some redeeming value; we'll highlight her absence in our closing argument. Perhaps the jurors will infer that her failure is a reflection of the damage it might do to Sturtevant's alibi. The defense will have a difficult time explaining why she wasn't produced."

"My chief concern, Asa," the attorney general continued, "is the increasing reluctance of jurors to find defendants guilty of murder in the first-degree. There is a persistent element of ambivalence among the general population about convicting anyone of a crime punishable by death."

"I agree, sir," French replied. "If not for the legislative changes prompted by you and Attorney General Allen over the past six years, the government would be at an even greater disadvantage in selecting a death-qualified jury."

"Still," Train suggested, "I wonder if it wouldn't be wise to abolish the death penalty altogether."

"You're not serious, sir," responded French.

"Well, one has to consider if the certainty of a sentence of life imprisonment would be more effectual in deterring men from murder than the mere possibility of punishment by death. If juries were permitted, by law, to relieve themselves of the terrible responsibility which they now feel in capital cases, growing out of the existence of the death penalty, conviction would be had where acquittals now take place. If an error has occurred in the trial and conviction of a man sentenced to imprisonment for life, that error can be measurably repaired to him; not so to the unfortunate being whose life has been taken. As our law now stands, secret murder in this community may possibly have become one of the safest of crimes."

***

Train's comments reflected the ongoing evolution of laws related to homicide in Massachusetts. In 1858, the Massachusetts legislature had abandoned the common-law definition of murder and separated the crime into two degrees. Rather than deciding whether the defendant, if guilty, had committed murder or the lesser crime of manslaughter, the jury could now determine what degree of murder the defendant had committed. First-degree murder was an offense committed with deliberately premeditated malice aforethought, or in the commission of, or attempt to commit, any crime punishable with death or imprisonment for life, or committed with extreme atrocity or cruelty. A defendant convicted of first-degree murder faced death. Second-degree murder was defined as an offense that did not fit the definition of murder in the first-degree and was punishable by life imprisonment. If the crime did not fall into any of the degrees of murder established by law, the jury could then consider a verdict of manslaughter.

Attorney General Charles Allen, Train's immediate predecessor, believed the prosecution was at a disadvantage in securing a "death-qualified" jury. Under existing law, a defense attorney could unconditionally dismiss up to twenty prospective jurors by what was termed a "peremptory challenge" if he merely suspected the individual might convict his client based on some real or supposed disposition. The prosecution, however, was prohibited from exercising this right.

In 1868, Allen testified before the state legislature that his failure in securing a murder conviction in a recent capital case was because of his inability to keep two men opposed to capital punishment off the jury. He pushed for larger jury pools and the right to exercise peremptory challenges. The following year, new legislation authorized the prosecution's use of five peremptory challenges in capital cases for which the attorney general had exclusive jurisdiction.

Train succeeded Allen as attorney general in 1872. He was a Framingham, Massachusetts, native, graduated from Brown University in 1837, and was admitted to the Suffolk County bar in 1841.

Train appealed to the state legislature for further reform. His first important trial, the prosecution of Leavitt Alley for the murder and dismemberment of Abijah Ellis, whose body parts were found in the Charles River floating in two wooden barrels, had ended in an acquittal.

"Experience has demonstrated," the attorney general testified, "that juries will return a verdict of guilty of murder in the second-degree, instead of in the first-degree, where there is the slightest ground, and sometimes when there is not, since such a verdict does not involve a possibility of taking the life of a prisoner."

The legislature agreed with Train and increased the number of peremptory challenges to ten, but Train was not entirely satisfied. He still believed that "'...the danger that the innocent may be executed instead of the guilty presses upon the juryman with fearful power,' and might lead him to vote for an acquittal when a conviction was warranted."

***

At 11:06 a.m. the court crier ordered all to rise as Judges Wells and Ames emerged from their chamber and assumed the bench. At the conclusion of the crier's opening proclamation, Judge Wells instructed clerk of court William Whitman to proceed with jury empanelment.

Fifty-eight men from Plymouth County answered to their names as the clerk read from a list. The court immediately excused three due to illness. When Whitman called the first eligible juror, Judge Wells addressed the remaining venire, or jury pool, and explained the law as it pertained to juror selection. Anyone, he instructed, who is related to the defendant or victims is ineligible to hear evidence and determine the fate of the prisoner. So, too, is any juror who has formed an opinion about the defendant's guilt or innocence, is biased, has conscientious scruples, or opposes capital punishment.

When Wells concluded, Attorney Harris rose from the defense table and objected to the government's intent to try the prisoner exclusively on the indictment charging him with the murder of Simeon Sturtevant. Harris claimed the defendant had a right to face trial on all three indictments at the same time. The court disagreed and ordered the trial to proceed on the sole indictment.

A combined twenty-four jurors were dismissed as a result of peremptory challenges by the prosecution and defense. Nineteen more of the remaining thirty-one prospective jurors were dismissed by the court, twelve for cause, five for bias, one for conscientious scruples, and one with an opinion of the defendant's guilt.

The twelve men remaining in the pool were sworn as jurors. They were Isaac Newton Hathaway of Marion; Joseph Taber of Mattapoisett; Daniel Hobart of Hingham; Ellis Purrington of Mattapoisett; Philip Pierce of Wareham; Nahum Reynolds of Brockton; Henry Bennett of Rochester; Benjamin Gammons of Rochester; Wellington Caldwell of East Bridgewater; Francis Arnold of Pembroke; Lucius Haywood of West Bridgewater; and George McLaughlin of Hanover.

The median age of the jurors was forty-nine years. The oldest among them was sixty-eight, the youngest twenty-six. Gammons, Caldwell, Arnold, Hayward, and McLaughlin were shoemakers; Reynolds and Bennett were farmers; Hathaway and Taber were fishermen; Pierce was a merchant, Parrington a carpenter, and Hobart a house painter. Judge Wells appointed Isaac Hathaway as jury foreman and ordered a recess until 2:30 p.m.

Chapter Ten: The Trial

Day One – Monday, June 29, 1874 – Afternoon Session

At two o'clock, deputies at the north entrance admitted spectators to fill the seats vacated by the jury pool. As soon as the courtroom had reached capacity, they denied further access, leaving dozens of disgruntled people milling about in the heat outside, waiting for a chance to fill a vacancy left by a departing spectator. Some found a modicum of relief in the shadow of the courthouse as the sun began its descent in the western sky.

Judge Wells had ordered the sequestration of all government and defense witnesses during preliminary proceedings, a practice designed to prevent each from hearing the testimony of others in an effort to minimize opportunities for fabrication and/or collusion. The court assigned two separate waiting rooms for witnesses outside the courtroom – one for men and one for women, as custom dictated. The witnesses were prohibited from discussing their testimony before or after being examined and were kept under the watchful eyes of posted deputies. Scientific and medical witnesses were excluded from sequestration and were permitted to sit within the bar enclosure.

The court was called to order and Judge Wells instructed Clerk Whitman to read the indictment against the defendant for the murder of Simeon Sturtevant. Sturtevant listened intently in the prisoner's dock, stroking and twisting his moustache with his right hand. When Whitman concluded, Wells motioned to the prosecution table and District Attorney Asa French rose to present the government's opening statement.

"May it please Your Honors, and you, Mr. Foreman, and gentlemen of the jury, the duty of the hour was not chosen but thrust upon all concerned," French began. "The prisoner stands charged with a fearful

109

crime, which the government must prove, if possible. The responsibility for determining the prisoner's guilt rests solely with the jury.

"There are two propositions in the indictment," French continued. "One, that Simeon Sturtevant was murdered. The other, that William E. Sturtevant was the perpetrator.

"First, was Simeon Sturtevant murdered?

"In the old house at Halifax lived two brothers and Miss Buckley, in very comfortable circumstances, economical and saving, with money always at hand. On Sunday night, the 15th of February, a friend, Mr. Thompson, called at the Sturtevant house. He was the last to see the three alive.

"At eight o'clock the next morning, one Stephen Lull found the dead body of Miss Buckley near the house. Neighbors soon after came, and all entered the house, and near the door found the body of Thomas Sturtevant stone dead. In one of the front rooms was found upon the bed the dead body of Simeon Sturtevant. All the bodies were covered with blood, and blood was all about. Apparently the same weapon had been used upon all the victims. Near the body of Miss Buckley was found a heavy birch stake, which had evidently been used in the murder, if established."

French drew closer to the jury box and posed his second question. Every eye in the courtroom was riveted on the prosecutor.

"Second, was the murder committed by William E. Sturtevant?

"In the room where Simeon Sturtevant lay, a closet had been rifled and its contents scattered. Other rooms showed similar signs, and the fact of a hasty robbery was evident. The robber made short work, leaving from some cause soon after commencing, and no doubt the murder was caused by the desire to become possessed of the money. Scrip of a very rare kind was found in a bureau drawer.

"On the following Tuesday, Officer Pratt visited William E. Sturtevant at his place of business in South Abington for the first time. Pratt saw evidences of guilt in blood-stained clothing and scrip of the same issue found in the bureau drawer and of the same general appearance.

"At the house of the prisoner, a thorough search was made for the prisoner's overcoat. It could not be found at this visit, but Officers Pinkham and Philbrick soon afterwards found it in the same house, covered with blood – probably the blood of Simeon Sturtevant.

"Mr. Pratt next visited the scene of the murder with William E. Sturtevant. From place to place the officer and his companion went during the day until towards night. William E. Sturtevant was informed that he was a prisoner charged with the murder of his relatives. After his arrest, on being searched, money was found upon him, which he alleged was bounty money got during the war. On Wednesday, he was taken to Plymouth and fully committed.

"While up to the time of the commission of the crime he had hardly any money, on the day after he had between $300 and $400, and paid bills which had been long standing because of his inability to pay."

French stepped back from the jury box and, after briefly consulting with Attorney General Train, called for his first witness, Boston architect and surveyor Luther Briggs.

Briggs testified that he had gone to the crime scene four days after the bodies of the victims had been discovered and had prepared plans and surveys of the house and property. DA French went to the prosecution table, retrieved several documents, and presented them to Briggs. The witness identified them as the renderings he had prepared under the direction of state constables.

"Who was with you when you conducted your surveys?" French asked.

"Constables Pinkham and Philbrick and several others," Briggs replied.

"Looking at the plans in your hands, can you tell us the distance you measured from the Sturtevant house to the home of Zebadiah Thompson?"

"Thompson's house is one hundred and sixty-six feet from the Sturtevant house on the same side of the road."

"And from Sturtevants' to the house of Thompson's neighbor, John Holmes?"

"I measured a distance of one hundred thirty feet diagonally opposite."

French asked Briggs to consult a third plan encompassing a larger area around the Sturtevant house.

"How far away from the house was Mary Buckley's body found?" asked French.

"I calculated a distance of six hundred twenty-one feet," said Briggs.

Briggs indicated that the road in front of the house runs northeast and southwest and that Simeon Sturtevant's body was found in the southwest corner of the house.

At French's request, Judge Wells admitted the plans as evidence and instructed the clerk to mark them as government exhibits. When

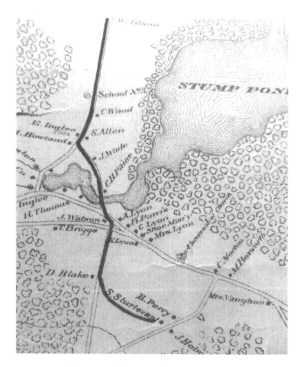

Suspected route of the murderer

defense counsel indicated they had no questions for the witness, Judge Wells dismissed him and Briggs stepped down from the stand.

Charles Paine, a Halifax civil engineer and county commissioner, was the government's next witness. French showed him a map depicting certain parts of Halifax and Hanson and asked him to identify it. Paine acknowledged it was a drawing he had prepared at the request of state constables.

"Did you calculate any distances from Hanson to Halifax?" French inquired.

"Yes, I did," Paine replied and indicated the distance from Keene's Corner in Hanson, where the defendant lived, to the Sturtevant house in Halifax was four-and-one-half miles, fifteen rods.

"Is this the most direct route?"

"Yes," said Paine.

When asked if he had considered other routes, Paine identified a secondary route through Hanson that added two miles and a third through Bridgewater that was a half mile further than the first route.

"Did you measure the distance from the defendant's house to Mrs. Josselyn's property?"

"Yes, I did. I calculated the distance as forty-three rods (709 feet)."

When French indicated he had no further questions, defense attorney Harris approached the witness.

Harris intended with his first questions to establish that someone would have seen the defendant if he had walked from Hanson to Halifax along the direct route Paine had described.

"How many homes exist between the defendant's house in Hanson and the Halifax house?" asked Harris.

"Sixteen," Paine answered.

"Were you out during the evening of Sunday, February 15 ?"

"Yes."

"Do you recall how dark it was that night?"

"It was dark, but not extremely so. Even while I was riding in the darkest areas I could still see the ruts in the road."

Harris next intended to begin dispelling the notion that the defendant was well acquainted with the inside of the Sturtevant house and knew where the brothers kept their money.

"Did you complete an inventory of property found inside the house?"

"Yes," replied Paine. "In a trunk marked 'S.S.' I found $615.52 in specie and notes amounting to $2,142.39. In another trunk marked 'T.S.' was a pocket book containing $860 in bills and $268.55 in specie."

"No further questions."

"You may step down, Mr. Paine," Judge Wells instructed.

The government called Albert Chamberlain, the North Abington photographer retained by Constable Pratt to document the crime scene a few days after the murders. Chamberlain was summoned from the witness room by a deputy and directed to the witness stand. By this time the heat was stifling inside the crowded courtroom. Jurors and spectators wiped their brows and necks with handkerchiefs and frantically waved fans to cool themselves. Water was in constant demand.

DA French approached him with a series of photographs and he identified each as images he had taken of the interior and exterior of the Sturtevant house, the path leading to Dan Blake's, and the place where Mary Buckley's body was discovered.

French requested that the photographs be admitted as evidence and the court so ordered. Judge Wells dismissed Chamberlain when Harris waived cross-examination.

Zebadiah Thompson, the Sturtevants' next door neighbor, was the next witness for the government. Thompson was the last person to converse with Simeon Sturtevant and Mary Buckley before their deaths.

"Mr. Thompson," DA French began. "When was the last time you saw the Sturtevant brothers and Mary Buckley alive?"

"I visited the Sturtevants at about six-thirty on Sunday evening.

Simeon carried in an armful of wood for Miss Buckley to build a fire in his bedroom. Miss Buckley tried to light a lamp and I gave her a match. The lights were on there until at least nine o'clock when I looked out from the door in my house and noticed a lamp flickering in the porch."

"Did you see Thomas Sturtevant that evening?"

"No, I did not."

Asked about the Sturtevants' nighttime habits, Thompson said he had seen lights on in the house as late as ten o'clock.

The defense had no questions for the witness and Thompson was excused. Before the government called its next witness, Judge Wells allowed the jurors to remove their coats and loosen their ties.

Stephen Lull took the stand and, after he was sworn, testified that he lived in Halifax, about three-quarters of a mile from the Sturtevant house.

"Were you in the area of the Sturtevant house on Monday morning, February 16th, at about eight o'clock?"

"Yes, I had risen at sunrise, took breakfast, and left my house for Daniel Blake's. I'm a shoemaker and had several tools for Blake to sharpen. There is a path alongside the Sturtevant place that leads through a field to Blake's house. When I had gone about thirty-five or forty rods along the path, I noticed something in the grass fifteen feet off the path. When I went closer, I saw that it was the body of a woman, lying on her left side, and apparently dead."

"Did you recognize her?"

"No, the right side of her head and face were bludgeoned and bloody and the left side of her face was imbedded in the earth."

"What did you do next?"

"I ran back along the path to John Holmes's house and knocked on the door. John was absent, but his wife, Lucy, and daughter, Edith, were there. I told them what I had found and asked them to come back with me."

"What happened next?" French asked.

115

"We went back to the Sturtevant house and rapped on the front door. No one responded, so we went out to the path to the body in the field. Lucy recognized the body immediately by the clothes she was wearing as Mary Buckley, the Sturtevants' housekeeper. I sent Edith to Daniel Blake's house to alert him and Edwin Inglee, the chairman of the selectmen."

"What did you and Mrs. Holmes do next?"

"We waited by Miss Buckley's body for Blake and Inglee."

"Did Blake and Inglee arrive?"

"Yes, Daniel Blake returned with Edith. He had sent his son for Inglee. Lucy sent Edith home and accompanied Blake and I to the house. We went to the porch door in the rear and found it unlocked. When we stepped in, we saw Thomas Sturtevant lying on his left side in a pool of blood."

"Did you notice any wounds?"

"Yes, the right side of the back of Thomas's skull was crushed."

Lull said that they exited the porch and closed the door. He went to the barn with Blake and noticed that there was a feed of hay in front of each cow but it was too far away for them to reach.

"Did you find anything else in the barn?"

"No, we returned to the house and found that Inglee had arrived. We led him to the porch and Thomas's body. From there we entered the house and found Simeon, terribly mutilated, lying in the bed in his room. The walls and bed clothing were freely spattered with blood."

"What else did you notice in Simeon's room?"

"The door of a closet opposite the foot of Simeon's bed was opened and coins were scattered on the floor near it. The closet was in confusion."

"Did you inspect the rest of the house?"

"Yes, we next went into the sitting room and found a trunk moved away from the wall. It was unstrapped, but locked. In one corner of the room stood a bureau with the upper drawer partly pulled out. Nickel pieces, copper coins, and an open, empty pocket book were on the floor

116

nearby. We left the sitting room and went up the stairs to the second floor but didn't find anything unusual there."

Lull explained that he and the others went back downstairs and removed the bodies to the kitchen. Six or seven people were still there when he left the house at about noon.

"Did you ask Ephraim Thompson to do something before you left?"

"Yes, I asked him to recover the stake that was near the spot where Miss Buckley was found."

DA French went to the prosecution table, picked up the murder weapon, and presented it to the witness. Lull identified it as the stake he had found lying next to Mary Buckley's body. He added that it was bloody when he first saw it.

"Thank you, Mr. Lull. I have no further questions. Your Honor, I ask that the stake be admitted as a government exhibit."

"So ordered," said Judge Wells.

French took his seat at the prosecution table, nodded to the defense, and said, "Your witness."

Attorney Keith got to his feet, retrieved one of the plans prepared by Luther Briggs, and handed it to Lull.

Lull pointed out his home on the plan at Keith's request.

"Which route did you follow on Monday, February 16th?"

"Rather than following the roadway, I went across several lots in the direction of Daniel Blake's house."

"Why and for what purpose did you go that way?"

"It was a shorter distance. I was on my way to Blake's to have him sharpen some tools I use as a shoemaker."

"Was there any snow on the ground?"

"Yes, there had been a light fall of snow overnight. I don't know what time it fell, but when I rose at seven o'clock in the morning, the snow was there.

"Where exactly did you access the path?"

"I passed between the house and a wood-house one length of fence from it. I struck the path between the house and barn."

Harris asked Lull if he had seen any tracks in the roadway or along the path on the way to Blakes and Lull said no.

"Was the barn door open or closed?"

"It was closed."

"What happened next?"

"I continued along the path towards Blake's house and reached the body of Miss Buckley."

"Did you notice any tracks around the body at that time?"

"No."

"What did you do after you found the body?"

"I first informed Mrs. Holmes and her daughter. I then sent to Mr. Inglee by way of Mr. Blake's house."

"How often do you use the path you took?"

"The path is very familiar to me."

"Did you notice any footprints around the Sturtevant house?"

"No, but I didn't look for any."

"Did you see any near Miss Buckley's body?" Harris asked.

"I walked around the body without touching it at the time and saw no tracks near it," Lull replied. "The ground was soft near the body, but no footprints would have been made if one had walked in the path."

"How far from the path was the body?"

"It was about fifteen feet away."

"In what condition did you find her?"

"Her body was rigid and cold. She was fully dressed and wore rubber overshoes over leathers, a cloak, which was fastened, and a cloud tied upon the head of red and white stuff. Her gown was gathered up and pinned in more than one place."

Keith paused momentarily and Lull glanced at Sturtevant in the dock. The prisoner stared blankly.

"When did Inglee arrive?"

"He arrived about half past eight or a little later. It was after we had found Thomas's body."

"Do you know if Thomas and Simeon quarreled frequently?"

DA French rose and objected to Keith's question.

"Your Honors," Keith argued, "I wish to prove that Simeon had frequently quarreled with his brother, threatened his life, and was of unsound mind. It is my belief that the discoverers of the murder thought Simeon to be the murderer until they found him dead."

"Objection overruled," said Judge Wells and turned to Lull. "You may answer the question, Mr. Lull."

"Simeon and Thomas were not, to my knowledge, in the habit of frequent altercations."

This was not the answer Keith was looking for, so he moved on.

"Did you find any scrip in the pocket book you found?"

"No, the pocket book was lying open. There was no scrip in the pocket book, or in the drawer or the room."

Lull went on to tell the court that he and three or four others had entered Simeon's room. During a conversation they agreed that a robbery had taken place.

"Did someone open the bureau drawer in the sitting room or was it already opened?"

"Ephraim Thompson opened the drawer. I looked in before he touched anything and noticed there were writing papers inside."

"What else did you find in the closet in Simeon's bedroom?"

"There was a watch hanging under a lower shelf, loose papers, and an open pocket book. I examined everything but touched nothing."

"Where did you go after you left Simeon's room?"

"I went upstairs and found no signs of disturbance."

"Where else in the house did you go?"

"I went into the northeast room and saw two trunks on the floor. Neither were disturbed."

"Did you notice any blood in any other rooms in the house?"

"No, there was no blood in the house except in the rooms where Thomas and Simeon were found."

Lull acknowledged that he had been inside the Sturtevant house on previous occasions and used the path between the house and Blake's often, as much as a dozen times a year.

"Do you consider it unusual that no tracks were found about the house and near Miss Buckley's body?"

"The ground would receive tracks that morning in some places."

At the conclusion of Lull's testimony, Judge Wells excused him from the stand and ordered court adjourned until nine o'clock the next morning.

Chapter Eleven: The Trial

Day Two – Tuesday, June 30, 1874 – Morning Session

Court opened on Tuesday morning, June 30, after deputies had placed the prisoner in the dock, the jury had filed in, and Justices Wells and Ames had taken their places at the bench. Every seat in the gallery was occupied and about a dozen additional spectators stood in the back of the courtroom. Temperatures had fallen slightly from the day before and a fresh wind blew from the northwest under fair skies.

District Attorney French called Lucy Holmes, the Sturtevant neighbor who had accompanied Stephen Lull to Mary Buckley's body. Lucy told the court she had lived nearly opposite the Sturtevant house for the past twenty-one years.

"When did you last see the Sturtevants and Miss Buckley before the murders?"

"Thomas Sturtevant was at my house on Sunday morning. I didn't see Simeon or Miss Buckley that day."

"What do you recall about Sunday night?"

"I noticed a light in the Sturtevant house just before I retired between eight and nine on Sunday night."

Lucy explained that she had first heard of the body off the path when Stephen Lull came to her house on Monday morning and told her.

"What did you do?"

"I went with Lull and my daughter Edith to the place where he found Miss Buckley. The body was near the path between the Sturtevant house and Mr. Blake's house."

"How did you know it was Miss Buckley?"

"I recognized her by the dress. Her head was neatly enveloped in the cloud she wore, so that I should not have recognized her but for her dress."

"Did you notice anything else?"

"Yes, I saw a stake with blood upon it near the body."

French took the stake admitted as a government exhibit during Stephen Lull's testimony and presented it to the witness.

"Do you recognize this stake?"

"Yes, it is the same stake I saw lying next to Miss Buckley's body."

French returned the stake to the evidence table and asked the witness to tell the court what happened next.

"Mr. Lull sent my daughter Edith for Mr. Inglee. She returned with Mr. Blake and his wife. We went into the house and we saw the body of Thomas lying on his left side in a pool of blood upon the floor. A lantern and a bucket of meal and water were upset near him. A small piece of candle was in the lantern. There was a cage with a parrot in it on a stand near the head of Thomas. It was a talking parrot."

"Did you go into any other part of the house at this time?"

"No, not until Mr. Inglee arrived. Then we went into the room in the front of the house, occupied by Simeon. We all went to the door of Simeon's room together. I saw Simeon lying upon the backside of the bed, on his back, covered with blood, and blood spatters around the room."

"Did you go inside the room?"

"No, I didn't. I looked in from the doorway. The others went in."

Lucy testified that she was in the sitting room in the house and saw the bureau there with the top drawer closed and a piece of paper protruding from it. She also stated that she saw two coins on the floor and that the front entryway door was closed.

Attorney Harris began his cross-examination by asking Lucy if everyone had gone into the house the same way. Lucy testified that they had and denied anyone had used the front entry to gain access to the sitting room.

"Did you notice any bloodstains on the door of Simeon's room?"

"No."

"Did you see someone open the bureau drawer in the sitting room?"

"Yes. Ephraim Thompson opened the drawer."

"For what purpose?" Harris asked.

"We were all searching for evidences of robbery."

"Did you look inside the drawer?"

"Yes. I saw an open pocket book in the drawer, but no money. I saw the same pocket book afterwards at my house in the possession of Mr. Thompson. There were spots on it which I called bloodstains."

Lucy responded to Harris's final question by stating that the ground was soft on Monday morning.

Judge Wells excused Lucy from the stand and the government called her daughter, Edith. Edith corroborated the testimony given by her mother and Stephen Lull. She stated that after she returned to the Sturtevant house with Blake and his wife she went immediately home.

Daniel Blake followed Edith on the witness stand. After being sworn, he glanced at the prisoner's dock and was met with a baleful glare from his nephew.

"Mr. Blake, please tell the court where you live in relation to the Sturtevant house in Halifax," French began.

"I live about a quarter mile from the Sturtevant's house. There is a path between my house and theirs that both families use."

"What is your relationship with the Sturtevants?"

"I am related by marriage. My wife is their niece."

Sturtevant shifted on the bench in the dock and kept his eyes fastened on Blake as he testified.

"When was the last time you saw Simeon, Thomas, and Mary Buckley alive?" French asked.

"I spoke with all of them on Sunday afternoon between four and five o'clock."

"How did you come to hear about the murders?"

"Edith Holmes first told me of the murders at half past eight Monday morning. I went to the house of the Sturtevants and found Mr. Lull and Mrs. Holmes standing in the path and Miss Buckley's body lying nearby, nearly parallel with the path. There was a stake near the body. One end was bloody."

French retrieved the stake previously submitted in evidence and Blake identified it. He said he had last seen the stake when Ephraim Thompson brought it into the Sturtevant house.

"Please tell the court what happened next."

"We left Buckley's body and went to the house. We went inside the porch and saw Thomas's body lying there. The body was lying with the head near the east door. He had a wound on the right side of the back of his head."

"What else did you notice about the room?"

"There was a parrot in the room, a talking parrot. There was a hand lamp on the table with some oil in it. A lantern lay by the side of the body with a piece of candle in it."

Blake said they didn't enter the house at that time. They waited for Inglee and when he arrived they went inside through the porch to the front room where they found Simeon dead. He said he saw blood on the wall over the mantelpiece, on the ceiling, and on the bed.

"What else did you see?"

"In a closet in one corner of the room I saw a watch hanging. Ephraim Thompson met us in the house and we went into the sitting room. I saw a bureau with the top drawer closed and a piece of paper protruding. There were coins on the floor in front of the bureau. Thompson opened the drawer and I saw an open pocket book. The drawer was in confusion. I saw twenty dollars in bills, one ten and two fives, in the drawer, along with some scrip. There were two dollars found in the cupboard in Simeon's room and notes of hand in pocket books."

"Was any other money found?"

"Yes. On Friday nickels were found out in the field near the gap in the fence. Constable Pratt and Mr. Keene picked up each piece."

"Do you know the defendant?"

"Yes, he has worked for me as a shoemaker and a wood chopper."

"Which hand did he use to chop wood?"

"He held his axe habitually right hand foremost."

"Your Honors, the defense objects to the witness's last statement," Harris interrupted.

"We will allow it," ruled Judge Wells.

"Please tell the court when the defendant worked for you and how much you paid him for his services."

"He worked for me from November 1871 to May 18, 1873. From January 28 to May 18, 1873, he earned $199.20. He told me he was trying to lay up a dollar a week until he had $100 for a rainy day. He placed his money in a box, and in February he smashed the box up. It had six dollars in it."

DA French returned to the prosecution table, sat down, and conferred briefly with Attorney General Train.

"I have no further questions, Your Honor," said French.

Attorney Harris's chair scraped loudly on the floor as he rose and pushed it away from the defense table. He began by asking Blake where he lived.

"I have, since the death of the Sturtevants, bought their place, and am now living upon it. I went there to live a fortnight after the funeral."

Harris picked up one of the photographs previously entered as evidence and marked as a government exhibit.

"I show you one of the photographic views taken of the bureau in the sitting room. Is this how the bureau appeared when you first searched the house on Monday, the sixteenth of February?"

"The photograph was taken under the direction of Officer Pratt the day after the murders. I fixed the bureau as nearly as possible as it was on the sixteenth."

"Do you know where the defendant's father resides?"

"Yes, he lives in Lewiston, Maine."

"How long had you known the Sturtevant brothers?"

"I had known them for fifteen years."

Harris once again introduced a line of questioning intended to show animosity between Thomas and Simeon Sturtevant. French objected and the court sustained, ruling that the question would not be allowed until further testimony proved it competent.

Harris informed the court that he had no further questions for the witness. Judge Wells excused Blake and called for a ten minute recess. When the trial resumed, the government called Halifax storekeeper and selectman Edwin Inglee as its next witness.

Inglee testified that he lived one mile from the Sturtevant house. He was acquainted with the prisoner and knew that he lived in South Hanson at the time of the murders.

"When did you find out about the murders?" French began.

"I first learned of the death of the victims on Monday morning. Daniel Blake's boy informed me. I harnessed my horse and went over to the house and arrived at half past eight o'clock. When I drove up, Mr. Lull, Mr. Blake, and Mr. Bosworth stood there. Lull and Blake went into the house with me. We found the body of Thomas in the porch, laying on his left side, with his head near the east door, the door nearest Mr. Holmes's house. We went in at the west door, nearest the path."

"What else did you see in the porch?"

"There was a table in the room, a lantern on the floor, a lamp on the table nearly half full of oil."

"Where did you go next?"

"We went into the west front room. On the bed lay Simeon Sturtevant with his face smashed in, the bed covered with blood and blood over the head of the bed and upon the wall and at the foot. The blood was spattered on the ceiling like the rays of the sun."

"Please continue," French said.

"After Mr. Thompson came, we went down to the field and brought up the body of Miss Buckley. We laid the body in the kitchen and also brought in the body of Thomas. Mr. Lull washed the bodies."

"Did you see any money in the closet in Simeon's room?"

"No. I went into the sitting room at seven o'clock that evening with Mr. E. B. Thompson. In the upper drawer of the bureau was some scrip and bank bills. It appeared to be scrip of an old issue."

"How long were you there?"

"I stayed about two and one-half hours. There were eight or ten people there when I left."

"Did you see the prisoner sometime after you left the house?"

"Yes, I saw him on Tuesday evening at my house. Officers Pratt, Philbrick, and Pinkham were present."

"Did you speak with him at that time?"

"Yes, I had a conversation with him before his arrest. We talked upon business prospects. He said he never knew business so dull and that he had been often afoot because he had no money to pay his fare."

"How long were you with him?"

"We spoke for about three-quarters of an hour."

Attorney Harris approached the witness for cross-examination and asked Inglee how well he knew the Sturtevant brothers.

"I was well acquainted with them."

"Were they considered wealthy?"

"I knew their reputation for wealth. I was the town's assessor. They were considered well off."

"You know the prisoner?"

"Yes, I have known him a long time."

"Do you harbor any animosity toward him?" Harris asked, focusing on the jury.

"I have no feeling against the prisoner which I should not entertain against any person similarly accused."

"Did you realize he was a suspect when he came to your house with the officers?"

"I supposed when I met the prisoner that evening that he was under the surveillance of Mr. Pratt."

"On the day the bodies were found did you suggest to someone that the prisoner was responsible?"

"I think I stated to Mr. Pratt that I believed the prisoner the guilty person before I had seen the stake and the money."

"When you found Thomas's body did it appear to you that he had tried to defend himself?"

"There was no indication of a struggle by Thomas. The body lay as it fell. When his body was carried out I looked on the floor for a weapon, but didn't find one."

Inglee acknowledged that he was one of the administrators of Thomas and Simeon Sturtevant's estates. He identified Ephraim Thompson as the other.

"Do you remember who first entered the sitting room before you found Simeon?"

"I do not remember seeing anyone enter the sitting room before the body of Simeon was found. Myself, Mr. Lull, and Mr. Blake first entered the room of Simeon. When we left the room we went out of the house and waited for Mr. Thompson. We did not enter the sitting room at that time."

Inglee passed from the courtroom after this last question and District Attorney French called Ephraim Thompson to the stand. Thompson testified that Daniel Bosworth had first notified him of the murders on Monday morning at about nine o'clock. Thompson described the position of the bodies and the condition of the rooms inside the house. His testimony corroborated the statements made by previous witnesses.

"Did you notice any footprints outside the house?" French asked.

"On Monday forenoon I saw tracks indicating that some person had traveled in haste from the porch to the place where Miss Buckley was found."

French returned to his table and Harris began his cross-examination.

"Did you notice any other tracks outside the house?"

"No," said Thompson. "I did hear of a track by the side of the road on Monday afternoon. The tracks led away from the house. The print was quite deep."

"Will you tell the court how you would best describe the physical traits of the Sturtevant brothers?"

"Thomas was a strong, powerful man, but slow. Simeon was a very active man, unusually so, and of quick motion."

Judge Wells looked up at the wall clock and saw that it was well past one o'clock. He interrupted Harris, called a recess, and announced that court would resume at two-thirty.

Chapter Twelve: The Trial

Day Two – Tuesday, June 30, 1874 – Afternoon Session

Ephraim Thompson returned to the stand at 2:30 pm. and Harris continued his cross-examination. Thompson, one of the administrators of the Sturtevant estates, testified that he had found promissory notes given to the Sturtevants before their death and declared he could produce them if necessary. He further stated he had found no savings or other bank accounts among their effects.

Thompson was excused and DA French called Dr. Asa Millet as the government's next witness.

"Did you have occasion to go to the Sturtevant house in Halifax last February?"

"Yes," Millet responded. "I was called upon to assist at the autopsies of the Sturtevants and Mary Buckley. I went on the Tuesday morning following the discovery of the bodies and the autopsies took place at once. Drs. Brewster and Pillsbury assisted me. I took possession of the west front room and made the examination there. We examined Mary Buckley first, then Simeon, then Thomas."

"Please tell the court what you observed during the autopsy of Mary Buckley."

"The body of Miss Buckley was extremely rigid. There was no sign of injury upon the body below the neck. The right side of the head was crushed in, breaking the skull in two places. There was no other mark of violence except a small contusion upon the nose. The skin was not broken."

"Did the wound to her skull cause her death?"

"Yes."

"Did you determine the means by which the wound was inflicted?"

"Yes. It was a contused wound produced by a blunt instrument."

"Please describe the particulars of your examination on the body of Simeon Sturtevant."

"On the face was evidence of two or three distinct blows, all in the same direction. The man must have been lying on his back when he was struck. He must have been approached from the right side and given a right hand blow. All the blows were in this direction. The lower jaw was fractured on the left side, tearing the lip. The upper jaw was fractured, not cutting the lip. The bone of the nose was broken. The bone above the eye was crushed in. The flesh wound over the other eye cut through, but did not break the bone. The scalp was not cut through in any point."

"What did you find when you examined the brain?"

"I removed the brain and found it was injured by the bone being pressed down upon it. The wounds were necessarily fatal. There were marks of congestion in the lower brain. He must have died speedily."

"What did your post-mortem examination on the body of Thomas Sturtevant reveal?"

"I found no bruises except one on the back part of the scalp near the right ear. The process was crushed in two small pieces, while the scalp was not torn. This wound being at the base of the brain might cause instant paralysis of the whole body. The wound was a contused one and must have been made with a blunt instrument."

DA French showed Millet the stake recovered near the body of Mary Buckley and asked him if it could have been used to inflict the injuries on all three victims.

"It is not inconsistent that they were all struck with the same weapon, which might have been the stake."

Harris rose and asked the doctor if he could say with certainty that the stake in evidence was the stake used in the attacks.

"Any other stake would have produced the same result if heavy enough, or any similar weapon."

"Can you tell the court with certainty that the wounds were inflicted at the same time and by the same weapon?"

"Nothing in the autopsy would have disclosed the fact if the wounds had been made some hours apart, and by different weapons of the same character."

Millet was excused and the government called Jabez Thompson, Ephraim's son. Thompson testified that he had been at the Sturtevant house on Monday morning and had seen several pieces of scrip in the bureau drawer in the sitting room.

Thompson was followed by Daniel Bosworth, who was also present at the crime scene on Monday morning. He corroborated the testimony of the previous witness and others about conditions found within and without the house.

Judah Keene of East Bridgewater took the stand and testified that Halifax selectman Bourne had placed him in charge of the Sturtevant house from Monday, February 16, until Monday, February 23. He told the court he had removed scrip on Tuesday and Wednesday from the top drawer of the bureau in the sitting room, placed it in a small box, and locked it up in a smaller drawer in the house.

French showed the witness several pieces of scrip and Keene identified it as the scrip he had removed from the bureau and placed in the box on the aforementioned Wednesday. French then showed Keene twenty-five and fifty cent pieces issued in 1863 and he identified these as scrip he had taken from the bureau on Tuesday. French submitted the scrip for evidence and the court ordered all of the pieces marked as government exhibits.

"Did you find any other money during the time you were in charge of the house?" French inquired.

"Yes," said Keene. "On Friday I made examination of the path leading from the house to Daniel Blake's. Officers Philbrick, Pinkham, and Pratt, and a Boston gentleman were with me. We found coins near the gap in the fence."

Defense attorney Harris approached Keene and asked him how long he had remained at the Sturtevant house.

"I remained until after the inquest."

"Did you tell someone about what you had found in the bureau drawer and that it was scrip issued in 1863?"

"I never told any man that I found scrip dated 1863."

"Were you present when officials brought the defendant to the Sturtevant house to view the scene?"

"I never saw William Sturtevant during the week that I was there. I heard he had been there."

Keene was excused and the government called Philip Kingman. Kingman identified himself as a deputy sheriff and county coroner and stated that he had conducted the inquest into the deaths of the Sturtevants and Miss Buckley. He testified that he went to the Sturtevant house on Tuesday morning and immediately empaneled a jury.

"Did you have occasion to examine the bureau in the sitting room while you were there?"

"Yes, I was with Mr. Inglee and Mr. Paine in the afternoon and inspected the top drawer. It was in confusion, as was the whole house. Bills were handed me as money from that drawer. The scrip that I got from there I placed in a bag with some silver coin and deposited it in a savings bank."

"Did you receive any other money?"

"Yes," Kingman answered. "After the funeral Mr. Keene went to the bureau and handed me some scrip which he took from a smaller drawer in the bureau, which he unlocked for the purpose."

Once more the district attorney retrieved the cart stake from the exhibit table and showed it to Kingman. Kingman identified it as the same stake found on the morning of the murders and presented to the jury as evidence during the inquest. He was then excused with no cross-examination by the defense.

With the next witnesses the government intended to demonstrate for the jury that prior to the murders the defendant was in dire financial straits. Other witnesses would establish that the defendant's financial condition had changed drastically after the murders.

French called Bridgewater shoemaker Charles Brown. Brown testified that he had employed the defendant from the end of March 1873 until June 7, and from July 12 until September 6. The witness stated that he paid Sturtevant about $135 for his work.

Edward Edson, an East Bridgewater shoemaker, stated that Sturtevant had been in his employ from September 27, 1873 until December 10, 1873 in Bridgewater. He testified that he had paid grocer John Drayton fifteen dollars on behalf of the defendant to settle a debt. Sturtevant earned an additional $34.52, which the witness stated he still owed the defendant.

When cross-examined by Attorney Harris, Edson stated that some of the work Sturtevant did was for Frank Bourne of South Hanson. He also testified that Sturtevant and his wife, Abbie, boarded with Abbie's mother in Hanson while he worked for him. What Edson failed to disclose during cross-examination was that Abbie Sturtevant was his niece, the daughter of his sister, Lucy Edson Parrish.

Henry Blake, the South Abington boot and shoe manufacturer, testified the defendant had worked for him continuously from February 2 until his arrest on February 17. He had paid Sturtevant ten dollars in advance on February second. By the sixteenth of February, he owed Sturtevant an additional twenty-one dollars and forty cents.

Grocer John Drayton of South Hanson was called. Drayton testified that the defendant lived about a quarter-mile southeast of his store. Sturtevant had visited his store on Saturday evening, February 14, and bought a fish for forty-two cents on credit.

"Were there any other transactions between you and the defendant at your store?" DA French asked.

"Yes, he came into the store on the seventh of February," Drayton replied. "I have many charges against him between the seventh and the fourteenth."

"How much is he in arrears?"

"He owes me forty-seven dollars. It has been running since the fall before. He had made some payments. I never asked him for pay. Mr. Edson paid me fifteen dollars on his account, and I was promised the remainder. Sturtevant told me he could not pay, as he could not get his money. He spoke of this more than once."

"Did the defendant return to your store after the fourteenth?" asked French.

"Yes, he bought of me on Sunday, the fifteenth," said Drayton.

"Did he pay you on that day?"

"No, he paid me the following evening with two ten-cent scrip."

The district attorney picked up some scrip from the prosecution table and asked Drayton to identify it. Drayton drew the court's attention to his signature on the scrip.

"This is the same scrip I received from Sturtevant on Monday and turned over to Mr. Pinkham on Tuesday," Drayton testified.

Attorney Harris began his cross-examination of Drayton by asking if the defendant had purchased anything from him when he visited the store on February 7.

"I sold Sturtevant a beef shin weighing eleven and a half pounds on credit that evening and marked the sale in my book. I sawed the bone in my back room and he carried it off," Drayton answered.

"Was anyone in the store during this transaction?"

"I don't recollect anyone being there."

"Are you sure the defendant was in your store on the fifteenth of February? Wasn't it the fourteenth?"

"No, I'm sure I have the right date. James Brewster was in my store on the evening of the fourteenth. I didn't sell any meat to Sturtevant on that evening."

"When did Officer Pratt first come to your store?"

"He came one or two days after the murders."

"Did you tell Pratt at that time that you had sold meat to Sturtevant on the Saturday night preceding the murder and that Sturtevant had paid for it?"

"I did not."

"Are you certain that you received the two ten-cent scrip from the defendant on Monday night the sixteenth?"

"Yes. There were several persons present when he made the payment. I noticed the money before I put it in the money drawer. I kept it in a separate compartment."

"Why did you do that?" Harris inquired.

"I put it in a separate compartment because it was different from anything I had seen," Drayton replied.

"You're not sure which day it was that Officer Pratt came to your store?"

"The officer came to my store on Tuesday."

"Did he just happen to drop by, or did you send for him?"

"Martin Howland sent him. I had told Mr. Howland about the scrip."

"I have no further questions for this witness, Your Honor," Harris announced and glanced at the jury before returning to his seat at the defense table.

"You may step down, Mr. Drayton," Judge Wells said.

Prosecution witness Frank Osborne was called and he testified that he had worked with the defendant at Henry Blake's shoe shop in South Abington.

"What did Sturtevant do in the shop?" the district attorney asked.

"He tacked on soles for three or four weeks. From him the work came to me."

"When did you last work with him?"

"He was at work in the shop all day Monday, February 16, and came Tuesday morning."

"Did you notice anything unusual about his work on those days?"

"Yes, on these occasions there was a peculiarity in his work," Osborne related. "The soles were on one-sided. He was a very good workman for this kind of work. I called his attention to it, and showed him the bad work. He said he would do better. I spoke of more than one shoe. I never had to speak to him before for the purpose."

"Did the defendant settle a debt with you on Monday, February 16?"

"Yes, on Monday morning he paid me seventy-five cents which he owed me for milk. He had owed me for two to four months. It was in twenty-five cent pieces, three of them."

"What became of them?"

"I did not keep them. They were taken from me by Officer Pratt."

The district attorney showed the witness three twenty-five cent pieces of scrip and the witness stated that they resembled the scrip paid him by Sturtevant.

On cross-examination Osborne testified that he was not the defendant's supervisor at the shop and admitted that it was an everyday occurrence for workmen to make mistakes in their work.

Harris asked him what had drawn his attention to the scrip Sturtevant had given him.

"I noticed that the money paid me was of a different appearance. One of them was of a kind I had not seen for a long time. The shortest piece was the one Officer Pratt first intimated to me that this money should be used in the case of William E. Sturtevant. This was two or three days after they were paid me."

"Had the defendant worked for you before?"

"Yes, at two different times – three years ago, and one year ago last fall. I cannot say how much he earned while he worked for me. Think it was more than $12 a week and I paid him all. He was an industrious man. He had worked for Mr. Blake in South Abington about five weeks at the time of his arrest."

"How did he come and go from work at South Abington?"

"Sometimes he went home on the cars; sometimes he walked. The cars came along about six, or a few minutes past."

"Was the defendant absent from work during the week prior to the murder?"

"No, he was there every day."

"Did you ever hear that the defendant had sustained an injury prior

137

to his arrest?" asked Harris.

"Yes, I heard the prisoner had been kicked by a horse," Osborne replied.

"Did you ever notice any blood on his clothing?"

"No."

DA French called William Copeland after Osborne was excused from the stand. Copeland provided further evidence of Sturtevant's difficult financial position, testifying that on February 7th, he had sold Sturtevant four dollars' worth of coal. Sturtevant wanted to buy one-half ton on credit, but Copeland "would not trust him."

French called another of Sturtevant's co-workers at Blake's shoe shop. William Hill testified that he saw Sturtevant at the shop on Monday, February 16. Sturtevant had taken the train that morning and had walked with him from the depot to Blake's on South Avenue. He stated he saw the defendant again the next morning but Sturtevant had walked from home to the shop.

"Was the defendant in debt to you?"

"I lent him money at the time of the funeral of his grandmother. I cannot remember when that was. (Sturtevant's paternal grandmother, Lucinda Sturtevant, died on January 30, 1874). The amount was between seventy-five and eighty cents."

"How far is Blake's shop from the depot?"

"It's two-thirds of a mile."

"Did you have a conversation with the defendant during the walk from the depot to the shop on Monday morning?"

"Yes, I told him I didn't think there would be much work at the shop that day. Sturtevant told me he did not care, that he was tired, as he had walked four miles from his house in Hanson to Northville in East Bridgewater the day before."

On cross-examination, the witness acknowledged that he knew Daniel T. Blanchard of the Northville section of East Bridgewater and stated that he believed Blanchard was related to Sturtevant by marriage.

"If Sturtevant had walked to Northville on Sunday, would he have passed by the Sturtevant house in Halifax?" Attorney Harris asked the witness.

"No. If Sturtevant walked from his home in South Hanson to Northville, he would have taken a route directly away from Halifax."

"Did Sturtevant ever pay back his debt to you?"

"Yes, he paid me the borrowed money a few days after it was lent."

On re-direct examination, DA French asked Hill if it was unusual for the defendant to walk from home to Blake's shop. The witness stated that Sturtevant often walked and seldom took the train.

Sturtevant nodded to Hill and smiled as he left the witness stand.

The district attorney called fifty-two-year-old Halifax shoemaker Cyrus Wood. Wood had gone to the Sturtevant house at about ten o'clock on the day of the murders. He testified that he had joined others in search of coins and other evidence near the house and, on the path, found three coins that he later gave to Constable Crocker.

The defense had no questions for Wood and he was excused. French called another Halifax shoemaker, Horace Thomas. Thomas lived a few doors down from Cyrus Wood near Stump Pond and Inglee's store. Thomas acknowledged that he, too, had been at the Sturtevant house on the Tuesday after the murders, had found a coin along the path, and turned it over to Crocker.

Constable William Crocker took the stand and was duly sworn. He testified that he had first heard about the murders at nine o'clock on Monday morning and had gone directly to the Sturtevant house. Later that day he received two five-cent pieces and a one-cent piece from Cyrus Wood and, on Tuesday, one coin from Horace Thomas. Both men had found the coins by the gap in the fence on the Sturtevant property. He had the men point out where they had found the coins. While there he noticed some tracks pointing in the direction of Edwin Inglee's general store. Crocker brought the tracks to the attention of Officers Pratt and Collingwood and was present when Pratt measured the deepest footprint.

The defense waived cross-examination.

Lydia Reed of South Hanson was the government's next witness. She stated she had known the defendant since last November and that he occupied part of the same house where she resided in South Hanson.

"Did you see the defendant at South Hanson on Sunday, February 16?" DA French began.

"Yes, I saw him in the dooryard of the house on the afternoon of the day of the murder," Reed replied. "I left for the day and returned at about nine or ten at night."

"Do you know if any of the Sturtevant family was awake at that time?"

"No."

"Do you remember hearing anything unusual during the night?"

"Twice in the night I heard a noise, but I don't know when. It sounded like the lifting of stove covers."

"What time did you awaken on Monday morning?"

"I rose at five o'clock and heard the Sturtevants in the other part of the house. I saw Mrs. Sturtevant through an open door. I had never known them to rise so early."

Attorney Harris asked the witness on cross-examination if she ordinarily rose so early in the morning. She acknowledged that she did. Challenging her veracity, he asked her to describe the stove the Sturtevants used. She could only say that they burned coal in it.

"How often had you heard the stove covers rattle in the night?" Harris posed.

"I never heard the noise before."

"Did you know when William Sturtevant was arrested?"

"No."

"Did you tell someone that Mrs. Sturtevant was a party to the murder?"

"I never said that," Reed protested, glancing nervously at Sturtevant in the dock. "I may have said that there was bloody money found in the closet by the stove."

"How long after the defendant was arrested did Mrs. Sturtevant and her child leave the house?"

"The furniture was removed on the Friday following William's arrest. Mrs. Sturtevant was not well about that time."

Harris turned to the incident with the hen hawk to raise doubt in the jury's mind about the bloodstains found on his clothing by the police after the murder.

"Do you know anything about the defendant and an incident with a hen hawk?"

"I have heard that sometime before the murder was committed, the prisoner cut off the head of a hawk in the yard."

Harris indicated he had no other questions and DA French called William Jefferson, the South Hanson sawyer, to the stand. Jefferson testified that he lived in South Hanson last February, "about four stone's throws" from the house of William Sturtevant.

For the fifth time, French retrieved the stake from the evidence table and asked Jefferson to identify it.

"Do you recognize this stake?" French asked.

"I must have cut this stake on the third of January. I cut others on the same day in different places, all for the same cart."

"How do you know it's the one you cut in January?"

"I recognize the stake by the marks made by a small hatchet which I had at the time. I sharpened this stake upon the small end because my hatchet was dull."

Jefferson explained that he had cut the stakes for Widow Josselyn's hay cart.

"Did you see the cart at Mrs. Josselyn's on Sunday, February 15?" asked French.

"No, but I saw it there frequently," Jefferson answered.

"Did you see the cart there on Monday, February 16?"

"No, I did not."

"When did you next see this stake?"

"A constable brought the stake to my house, and after I told him I had cut it, he asked me to show him the place where it was cut."

"Please continue," French prompted.

"I recollected at once where I cut the stake when I saw it. I went with the constable and found the stump."

The district attorney went back to the prosecution table and returned with a stump and Jefferson identified it as the one from which he had cut the stake. The stump was admitted as a government exhibit.

"Mr. Jefferson, do you know the prisoner?" French inquired.

"Yes, I have known the prisoner by sight for two years."

"Have you ever spoken with him?"

"Yes, I had a conversation with him not exceeding six days before the murder. I met him on the road and invited him to ride. I asked him why he walked, and he said it was hard times and he had not money to ride."

Judge Wells looked up at the courtroom clock and saw that it was nearly seven o'clock.

"Mr. French, I'm going to interrupt you here. Court will adjourn until nine o'clock tomorrow morning. The jury is dismissed."

Chapter Thirteen: The Trial

Day Three – Wednesday, July 1, 1874 – Morning Session

As on the previous days, deputies marched Sturtevant to the courtroom and secured him in the prisoner's dock. Observers noted that Sturtevant had added a collar and tie to his attire, "effecting a great improvement in his not very prepossessing appearance," according to the *Boston Journal*. The *Journal* correspondent noted that the prisoner had been attentive and "betraying no signs of nervousness" during the past two days of testimony. "In his cell, he evidently means to keep up his courage if it can be done by dancing the single shuffle, speaking to other prisoners in a cheerful manner, and making other manifestations of good spirits and unconcern."

The jury filed in promptly at nine o'clock. Judges Wells and Ames called the court to order and the government re-called William Jefferson. Attorney General Train took up the direct examination.

"Mr. Jefferson, yesterday you testified that a constable accompanied you to the place where you cut the stake now in evidence. Please tell the court who that was."

"Mr. Philbrick went with me to the place where the stake was cut."

"Thank you, sir. I have no further questions."

Judge Wells dismissed Jefferson after Attorney Harris indicated he had no questions and Train called Sturtevant's uncle, Joseph Dow of South Hanson. Dow identified himself after being sworn and Train asked him if he knew the prisoner and if he had had a conversation with him after the murder.

"I know the prisoner. I saw him after the murder on Tuesday morning at his house and talked with him about it. He asked me if I had heard of the murder and what I supposed they were murdered for. I told him I thought they were murdered for money."

"How did he respond?"

"He said he did not think they had much money by them except $600 that George Hayward of Halifax had paid them."

"Have you ever heard the prisoner refer to bounty money he had received?"

"I have heard William Sturtevant refer since the war to $800 which he received as bounty money from the war. He said he had loaned it to a woman two or three years ago and lost it all. The woman lived in Providence."

Several jurors raised their eyebrows and shifted in their seats. Dow had just confirmed that Sturtevant knew there was at least $600 in the house and they had no reason to doubt his testimony. Dow's statements also contradicted the prisoner's claim, as presented in the district attorney's opening statement, that the money taken from him by Constable Pratt was from the proceeds of his bounty. Dow was now testifying that the prisoner had lost his bounty money years ago.

Attorney Harris began his cross-examination and quickly changed the subject.

"What time did you arrive at the prisoner's house on Tuesday morning?"

"I went to Sturtevant's house on Tuesday morning at about 4:30 a.m. and called him up (woke him)."

"Are you sure it wasn't you who brought up the murders during your conversation?"

"I did not ask him if he had heard of the murders."

"How far do you live from Sturtevant's house?"

"I live two and a half miles away."

"Who first mentioned the money?" Harris asked.

"Mr. Sturtevant first mentioned the matter of money and spoke of his own accord," Dow related. "I knew before this that George Hayward had paid the Sturtevants money but did not know it until after I heard of the murder."

"Are you related to the Sturtevant family?"

"Yes, my wife is a sister of the prisoner's father. She is an heir of the property and has already received a payment from the property."

"Did you talk about anything else with the prisoner on Tuesday morning?"

"I had not much talk with the prisoner on Tuesday morning on other subjects than the murder."

"Was the prisoner awake when you went to his house at 4:30?"

"There was no light when I approached the house. I have no reason to think he was up until I called him."

"Has the prisoner ever worked for you?"

"Yes, he has worked for me at different times, the last time a year ago last fall for a few weeks. My business is shoemaking and I paid him about $2 a day."

"What was his situation at that time?"

"He was married, but not keeping house. He boarded with his wife's mother."

Sturtevant motioned to Harris.

"May I have a word with my client, Your Honors?"

"You may," Judge Wells replied.

Sturtevant leaned out from the dock and whispered in his attorney's ear. Sturtevant had remembered another occasion that might explain the bloodstains on his clothing.

Harris turned his attention back to Dow and asked him if he had ever helped the prisoner butcher a pig.

"Yes, I remember butchering a pig about Thanksgiving time, but cannot fix the date. The prisoner helped me cut it up."

On re-direct, Attorney General Train asked Dow why he was at Sturtevant's house at such an early hour on Tuesday.

"I was going to meet the freight train on the Tuesday morning I saw Sturtevant to ship some shoes. I went to the South Hanson depot first, but the train was late and I did not wait for it. I stopped by Sturtevant's on the way back."

Sturtevant glowered at Dow as he stepped down from the stand and left the courtroom.

The government called George Hayward of Halifax. Once sworn, Hayward confirmed he had paid Thomas Sturtevant $595 on January 16, 1874.

On cross-examination Hayward testified that the transaction took place in a back room at Thomas Sturtevant's house. Simeon and Mary Buckley were present.

"I took up the note," said Hayward. "Interest was computed upon it. The note was destroyed as soon as paid."

Hayward, a thirty-two-year-old married farmer with two children, explained that the note was three years and two months old and that he had borrowed money from Thomas to purchase property.

"How long were you at the house that day?" asked Harris.

"I was there three hours."

"Did anyone leave the room?"

"No person left the room while I was there except Thomas when he went for the note."

Hayward testified that he was there for an hour before he paid the money. He had placed it on a table in one hundred dollar piles.

"Did you see Thomas put the money away?"

"No."

"Did you tell anyone about the payment?"

"I talked with no person about the payment until Tuesday after the murder."

"Did you mention it to Officer Pratt?"

"No."

"Who did you speak to about the money after Tuesday?"

"Ephraim Thompson has asked me about the kind of money paid. I have told a number what kind of money it was and what denominations the bills were."

"What were those denominations?"

"There were $5, $10, $20, and other denominations. The highest denomination was a $20 bill."

Harris indicated he had no further questions for the witness, as did the attorney general. Hayward was excused and Train called Dr. Edward Wood of Cambridge, a Harvard professor and reputed expert in the analysis of blood. He was a graduate of Harvard College, class of 1867, and an 1871 graduate of Harvard Medical School. He was appointed a professor at the college immediately after receiving his medical degree.

Wood testified he had received evidence submitted to him for chemical analysis by officers Pratt, Philbrick, and Pinkham.

"Please tell the court what items were delivered to you and when."

"On February 21, the officers brought me a black felt hat, a gray double-breasted overcoat, a gray vest, a button shirt, a paper collar, a pair of congress boots, a piece of a pillow case, three pieces of wallpaper, and a piece of brown paper. On February 25, Pinkham and Philbrick brought me a cart stake. On March 7, Pratt delivered a pair of pants and a wallet. On April 21, Pratt delivered a one-dollar bill and a five-dollar bill. On April 25, Pratt brought to me a one-hundred-dollar bill of the Suffolk Franklin Bank of Boston, and on the twenty-third of May, a piece of a door casing. All of the articles are here in court today."

Train retrieved the gray, double-breasted overcoat from the prosecution table and presented it to the witness. Wood identified it as the coat he had received on February 21.

"Did you conduct a scientific examination of the overcoat?"

"Yes."

"What did you find?"

"On the overcoat there were twenty-one stains, numbered for examination, four of which were not blood as the rest are."

"How many of these stains did you examine?"

"I subjected thirteen of the stains to chemical testing to obtain crystals and a microscopic test for the corpuscles. All were certainly blood stains."

"Do the stains have the same appearance as when you first examined them?"

147

"The stains are darker now than when first brought to me. They are not so distinct. I shaved off the stains for testing with a sharp instrument. The stains were spatters."

Wood pointed out each of the stains he had found on the coat to the jury. He focused on a particular stain he had detected on the right hand side of the coat below the lower button hole.

"I wish to inquire what the stains upon the coat would indicate as to the direction from which the blood came," Train said.

Attorney Harris immediately objected.

"Your Honor, this question is beyond the scope of the witness's expertise. It has no relation to chemistry or any other branch of science."

Judge Wells turned to the witness and asked him, "Is the coat in the same condition now as then in that respect? Did it show anything then that it does not show now?"

"It did," Wood responded. "The natural rubbing from being handled has removed a portion. It could only be noticed, also, by the use of a lens."

"The natural rubbing of the coat has partially obliterated the blood?" Wells prompted.

"It has obliterated a portion of it; it can't be seen as distinctly."

Directing his attention to Attorney General Train, Wells said, "I think your first inquiry would be, whether there was anything discovered that indicated anything of the sort."

Train then asked Wood, "At the time you made your first examination, was there anything discoverable that indicated the direction from which the stains had come that you found upon the coat?"

"Yes, sir," Wood responded.

"What?"

"The appearance of the stains," replied the physician.

"Will you tell us what direction they had come from?"

Harris objected once more and said, "So far as the stains are concerned that are upon the coat, the jury can judge as well as he can."

"I think the witness can describe what it was that he saw that indicated the direction, and show what it was, rather than to give a general opinion as to what the direction was," Judge Wells ruled.

"I wish to reserve an exception," Harris said, "so far as the stains that are now upon the coat are concerned, and which the witness says are the same now that they were then, excepting the change resulting from the natural handling of the coat."

"I understand, also," Wells replied, "that he says that there were indications then that are not apparent now, that he examined it with a lens, and that that aided his examination. It is in that view that he is allowed to describe what the indications were which indicated the direction."

"What is not there now, we do not object to the witness describing; but so far as anything now visible, indicating which direction the blood came, is concerned, we object to that. We think the distinction should be observed by the witness; and unless Your Honors are of a different opinion, we ask that he may be confined to that," Harris argued.

Wells and Ames overruled Harris's objection. Judge Wells said, "We think he may give the whole description, as it was found. Dr. Wood, you may answer the question."

Harris, Keith, and Lord conferred in low tones at the defense table.

"It is an oval stain between one-eighth and one-fourth of an inch long, and one inch from the edge of the coat, on the right hand side, front, and three and three-fourths inches below the last buttonhole, the bottom button hole. The direction of the stain is diagonal. Using my own coat as an illustration, the stain lay in this direction (illustrating). The upper portion of the stain contained more blood than the lower, which it does not contain now, on account of its having been rubbed off," Wood explained.

"What does that indicate as to the direction?" Train asked.

Harris rose again.

"One moment," he argued. "If it is chemistry, we do not object; if it is anything else, we do."

"I think if the witness explains the reasons at the same time that he gives the result he may do so," Judge Wells ruled. Exasperated, Harris sat down.

"If the force of a stream of fluid," Wood testified, "whatever it may be, and especially blood, be from below upward, the heaviest portion of the drop will stop at the further end of the stain; if from above downward, it will stop below."

Harris was not satisfied. "That is pure opinion as to a matter of mechanics, not chemistry," he said. "Any butcher is just as good an expert on that as this witness."

Wells again overruled Harris and said, "The evidence is admitted subject to exception."

Wood concluded his answer by indicating that the direction of the stain could only be seen with a lens because of its size.

"Now, you have described one, the direction of which was upward and diagonal. Is there any other?" Train asked.

"Not upon the coat," Wood answered.

Wood returned the coat to Train, and Train submitted it to the jury for inspection. After the last juror examined it, Train offered the overcoat as evidence and the court ordered it marked as a government exhibit.

Train presented Wood with the defendant's paper collar and black felt hat, and a piece of bloodstained cloth. Wood confirmed he had received all three items from state investigators on February 21. He found two stains on the collar and eleven stains on the hat. He acknowledged that with the passage of time the stains on the hat had become darker and more indistinct and one or two had disappeared.

He identified the cloth as part of the pillowcase seized as evidence from Simeon's bed. He testified that the chemical and microscopic tests he had applied to the collar, hat, and cloth all confirmed the presence of blood.

The court admitted the collar, hat, and pillowcase sample as evidence without objection from the defense.

"Did you find any bloods stains when you examined the pants and the shirt?" Train asked.

"I did not."

Attorney General Train presented Wood with a piece of wallpaper and asked him to identify it.

"This piece of wallpaper is the same as that delivered to me by the state officers. It is said to have come from over the head of the [Simeon's] bed."

"What were the results of your analysis?"

"I found the stains on the wallpaper to be of blood and muscular tissue."

Train handed Wood a second and third piece of wallpaper and asked him to identify each.

"These came from over the mantelpiece and I confirmed, through testing, the presence of blood from the stains that appear on it."

Train moved to have the wallpaper entered into evidence, and with no objection from the defense, the three pieces were admitted and marked as government exhibits.

Train picked up the cart stake from the evidence table. Wood identified it as the stake submitted to him by Philbrick and Pinkham on February twenty-fifth. He told the court he examined the stake and found bloodstains and fragments of bone, one as large as a pea, imbedded in it. Wood had the fragments in his possession in a small paper box and gave them to Train for viewing by the jury. Train returned the stake to the evidence table and after a motion to the court, the bone fragments were also admitted as evidence.

Train then presented the witness with the vest, boots, and the portion of the door casing submitted to him by the officers. Wood testified that his examination revealed no blood on these articles. He also testified that he had examined several hairs on the boots and was of the opinion that some were human and others were not. Although some experts had microscopically shown hairs that had been found at a crime scene were consistent with a victim's hair as early as 1851, Wood was reluctant to assert that the hairs on the boots belonged to the murdered brothers and their housekeeper.

Train turned his attention to the currency seized by the officers and submitted to Wood last April. Wood told the court that he found stains on the one-dollar bill but none were blood. He did find a bloodstain on the right end of the face of the five-dollar bill. The bill was dated December 14, 1864. On the one-hundred-dollar bill, issued by the Suffolk National Bank on December 22, 1864, he found a bloodstain on the lower left hand corner of the face. All were entered into evidence.

"What is your expert opinion as to all of the bloodstains you tested?"

"In all of the stains I have examined, the globules are of exactly the same size, appearance, and character rendering it certain in all human probability that they are all of the same kind. They also correspond with those of my own blood, which I have taken. In all probability, these stains are all the same kind and are human."

Attorney Harris objected to Wood's opinion as to the stains being human as opposed to animal and was overruled by the court.

"When did you receive the one-hundred-dollar bill from the state officers?" Harris asked the professor on cross-examination.

"The bill was given to me on April 25, 1874."

"Do you recall a time recently when Attorney Keith and I visited your office?"

"I remember receiving from yourself and Mr. Keith a visit about four weeks since, in which I stated that all the money I showed you contained no bloodstains."

"And yet you testify today that you did in fact, find bloodstains, is that not true?"

"I acted under instructions [from the police] and do not hold myself responsible for any ideas you might have formed from answers. I did not say I had showed you all the money."

152

Wood underwent a sharp cross-examination about the scientific theories of determining the difference between human and animal blood.

"Do other experts in the field of chemistry believe that science can prove the difference between human and animal blood?" Harris posed.

"There is a wide difference of opinion between equally good authorities as to the possibility of making a distinction."

Wood was excused and Dr. Henry Bowditch, assistant professor of physiology at Harvard Medical School, took the stand to testify on behalf of the government. After he described his qualifications in the study of blood and chemistry he testified to receiving articles during the previous spring from Dr. Wood. Train showed Bowditch the articles of clothing, pillowcase fabric, wallpaper, paper bills, and the cart stake previously admitted in evidence and Bowditch confirmed they were the same articles he had received from Dr. Wood.

"What did you do with these articles?"

"I subjected them to the Haemin crystal test and the microscope test." (A crystal of salt and acetic acid is added to dried blood on a glass slide and heated. When cooled, crystals of rhombic rods form and confirm the presence of blood.) "On the hat, coat, pillow case, and paper collar I found human blood. On the cart stake I found blood and a piece of bone and adhering to the bone a small fragment of muscular tissue."

"Did you form an opinion as to the nature of the bloodstains?"

"Yes, my conclusions, from the measurements and other tests are consistent with the theory that the stains were human blood."

Train yielded his witness to Attorney Harris and on cross-examination, Bowditch conceded that not all experts were convinced that human and animal blood can be differentiated. He also admitted that it was very difficult to determine with certainty the presence of human blood in a dried specimen.

***

Analytical chemists testifying about blood evidence during this period were seeking to establish the validity of scientific testing. The courts were skeptical and reluctant to accept the idea that science could conclusively discern the differences, beyond a reasonable doubt, between human blood and the blood of animals.

In 1868, the issue was contested during the murder trial of Samuel Andrews. State Constable George Pratt had arrested Andrews and participated in his trial so he was not surprised when blood and its properties became a focal point of the Sturtevant defense. Chemists testified about the process used at that time to determine the presence of human blood on a number of exhibits offered by the commonwealth. A chemical analysis called the guaiacum test involved placing a suspected stain into a mixture of glacial acetic acid and chloride of sodium. The test positively confirmed the presence of blood but fell short of determining if the blood was human or animal.

The contemporary technique for differentiating between human and animal blood consisted of soaking the bloodstained item in glycerin and water for several hours and then scraping a sample of the stain onto a microscope slide. The chemist inspected the sample for particles of starch and fat globules and circular, biconcave, disc-like bodies that corresponded in shape and size to human, red blood corpuscles. The chemist compared those corpuscles with known blood corpuscle samples from humans, horses, cows, dogs, rabbits, and pigs by inspecting their shape and measuring their size. Unfortunately, the size and shape of the human corpuscle varied so much that chemists could not be conclusive in stating that a bloodstain was, in fact, human blood.

As late as 1895, Joseph H. Linsley, MD, professor of pathology and bacteriology at the University of Vermont, published an article in *Medical Record – A Weekly Journal of Medicine and Surgery* about the scientific examination of suspected human bloodstains. Linsley asserted that microscopic examinations used to measure the exact size of corpuscles in blood specimens could not conclusively determine whether the specimens were human blood. He found it regrettable that certain medical men, posing as experts, would offer testimony and declare they could positively identify a suspected bloodstain as originating from a human source.

In 1901, Dr. Paul Uhlenhuth, a German bacteriologist, developed the precipitin test, a fail-safe chemical method for distinguishing human blood from animal blood by the presence of unique proteins. The modern system for blood typing (ABO groups) was established the same year. Present-day forensic scientists still use the precipitin test to confirm human origin.

***

The last witness for the government before the noon recess was Cyrus Bates, the South Hanson stationmaster. Bates testified that the prisoner appeared at the depot on Saturday, February 14, and bought two railway tickets on credit.

"Did he pay you for them at a later time?"

"He paid for them on the next Monday, when he bought two more and paid for all with fifty-cent scrip."

"How often did you see him at the depot?"

"I saw him frequently, every night and morning nearly."

"Where is the scrip he paid you with now?"

"I don't have it and do not know what became of it."

Attorney Harris approached and asked the witness on cross-examination if it wasn't possible that the prisoner had paid him on Saturday evening and not on Monday.

"The prisoner did not pay me for the two tickets on Saturday evening."

"Did you make note of the time and date he paid you?"

"I did not make any charge or memorandum of the matter."

"What is your opinion of the prisoner?"

"I have no feeling against the prisoner."

"Did you ever tell anyone that you thought he was guilty of the murders?" Harris demanded, his voice rising.

"I think I never expressed an opinion of his guilt."

"Did you speak with Officer Pratt about the prisoner?"

"Yes, I spoke with him on Tuesday, but I did not tell him about the railroad tickets which the prisoner had bought."

"Are you sure of the number of tickets you sold to the prisoner?"

"I sold him only four tickets in all on Saturday and Monday."

Judge Wells looked over at the jury box and could see that some of the jurors had grown listless. He looked up at the courtroom's wall clock and called a recess.

Chapter Fourteen: The Trial

Day Three – Wednesday, July 1, 1874 – Afternoon Session

Spectators chattered excitedly in the gallery waiting for court to reconvene. All were anxious to hear the testimony of state investigators who were expected to be called next. At two-thirty, District Attorney French summoned State Deputy Constable George Pratt of Abington to the stand. A hush fell among the gallery, interrupted only by an occasional muffled cough.

Pratt testified that he had been a constable for eight years and, before that, he had been a shoe cutter.

"When did you first learn of the Halifax murders?"

"I was notified on Monday, February 16, and arrived at the Sturtevant house at about three or four o'clock."

"What did you see when you arrived at the house?"

Hushed silence prevailed in the gallery as spectators and the prisoner leaned forward and listened intently.

"When I arrived there I saw on the floor of the kitchen the bodies of the people killed. I was taken next into the front bedroom where on the wall at the head of the bed and on the bed and on the wall over the bed were spatters of blood."

The district attorney picked up several photographs, previously admitted, from the evidence table and asked Pratt to identify them.

"These are the photographs taken inside the Sturtevant house by Mr. Chamberlain in my presence."

"I draw your attention to the photograph of the front bedroom. Is it a fair representation of what you saw on the day you first responded to the scene?"

Pratt paused to look at the photograph. When he first entered the room the wallpaper was intact above the bed. He knew that Pinkham and Philbrick had removed several pieces for chemical analysis.

"When I first saw the room the paper was all on the wall at the back of the bed, and spattered with blood."

"Did you see any blood on the floor?"

"No, I did not."

"Where in the house did you go next and what did you observe?"

"I went to the sitting room and saw a bureau, some chairs, and a trunk. I saw nothing on the floor. I looked in at the top bureau drawer but took nothing from it. I took hold of one piece of scrip. There were more pieces of scrip there. I left the pieces I handled. It was of the old issue."

"How long did you remain at the house?"

"I was about the house until sunset and from there I went to the nearest house."

"Please tell the court what happened the next day."

"On Tuesday morning I went to South Abington to the shop of Henry Blake. I saw the prisoner there. He came down from his workplace to the counting room."

"What was the gist of your conversation with him in the counting room at that time?"

"I told him I was going down to the scene of the murder and asked him to tell me what he knew about it. He said the people were his uncles. He said they were not in the habit of keeping money in the house, that they were farmers and it took all the money they could earn to pay taxes. He said the woman was not a relative.

"I saw upon his collar what I thought was a small blood spot. He was in his shirt sleeves and I sent him for his coat. He went and got his undercoat and when he returned he said it was a horrible murder and he would do what he could to assist me. He said he could prove he was all right Sunday as he spent the day with Daniel Blanchard of East Bridgewater and got back home at five o'clock. He said that two young ladies named Drayton and Bonney were at his house and stayed until nine o'clock. He went to bed when they left."

"Please continue," French said as he poured a glass of water at the prosecution table.

"I took his hat from his head and thought I saw blood upon it. He thought it looked like blood but could not account for its being there. When I asked him for his shoe size, he told me that he wore seven- or eight-sized shoes. I had a measure which I had fitted to a footprint on Monday afternoon [at the Sturtevant house] and I tried it on one of his shoes. It did not fit. I asked if he had any other shoes and he told me he had a pair of congress boots at home which he did not wear as they did not fit."

"Did he tell you when he had last worn them?"

"He said he hadn't worn them in two months."

"What happened next?"

"He went with me to Dr. Copeland's office [in South Abington]. He did not have his overcoat. I borrowed a magnifying glass and the doctor and I examined his collar and hat. The prisoner examined it and said it looked like blood. He said if it was blood he must have got it on the Saturday night before when he bought a shin from Mr. Drayton. He said he had worn the collar since Sunday morning."

This statement was not lost on the jury. Drayton had testified previously that Sturtevant had bought the beef shin from him on Saturday evening, the seventh of February, not on Saturday, February 14th, the night before the murders.

French showed Pratt the hat and collar previously entered into evidence and he identified both as the same articles he had examined on the day in question. He had placed his mark on both articles when he seized them.

"Where was the prisoner's overcoat at this time?"

"He said his overcoat was down to his house, that it was an old, ragged coat which he wore to and from the shop. I borrowed a coat and hat for him and took his. I searched the pockets of the undercoat and found a small, black book (wallet) containing scrip, postage stamps, and nickels.

"Did you seize the stamps and money at that time?"

"Yes, there were nine postage stamps. I took part of the scrip from him – four pieces, two twenty-five cent pieces, one ten-cent piece, and one three-cent piece."

"What became of the stamps?"

"I have the postage stamps now."

"What did you do next?"

"I next went to his house at Keene's Corner in Hanson. Dr. Copeland went with us. I found his wife there when we arrived. While at his house he stepped into an adjoining room to speak with his wife.

"I went to his bedroom and examined his clothes with the doctor's magnifying glass. In a trunk was a suit of black which he said he wore on Sunday."

"What about his overcoat?" French asked.

"His overcoat was not there. We could not find it. He said the overcoat must be up to the shop, as he had worn it the Friday before."

The district attorney went to the evidence table and picked up the congress boots submitted during the testimony of Dr. Wood.

"Do you recognize these boots?"

"Yes, those are the boots I saw at Sturtevant's house two days after the murders. They are the same boots officer Pinkham seized and later delivered to Dr. Wood."

"Where did you go next?" French asked as he placed the boots back on the table.

"We next went to the Sturtevant house in Halifax and arrived there about three or four o'clock in the afternoon. We drove up in front of the barn, all three in one carriage. Dr. Copeland hitched his horses to the fence about twenty feet from the barn doors. Sturtevant stepped into the barn by the front door. I went close behind him. As I stepped in he turned to come out. He made a motion as if he was putting something in his pocket. I saw something drop by the sill of the barn and went and picked it up. It was a roll of bills, in all amounting to $208."

A stunned look came upon the faces of Attorneys Keith and Harris and both looked in Sturtevant's direction. He had never told them about this money.

"What did you do with the bills?"

"I took some of them subsequently to Dr. Wood for examination – a one-dollar bill, a five-dollar bill and a twenty-dollar bill."

"Was the prisoner aware that you had found the money?"

"No, I did not tell him, and he did not see me pick it up."

"Please continue, Officer Pratt."

"We went into the house. He said he would like to see the bodies and I left him in the room with them for fifteen minutes while I went to the barn to look for more money. I didn't find any. When the prisoner came out of the room I told him we would go back to Blake's shop and get the overcoat. We went there and he looked for the coat and I looked for it but we could not find it. He said he thought some workman must have worn it away.

"At half past six we started to go to Mr. Inglee's. We got there at eight o'clock and found there Mr. Inglee, Mr. Pinkham, and a man I did not know, and perhaps some ladies. I left William Sturtevant with Mr. Inglee and went with Mr. Pinkham into an adjoining room where we joined Mr. Philbrick. After a conversation, we went back into the room where Sturtevant was and told him he was under arrest for the murder of the people at the Sturtevant house and that he need not answer any questions. The prisoner told Mr. Pinkham that he could ask him any question he saw fit."

Sturtevant scowled at Pratt. He never took his eyes off of him as he testified.

"Did Pinkham interrogate the defendant?"

"Pinkham questioned him and the prisoner stated that on Sunday he went to bed at ten o'clock, got up at twelve, shook the coal in the stove and put on fresh. He said he got up at five o'clock Monday and went to work for the day. He also stated that he did not spend any money on Monday or Tuesday. He said Miss Lydia Reed paid him eighty-five cents for making a pair of shoes and that on Saturday night he paid fifty cents for a shin which he paid for with between two and three dollars in scrip which belonged to his son [gifts from neighbors].

"Philbrick left the room momentarily and returned with the prisoner's overcoat and showed it to him. He acknowledged it as his own. We next searched him and found a five-dollar bill in a vest pocket. He was told to take off his pants and when he stooped down to push off his left shoe he threw a small roll under the end of the sofa. It proved to be a one-hundred-dollar bill and a twenty-dollar bill."

French showed the two bills in evidence to Pratt but he could not identify them as the same bills thrown under the sofa.

"What happened next?"

"The prisoner was asked where he got the money and he answered that it was bounty money, that it was not the same money he received for bounty but had been changed. He said that all the money he had had for some time was the money that I had taken from him at Dr. Copeland's."

"Did you bring the prisoner to Plymouth that night?"

"No, we stayed at Mr. Inglee's that evening and on Wednesday morning came to Plymouth and committed him."

"Have you had any conversation with the prisoner since he has been jailed?"

Defense Attorney Harris objected to any answers the prisoner may have given to Pratt during his interrogation at the jail. Harris argued that the prisoner did not have the benefit of counsel during the questioning and that Pratt did not inform the prisoner of his right to remain silent. The district attorney countered that Pratt and other officers had informed the prisoner when he was arrested on February 17 that he was not obliged to answer any questions and that the witness had voluntarily offered responses.

"Officer Pratt," Judge Wells began, "did you at any time prior to the prisoner's arrest advise him of his right not to answer your questions?"

"Yes, Your Honor, I advised him on two or three other occasions."

"Did you offer him any inducement or exert any influence upon him to answer your questions?"

"No, Your Honor."

"The court is satisfied that the prisoner was fully cognizant of his right to remain silent and the objection of Mr. Harris is overruled," Judge Wells pronounced. "Mr. French, you may continue your direct examination of the witness."

"Thank you, Your Honor," said French, and turned back to his witness.

"Officer Pratt, did you have conversation with the prisoner at the jail?"

"Yes, on February 22 I visited him at the jail and he told me that a few days before the murder he was talking with Frank Osborne when two strangers came along with a pair of horses. Sturtevant said they wanted him to 'stir up' the horses and when he tried, one of the horses kicked him and knocked him over. When he got up his nose began to bleed."

"Did he have an explanation for the one-hundred and the twenty-dollar bills?"

"He said that when he was at the Sturtevant house with me on the day he was arrested he removed the two bills from a box on the bureau. As for the other one-hundred-dollar bill that I seized from the sill at the barn, the prisoner explained that he had accumulated the money by saving a dollar at a time. He added that when he went 'Down East' with his wife, he changed a one-hundred-dollar bill for a man in a drinking shop in Portland.

"I questioned him about the scrip he had spent on Monday and Tuesday, and he again denied he had ever passed any on those two days."

"Did the prisoner ever tell you that Simeon Sturtevant had given him money?" French asked.

"Yes," Pratt replied. "He said all the change he had ever received from Simeon Sturtevant was a year ago, when he bought a rake off Simeon for forty cents, giving him a two-dollar bill and receiving one dollar and sixty cents in change."

"Did you return to the Sturtevant house in Halifax after the arrest?"

"Yes, sir. I was present on Friday. I saw the money picked up near the gap in the fence. Two or three pieces were first picked up, and I think Mr. Thompson picked up more. I have seven of the pieces picked up – two that Mr. Blake found and five that I picked up."

French showed Pratt the clothing admitted previously as evidence and he identified all as articles he and other officers had taken from the prisoner on the day of his arrest.

"Was there something unusual about the pants you seized from the prisoner?" French asked as he handed Pratt the prisoner's pants.

Pratt turned the pants inside out, turned to the jury, and inserted his finger through one of the pockets.

"Yes," said Pratt. "As you can see, there's a hole in the pocket."

"Was there any other money seized?"

"Yes, at the house of Mr. Inglee on Tuesday evening some scrip and nickels were taken from the prisoner. I have them now. I also received three pieces of money from Frank Osborne a few days after the murder."

Attorney Harris asked Pratt on cross-examination when he first conversed with the prisoner about the murder.

"I first talked with the prisoner relative to the murder on Tuesday, February 17, at about 10:30 a.m."

"What was his demeanor?"

"He appeared no different when I saw him than usual."

"Did he pale when you spoke about the murders?"

"No, he didn't. He was very ready to help me, more so than any man I have met during the investigation."

"What else did you discuss with him?"

"I asked him questions concerning his height, size of his shoe, color of his eyes, and so forth. At his shop and at Dr. Copeland's I tried the pattern [made from the impression of the footprint at the Sturtevant murder scene] on his shoe and remarked that it did not fit. The heel was not so long, but wider."

"Was he considered under arrest during this conversation?"

"I had no warrant for his arrest at that time, and no authority to detain him. He made no offer to escape or leave me."

"What did he say when you showed him the stain on his clothing at Dr. Copeland's office?"

"He said, 'It looks like blood.'"

"How long were you at Copeland's office?" asked Harris.

"Between one and two hours," Pratt answered.

"Was he cooperative at all times?"

"Yes. I noticed no hesitancy or evasion on his part. He was perfectly willing to answer anything."

"Are you sure of the time that he told you the girls left his home on Sunday evening?"

"Yes," said Pratt. "He said they left at nine o'clock and told me he went to bed after they left."

"Was there any discussion with the prisoner about a theft from Joel White?"

"There was. I talked to him in Blake's shop about the robbery of Joel White's gold."

"Have you returned to the prisoner's house since the arrest?"

"I have been there several times and have talked with Miss Reed on two occasions."

Judge Wells noticed that several jurors had become restless and called for a brief recess. When court resumed, Harris continued his examination of Pratt.

"I bring your attention to the incident at the Sturtevant barn," Harris began. "Had you lost sight of the prisoner at any time at the barn?"

"He was out of my sight perhaps half a minute," Pratt answered. "As he passed out I passed in. We met at the door. I turned round as he passed me, and was looking at him from behind when he dropped the roll of bills."

"Did Dr. Copeland see this?"

"No, he was at that moment putting blankets on his horses."

"What did the prisoner do after he allegedly dropped the bills?"

"He walked immediately towards the house."

"How many times was the prisoner in the house on that day?"

"I do not think the prisoner went into the house more than once."

"Who did you first tell about the prisoner's alleged actions at the barn?"

"The first person I told about finding the roll of bills was Dr. Copeland on the twenty-second of February."

Sturtevant motioned to Harris and whispered something in his ear. Harris changed course.

"Did you ask the prisoner any other questions at Inglee's house that you have not previously testified to?"

"I asked him that evening if he would state whether he took Joel White's gold, or was the murderer of the Sturtevants."

"What did he tell you?"

"He denied responsibility for both."

Sturtevant rolled his eyes. Harris asked Pratt again if the prisoner was free to leave at any time during the questioning prior to his arrest.

"There was nothing to hinder the prisoner leaving me at any time on Tuesday, except such prevention as I might use on my own authority. I had no warrant or instruction from a superior," Pratt said with irritation.

"Did you discuss the evidence you had gathered against the prisoner with anyone prior to this trial?"

"I have been asked a great many times what evidence I have against the prisoner. I never told anyone any point until I spoke to Dr. Copeland, and not after I told the district attorney."

"How many times have you interviewed the prisoner at the jail?"

"Three."

Harris stepped away. "I have no further questions for the witness, Your Honors."

"You may step down, Officer Pratt," Judge Wells advised.

166

Sturtevant had a sneer for Pratt as he crossed in front of the dock and left the courtroom.

DA French and Attorney General Train quietly conferred for a few moments before French called Dr. Horatio Copeland as his next witness.

"Have you seen the prisoner before?" French asked.

"I saw William Sturtevant on Tuesday, February 17, at my house. He came there with Officer Pratt."

Copeland corroborated the previous testimony of Officer Pratt as to what had transpired at his office, at the prisoner's house, and at the Sturtevant house in Halifax. He did offer new evidence of a conversation he had had with the prisoner at his house in South Hanson.

"When Officer Pratt was in another room looking for the overcoat, Sturtevant said to me that he had nothing to do with the murder. He said that the place to look for the murderer was at Frye's, on the Pete Hagan place (a resort for hard characters), which I think is in Bridgewater. He also told me that it would be found that he was not guilty, and the blood spots came from the shin of beef."

The defense had no questions for Dr. Copeland and the government called Ella Drayton, age seventeen, the daughter of South Hanson grocer John Drayton. She was visibly nervous when she took the stand.

Drayton testified that she lived near the prisoner's house and that at seven o'clock on Sunday evening, February 15, she and Mercy Bonney stopped in to visit the prisoner and his wife at their home. They stayed until 7:30 p.m.

On cross-examination she told defense counsel that she lived about a quarter mile from the prisoner's home and had only been there once before. She didn't notice anything unusual about the prisoner's demeanor during her visit on Sunday evening.

"Where did you go after you left the prisoner's house?"

"I went right home from there."

"Are you sure about the time you left?"

"It might have been later than half past seven when I went home."

Drayton was dismissed and the government called twenty-one-year-old Mercy Bonney. The witness stated that she was living in South Hanson on the fifteenth of last February and was at William Sturtevant's house on that evening with Ella Drayton. She told the court that she and Ella left the house at half past seven and that she went right home.

Attorney Harris, on cross-examination, asked her if the prisoner had seemed out of sorts during her visit. She testified by stating that he didn't seem out of sorts at all, but seemed his usual self.

Chapter Fifteen: The Trial

Day Four – Thursday, July 2, 1874 – Morning Session

As it had been throughout the trial, the courtroom was filled with spectators, the majority women. Fresh flowers had replaced the wilting bouquets of the day before. Newspaper reporters noticed that Sturtevant appeared to be in good spirits as deputies removed his restraints and placed him in the dock. Before the trial opened one reporter asked him how he felt.

"I'm as happy as a clam," the enthusiastic prisoner responded with a bright smile.

When court was called to order, the government called State Detective Hollis Pinkham. After being sworn, Pinkham identified himself and testified that he had been assigned to assist in the Sturtevant murder investigation by Chief Constable George Boynton.

Pinkham told the court the first step in his investigation brought him to the prisoner's home at Keene's Corner in South Hanson at about 4:00 p.m. on Tuesday, February 17. Sturtevant's wife, Abbie, and his twenty-month-old son, George, were present when he arrived at the modest, sparsely furnished, Cape-style home. He testified that he had searched the entire house and the attic.

"What did you find?"

"In the bedroom I found a coat hanging on a nail behind the bedroom door and a pair of congress boots, which I brought away."

French removed the overcoat and boots from the evidence table and asked Pinkham if he could identify them.

"Yes, those are the same boots and the same overcoat I took from the house."

"Are the boots in the same condition you found them?"

"No. When I found the boots they were very damp, as though they had been washed. I put my hand inside and found them very wet. There was not much mud upon them."

"Where did you go after you left the house?"

"I went to Edwin Inglee's place in Halifax. I got there about 7:00 p.m. Inglee, William Crocker, and, I think, Charles Paine were present. Pratt arrived soon after with the prisoner."

"What happened there?"

"At the house, Pratt placed Sturtevant under arrest and informed him that he was not obliged to answer questions. Sturtevant said, 'I am not guilty and can tell where I was.'"

"What did the prisoner tell you?"

"He said he was at Daniel Blanchard's through Sunday, that he came home at 5:00 p.m. and did not go out again that night. He told us he went to bed about 10:00 p.m. and got up again at midnight and fixed the fire. On Monday, he said, he got up at 5:00 a.m. and went to work, working all day.

"He said he spent no money on Monday but had on Saturday night when he bought a shin at Drayton's and paid fifty cents for it, and at the same time bought a fish which he did not pay for."

Again, testimony about Sturtevant's statements contradicted grocer John Drayton's assertion that the shin was purchased on the seventh of February and not the fourteenth.

"What else did he tell you?"

"He said that during the week before he had paid his house rent and bought some coal. He had received $15 from Mr. Whitmarsh that week. He told us that he had paid Mr. Drayton for some soap and apples in money, that he had paid the depot master for tickets on Monday. He also said he had received money from Mrs. Reed for work on shoes. He informed us that Mr. Pratt had taken some scrip and some postage stamps from him."

"Was there any discussion about postage stamps?"

"He said that while he was Down East he sent for some money to Mr. Dow who sent him $15, but he returned before the money arrived in Lisbon and the postmaster at that place, according to his instructions, re-mailed it to him, and those postage stamps were a part of the change after paying expenses."

"How did he explain having the scrip that Pratt seized?"

"He said the scrip belonged to his little child, given him by the neighbors, in an amount of $3 or $4. He could not name any person who had ever given the money."

"What happened next?" the district attorney inquired.

"I asked him if he had any money presently. He said he had none. I searched him and found in his right hand vest pocket a five-dollar bill. In taking off his pants he tried to pull off the left leg over his shoe, and took something from near the shoe and slipped it under the sofa. Philbrick stooped and picked up a one-hundred-dollar bill and a twenty-dollar bill," Pinkham responded.

French took the two bills from the evidence table, showed them to Pinkham, and he positively identified them as the same bills Philbrick had taken from under the sofa. French returned the bills to the table and asked Pinkham how Sturtevant explained the money.

"He said he took the five-dollar bill from a pocket book in his wife's work basket and the $120 was his bounty money. He hesitated very much while he said so and explained that the $120 was not the identical money but the proceeds of it. He said he had not the money with him when Mr. Pratt searched him and that he had taken the $120 also from his wife's work basket while Mr. Pratt and Dr. Copeland were in another room at his house. He explained that he took the money because he expected to be arrested and took it to employ counsel because he expected to be arrested from what Mr. Pratt had said to him and what the officer had found out."

"Did you question him about his overcoat?" French asked.

"He identified the overcoat as his own when I showed it to him," Pinkham responded. "He said the last time he wore it was on Friday (With this statement Sturtevant contradicted previous statements by Sturtevant to Pratt and others that he had purchased the beef shin on the

Saturday before the murders) and that he had not seen it since. He couldn't account for the stains on it, unless they had come from the beef shin. He remembered the wrapping paper in the closet and said it had been wrapped around the shin bone."

"What did he have to say about the boots?"

"He said he had not worn them at all on Sunday as they were large and hurt his feet."

"Did you notice any marks or scratches on his face or neck?"

"No."

"Please continue, Mr. Pinkham."

"We passed the night at Inglee's house. The next morning the prisoner was removed to Plymouth. On Wednesday morning Mr. Philbrick and myself went down to the road leading to Blake's house and near the gap in the fence we found a footprint, the track pointing towards Mr. Inglee's store. The left congress boot fitted that track exactly. The heel and toe were impressed. The whole footprint was defined. On Friday, I found a coin and picked it up."

French showed Pinkham the cart stake and he positively identified it as the stake found near the body of the Buckley woman.

Please describe for the court how you identified the cart stake."

"The result of the search for the place from whence the cart stake had been taken was that we found a cart having places for twelve stakes, eleven of which were present and one missing. We found the cart in front of Mrs. Josselyn's house, about thirty feet from the street in an open space with no fence next to the street. The stake we carried fitted the hole in the cart from which a stake was missing.

"As you look at the stake here admitted into evidence, does it look the same as it did when you first saw it?"

"On the bloody end of the stake when I first saw it there was fresh plastering."

"Were you able to determine where this fresh plastering may have originated?"

"There was an indentation in the plastering in Simeon's room."

"Thank you, Mr. Pinkham. I have no more questions. Your witness, Mr. Harris."

Harris approached the stand for cross-examination.

"How long were you at the prisoner's house on February 17?"

"I stayed at the house half or three-quarters of an hour."

"Did you speak with Mrs. Reed while you were there?

"Yes. I asked Mrs. Reed if she knew of the prisoner's whereabouts on Sunday. I think she told me she heard the stove covers rattle."

"Did you speak with Mr. Daland?"

"I have never seen Mr. Daland, who is reported to own the house and to live there, for whom Mrs. Reed is housekeeper."

"Did you ever make any attempt to locate Daland to ask if he heard the stove covers rattle?"

"No."

"What else did Mrs. Reed tell you during your visit?" Harris continued.

"She told me she saw Sturtevant in the yard just before sundown Sunday; that there were two young ladies there in the evening. She said she was awakened twice in the night. She also told me that she knew Sturtevant was up at five in the morning because he came to her to borrow a scraper to clear out the stove," Pinkham replied.

"Is your testimony here today influenced by the testimony of other witnesses?"

"I have not heard one word of testimony offered in this courtroom during this trial," Pinkham replied sternly.

"Did you take any notes about the events of Sturtevant's arrest and interrogation?"

"Sturtevant was very free to talk to me about the circumstances connected with the murder. I made no memorandum of the conversation which was held at Mr. Inglee's house on Tuesday night at that time. I rely upon my memory for the substance of the conversation."

"Did you make any memoranda after the conversation?"

"Yes. I made partial memoranda of the conversation sometime afterward."

"Did you read any memoranda prepared by Mr. Pratt?"

"I did not."

"Can you swear to the exact language of the conversation between you and the prisoner at Inglee's house?"

"No."

"Have you gone to Lisbon [Maine] to confirm the prisoner's story about the money he received from Mr. Dow?"

"I have not and don't know that anyone has."

"Was the prisoner's wife aware you had taken the defendant's overcoat?"

"I do not think the prisoner's wife saw me take the overcoat from the house."

"Did she give you permission for the search?"

"She made no objection to my searching the house."

"You stated on direct examination that you found indentations in the ceiling at the scene of the crime. Do you know if those marks are still there?"

"I have examined the ceiling at the Sturtevant house within a month and find no difference in the marks. They look just as fresh now as when I first saw them."

"The government alleges that the piece of the pillowcase submitted by you and others came from Simeon Sturtevant's room. Are you in agreement with this?"

"I do not know that the pillowcase from which I cut the piece examined by Dr. Wood came from Simeon's room."

Judge Wells called for a brief recess at this point and Pinkham stepped down. When the trial resumed, the government called State Detective Chase Philbrick.

Sworn, Philbrick identified himself and explained that he was called to assist the investigation of the Sturtevant murder on Monday, February 16, reaching the house at nine o'clock the same evening. That night he also visited Edwin Inglee's house and the next morning returned to the Sturtevant place. He remained there until 3:00 p.m.

"Mr. Philbrick," DA French began, "please tell the court when you first saw the cart stake now in evidence."

"The first I ever saw of the stake was on Tuesday evening when it stood in the corner of Simeon's room. It came into my possession at two o'clock that day, and I have had it ever since, except when Dr. Wood had it. It was in the same condition as now, except the blood showed somewhat plainer. Behind the door of Simeon's room I found a sliver which fitted a place in the end of the stake from which a fragment had been torn or broken."

French presented the stake and sliver to the witness and he identified both as the same stake and sliver he had found in Simeon's room. French asked the witness to fit the sliver into the stake and it fit precisely, although by this time the splinter, which was several inches long, had warped slightly.

"Did you find any indentations in the ceiling of the house?"

"In the back porch of the Sturtevant house I saw marks on the ceiling, as though partly made with a sharp instrument. In Simeon's room there were blood marks upon the ceiling, and freshly made indentations."

The remainder of Philbrick's testimony basically corroborated Detective Pinkham's, but before he was excused, DA French asked him a final question.

"Mr. Philbrick, will you please tell the court your best recollection of what the prisoner said as to his guilt or innocence at Mr. Inglee's house?"

"When Sturtevant was told he was under arrest he replied, 'I am all right. I did not murder those people. I have not been to their house but once for a year and that was at the funeral of my grandmother.'"

"Thank you, Mr. Philbrick. I have nothing further."

Attorney Harris questioned Philbrick at length and his answers were substantially the same as he had offered on direct examination.

Harris had the detective repeat his recollection of statements the prisoner had made regarding the stamps found in his possession by Constable Pratt, and questioned him about the comparison of the congress shoe and the tracks found across the road from Blake's at the gap in the fence.

"How can you be so sure that this congress boot," Harris asked, holding the boot aloft in his hand, "was the same boot that made the track?"

"The most prominent characteristic of the imprint was the line of leather on the sole that formed the re-lapping of the boot. When I saw that, and the fact that the print corresponded with the size of the boot, I was certain the boot had made the track."

Harris asked some additional questions, but none were of importance to the defense in overturning any previous evidence or testimony.

DA French felt a need to clarify Philbrick's testimony about the tracks so, as an added precaution, he recalled Constable Pratt to corroborate the detective's statements.

"Your Honors, may it please the court," Train said as Pratt left the courtroom, "unless something has been inadvertently omitted, the government rests its case."

Chapter Sixteen: The Trial

Day Four – Thursday, July 2, 1874 – Afternoon Session

Jesse Keith, junior counsel for the defense, rose at a signal from Judge Wells and addressed the jury with his opening argument when court resumed.

"May it please the court; gentlemen of the jury, the responsibilities of defense counsel in this case pales in comparison to those resting with the jury, who have life or death as the result of their faithful deliberations. You must, with the greatest care, consider all the circumstances of the case and exercise deliberate thought and action on all its details."

Keith recounted the leading features of the case, so unusual in the annals of crime. He reminded them of the readiness of the common mind to fix suspicion of guilt upon some person at the time of its commission, the terribly tragic nature of the crime, and the corresponding excitement resulting from it – all of which circumstances may have led to hasty and unwise opinion and action on the part of the public and those interested in discovering the perpetrator of this great crime.

"William E. Sturtevant had no fears of the result of the investigation. He rested confidently in his innocence. It has been indicated to some extent in the handling of the witnesses so far in the trial.

"We expect to explain to you the bloodstains which have been discovered on the clothes of the accused, and also that whoever committed the murder could not have escaped such trivial stains as those which have been examined here. We will further show you, by the testimony of experts, that it is impossible to determine whether dried blood has been extracted from human beings or from animals.

"We also propose to satisfy your minds as to the whereabouts of the prisoner on the Sunday afternoon and evening immediately preceding the tragedy and to give you his appearance and habits.

"We will explain the presence of a part of the money found on his person, and that the scrip which has been exhibited here is not as uncommon as is alleged.

"The condition of the ground in the vicinity of the Sturtevant house on that night was such that the prisoner could not have approached it without leaving certain marks of his presence imprinted close by the very threshold and all about. We will show you that the footprints that were discovered by the state officers were not made by any shoe the accused ever wore, and that it would be impossible to have those tracks identified after so long a time having elapsed between the time at which they are said to have been made and the time of their discovery.

"Remember that the life of a fellow being is in your hands. I warn you against receiving or retaining any impressions other than those which are derived from sworn testimony. On these and many other considerations I would ask for a verdict for the prisoner, a verdict you, gentlemen of the jury, can reflect upon with pleasure throughout the remainder of your lives and which should alike do justice to the prisoner and the Commonwealth."

Keith returned to the defense table and sat down. Attorneys Harris and Lord whispered congratulations to their colleague and Harris called the first defense witness.

Dr. Horace Chase of Boston left his seat inside the bar enclosure and took the stand. He had been a physician for ten years, he testified, had studied in Germany for seven years, and had specialized in the subject of bloodstains for the past twelve years. He had been called as an expert witness twice before in capital trials.

"Dr. Chase, please describe for the court the nature and characteristics of human blood."

"The characteristics of the red globules in fresh human blood are small, bi-concave bodies with a diameter of one three-thousandth to one five-thousands of an inch.""

"Is it possible to determine whether dried blood was human or animal?"

"It would be almost impossible to tell whether dried blood, whose globules were reduced from having lost their moisture, was human or animal."

"Is it possible to restore dried human blood to its original state, doctor?"

"To restore dried blood, a liquid must be added to restore the specific gravity of the natural fluid. The fluid may be made in many ways."

"What indications are displayed to show that the dried blood has been successfully restored to its original state?" Harris asked with his hands clasped behind his back.

"The time required to make satisfactory experiment with dried blood depends on how long it has been dry. The measurement of the restored corpuscles would determine whether the result was satisfactory or not," Chase answered.

"What will your measurement of the restored corpuscles indicate?"

"The size of the corpuscles is the distinctive feature between the blood of man and the blood of other animals of the same species. The restored corpuscles of dried human blood would be nearer that of the size of other animals than of man."

"Thank you, doctor. I have no other questions at this time."

Attorney General Train conferred with DA French then rose to approach the witness for cross-examination.

"Dr. Chase, have your studies indicated that it is possible to differentiate between the blood of man and the blood of animals when in a moist state?"

"I have no doubt that I can determine between the blood of other animals and man by the measurement test alone."

"And if the blood is in a dried state?"

"In two specimens of dried blood – one of which I knew to be

179

human – I should want the two to correspond very nearly to say they were both human."

"What measurement are you looking for in the restored globule?"

"I take an average from a number of tests."

"What are the parameters?"

"A measurement of between one five-thousandths and one fifty-four-hundredths of an inch," the physician replied.

"If a given fluid restores the globule in a known human blood stain, and also an unknown stain, to one fifty-four-hundredths of an inch, would these two specimens be of the same class?"

"I should regard as conclusive that it was the same species of blood but should rather have the measurement nearer if I was making the test."

Train concluded his cross-examination and Attorney Harris questioned the witness on re-direct.

"Does blood in a dried state reach a certain testing limit?"

"I have restored blood that has been dried three months, so that it corresponded exactly with fresh blood taken from my own body."

"How long does it take for you to restore such a specimen?"

"It sometimes takes six days."

"And what are the chances for success?"

"Perhaps twenty per cent of the corpuscles treated may be restored to original size."

"Thank you, Dr. Chase."

"Your Honors, the defense calls Dr. Joshua Treadwell."

Treadwell nodded to Dr. Chase as they passed by one another inside the bar. After he was sworn, Treadwell identified himself as a Harvard educated physician with specialized study in the area of bloodstains.

"Dr. Treadwell, in your expert opinion, what is an acceptable measurement of the human blood globule?" attorney Harris asked.

"The accepted diameter of the red globule in man is from one thirty-two hundredths to one five-thousandths of an inch. The theories differ slightly and corpuscles also vary. My own experience shows it to be one thirty-five to one thirty-six hundredths of an inch," said Treadwell.

"Would you find these levels acceptable in a specimen of dried blood?"

"In restoring dried blood, I wish to restore as nearly as possible the corpuscle to its original size."

"How does the length of time a specimen of blood has been dried affect your opinion?"

"If I had dried blood in my possession which after seven days treatment had only been restored to within one fifty-four hundredths to one six-thousandths of an inch, I should consider the result unsatisfactory."

Harris retrieved a book, *The Principles and Practice of Medical Jurisprudence*, written by Dr. Alfred Swaine Taylor and published in 1873, from the defense table and handed it to his witness.

"Does your opinion on this subject coincide with the views of Dr. Taylor as expressed in his book on medical jurisprudence?"

"It does," Treadwell replied.

"Would you please read aloud the paragraph I have marked inside the book?"

Attorney General Train immediately objected to the reading of any of the book's contents, and the court sustained his objection.

"Dr. Treadwell," Attorney General Train began his cross-examination, "if a fluid restores a globule in a known human blood stain and also an unknown stain to one fifty-four hundredths of an inch, would these two specimens be probably of the same class?"

"I should say there would be no probability about it. Nothing could be predicted upon it."

Attorney General Train indicated he had no other questions.

Attorney Harris called Daniel Blanchard, Sr., and followed with his wife, Lois. They lived opposite the home of their son, Daniel, Jr., on Washington near Oak Street in East Bridgewater. Both testified they had seen the prisoner leave their son's house on foot at four-thirty on Sunday afternoon, February 15. They said the prisoner was not wearing a coat over his black suit and had walked in the direction of South Hanson.

To the consternation of the defendant and his attorneys, Mrs. Blanchard, on cross-examination, contradicted Sturtevant's alleged statement to Pratt at Henry Blake's shoe shop that he hadn't worn his congress boots for two months. When Train showed her the congress boots in evidence, she stated they were similar to the boots Sturtevant was wearing on Sunday afternoon.

On re-direct by Attorney Harris, the witness, perhaps realizing adverse impact of her statement, admitted she could not say positively that the boots were the ones Sturtevant was wearing on the day in question.

Twenty-eight-year-old Daniel Blanchard, Jr. took the stand and confirmed he had lived in East Bridgewater at the South Abington town line the previous February with his wife, Lydia Parris Blanchard, Abbie Sturtevant's half-sister. He testified that Sturtevant had visited with him and his wife until four-thirty on Sunday, February 15, and corroborated the testimony of his parents by stating that the prisoner was wearing a black suit and no overcoat at the time. He said he did not recognize the congress boots in evidence.

Blanchard's wife Lydia, eighteen, verified her relationship with the prisoner's wife and said she too remembered Sturtevant wearing a black suit without an overcoat. To a question about the prisoner's demeanor during his visit she stated he seemed his usual self. On cross-examination she could not recall if the prisoner wore an overcoat that day, nor could she remember the type of shoes he wore.

Julius White, a twenty-five-year-old sawyer from South Hanson and relative of Joel White, testified he saw the prisoner on two occasions on Sunday, February 15. Sturtevant walked by his house at ten o'clock in the morning and stopped by at five in the afternoon to collect his milk pail. On cross-examination, White also failed to recollect what the prisoner was wearing at the time.

Helen Harding, who lived nearly opposite the home of Daniel

Blanchard in East Bridgewater, testified that she spoke with the prisoner on Sunday, February 15. When asked about his demeanor, the witness stated that the prisoner was cheerful and his conversation as usual. She also said on cross-examination that the prisoner was not wearing an overcoat.

The defense called Thomas Cook, a co-worker of Sturtevant's at Blake's shoe shop, to attest to the prisoner's work ethic. Cook testified that he had seen the prisoner on Monday, February 16, that he had come into work at the usual time, and had stayed the entire day.

"How did the prisoner typically get to work?"

"Sometimes he came afoot and sometimes he rode."

"What kind of worker would you consider him to be?"

"He was industrious. He worked every day but one during the time he was employed."

Charles Keene of Hanson testified that he knew the prisoner and lived near him in Keene's Corner. Keene testified that last December 8 he saw the prisoner kill a hen hawk with an axe.

Joel White of South Hanson was called by the defense and was asked if a certain amount of gold had been stolen from him. Before the witness could answer, Attorney General Train objected. He knew exactly where Harris was going with this line of questioning. Sturtevant had repeatedly denied to Constable Pratt that he had stolen the money from White. Now he wants to admit to the theft?

Attorney Harris addressed the court.

"Your Honors, almost a year ago this witness lost $200 in gold which he finally charged William Sturtevant with stealing. The prisoner does not deny the allegation. The defense asks that this witness's testimony on the subject might be heard to establish the fact that the money in the prisoner's possession could be accounted for on another theory than that he took it from the Sturtevant house."

"The government's objection is sustained and the witness will not be permitted to testify on the subject," Judge Wells ruled.

With their next witnesses, the defense continued its strategy of showing that the defendant's financial condition was not as dire as the government alleged. The first witness was Francis Bourne of Hanson, who testified that Sturtevant had worked for him two years before for a period of five days and that he paid him $12.60 for his services.

William Nash of Abington stated that the prisoner had worked for him for three or four weeks in September 1872. He paid him a total of $37.88.

Davis Gurney of Abington employed the prisoner in August and September 1872 as a bootmaker and paid him $33.75.

Horace Reed, also of Abington, retained the prisoner's services in February 1873 and paid him $12.12.

Harrison Packard of Packard Brothers, a country store in Halifax, testified that on or about January 20, 1874, he borrowed $600 from Thomas Sturtevant. The transaction took place in the afternoon inside the witness's store.

"Did you receive a note from Sturtevant for this loan?"

"Yes."

Harris showed the witness a noted signed by Thomas Sturtevant and Packard identified it as the same note he and Thomas had signed at his store. The court admitted the note as evidence.

"What were the denominations given you by Thomas Sturtevant?"

"There were no bills larger than twenty dollars."

"Had you ever borrowed money from Thomas before?"

"No, but I had traded with him."

To the surprise of many of the spectators in the courtroom, the defense called previous government witness Ephraim Thompson.

"Are you the administrator of the Simeon and Thomas Sturtevant estates?" Harris asked.

"I am," Thompson admitted.

"Did you make inventory of the money found in the Sturtevant's house in the aftermath of their murders?"

"Yes."

"Please tell the court what you found."

"I found $2,900 in the house within two days of the committal of the murders."

"I will ask you whether you had in fact made endeavors to ascertain what moneys could be traced to the possession of the Sturtevants, and what money they had paid out," Harris proposed.

Attorney General Train objected and insisted that Thompson's duty as administrator had nothing to do with the case and that none of the papers or ledgers found in the Sturtevants' house had been introduced as evidence. He further stated that Thompson had already testified during cross-examination on the second day of trial that he had found promissory notes but no savings or other bank accounts among the Sturtevant brothers' effects.

"I want to know whether the fact is not ascertained that this theory of the government is not supported, and I wish to show that investigation has been made, and it has been shown that there was no such fact," Harris argued. "They have not put in any refutation of it; yet they have opened a line of testimony from which they propose to show that these people were in the habit of keeping money, and that this prisoner knew it, and that that was the motive to the attempt upon their lives; and then they undertake to say that between $330 and $400 were stolen in that house by this party and taken away. We shall show the contrary of that. We shall show what was received and was accounted for. We shall be able to destroy, I think, the proposition that there was a large amount of money taken from that house."

"The court think [sic] that the fact cannot be established in that way," Judge Wells insisted.

"I limit the offer to the precise point," Harris argued, "that the investigation disclosed that there was not any such sum of money as is stated by the prosecution taken from that house; that there has been a thorough investigation made of the business relations and money transactions of these parties for a considerable period prior to their death, and also an investigation as to what was the disposition they had made of their money. Upon that investigation there is not found that there was any such sum of money unaccounted for as is said to have been taken by the prisoner."

"It is the same proposition, I think," Wells commented. "I think the amount of money that they may have had is not to be determined by information which the administrator may have obtained by inquiry or examination of the papers. Objection sustained."

Harris resumed and asked Thompson if he had found any ledgers or account books belonging to either of the Sturtevants. Thompson replied he had not.

"Did you find any bank books in their names on the premises?"

"I did not," said Thompson.

The defense called William Beal of Hanson. He testified that the prisoner had worked for him two years before as a shoemaker and he had paid the prisoner forty dollars for his work.

The court called a brief recess after excusing Beal and, when the trial resumed, Attorney Harris offered as evidence a copy of the 1862 Act of Congress, "The Legal Tender Act," which authorized the issuance of $150 million in United States [scrip] Notes. Harris asserted that all of the currency put into evidence by the government in the case was issued under the act. Harris read a portion of the act aloud and argued that, given the large amount issued by the United States, the scrip in evidence was not as rare as the Commonwealth alleged, but in fact was still in common circulation. Harris offered the copy of the Congressional Act as evidence and Judge Wells ordered it admitted and marked as a defense exhibit.

Attorney Harris advised the court that he had sent a constable to check on the condition of the defendant's wife.

"Your Honors, the constable tells me that Mrs. Sturtevant is still indisposed and unable to appear as a witness. We will send for her again in the hopes that her health has improved. I have spoken with her on several occasions. She will testify that her husband came home on Sunday night, went to bed at nine o'clock, and got up the next morning. She informs me that she is a sound sleeper and heard or knew nothing of his getting up in the night.

"We regret that Mrs. Sturtevant has been unable to testify to these facts, but we are content at this point, Your Honors," Harris continued, "to rest our case."

"The court will adjourn. The prosecution and defense will present closing arguments when court reconvenes at 9 o'clock tomorrow morning," Judge Wells instructed. "Witnesses are hereby dismissed. Gentlemen of the jury, you are not to discuss the evidence among yourselves until the government and the defense have concluded their closing summations and you have been dismissed for deliberation."

Chapter Seventeen: The Trial

Day Five – Friday, July 3, 1874 – Morning Session

Closing Argument of the Defense

Into the late evening and early morning hours Attorneys Harris and Keith pored over the evidence and enhanced the argument they hoped would convince the jury to exonerate their client. The two men had decided early on that senior counsel Harris would present the closing statement. Harris was ill and had struggled throughout the trial with a renal condition that had weakened him, but he insisted on assuming the responsibility.

"May it please Your Honors, and you Mr. Foreman, and gentlemen of the jury," Attorney Harris began solemnly, his hands clasped behind his back. "The government says that this prisoner, of his malice aforethought, of deliberate purpose and studied plan, for the purpose of possessing himself of certain monies, commits this most atrocious crime; that he carefully marked out the route he would travel; that he knew the road well; that he reasoned closely upon all the preliminaries. The prisoner is shown to be an undersized man; Thomas Sturtevant is represented as a large, muscular man, Simeon as a man of remarkable agility, while of the person of Mary Buckley little is known. Knowing all these facts, and the premises upon which he was about to act, the height of the rooms, and every incident connected with the scene, this prisoner deliberately set out, armed with no other weapon than a stake, four-and-a-half-feet long, to perform this great crime. In every and all respects the theories are improbable.

"Another principal theory advanced by the government is that the prisoner was a poor man up to the night before the murder, and had money in plenty on the day after, and that he must have obtained his

188

money in this way, as they would show he had disposed of all his money before the Saturday night previous, we deny this in all its parts. The government has shown nothing of the kind, all sympathy of the community is with the government in this case, every means possible have [*sic*] been afforded them to follow it up, but nothing of the kind has been proved. We have shown that money was honestly paid the prisoner during the two years before this murder was committed, amounting to $507, honestly earned and paid him, which they have in no way accounted for as being paid away.

"It is important that when we go into the dark we should be sure that we have a solid foundation on which to place our feet, and if the government is to prove the statement alleged why have they not accounted for the disposal of the money he honestly earned and received? The government have [*sic*] not shown the first proposition on which they stand.

"It is asserted that the prisoner committed the crime in a deliberate manner. Every day improbable things occur," the lawyer pointed out, his arms now akimbo. "But, because improbable, it does not follow they can be traced. It is proved, perhaps, that the crime was committed but in no sense have [*sic*] the government shown that *this man* was the perpetrator. There is doubt, and this prisoner must have the benefit of it.

"It is asserted that the motive for the crime was robbery; that the same hand struck the blow which ended the life of each victim. It is improbable if he knew the premises as asserted that he should have taken such a terribly roundabout way, including murder, to go at it, when he might so easily, if he knew the premises, have got at it without detection. Nor have the government shown that the prisoner ever knew there was money in the house. The prisoner is a poor fellow, knocked about the world and of no particular esteem, but he has practical everyday common sense and, if he went there at all, went to get something he knew was there. The evidences of robbing, so far as shown, prove it to have been committed by someone who did not know the premises or how to get at the money.

"If this man is the murderer, what sort of preparation did he make for the crime? He spent the day Sunday four-and-one-half miles from home, and walked all the way, going and coming, his appearance was in no way unusual, there were no movements uncommon or suspicious. He had not so much of a weapon as a pocketknife; he had been at work steadily for a month before the murder was done. Can it be that all this time that terrible crime was seething in his mind? He was free and merry on the Sunday, no indications of any such purpose, even the slightest, are even claimed to have been apparent.

"Four cardinal points are put forth by the government, on which they rest their convictions – the stake, the footprints, the money, and the bloody clothes. I ask you to consider the words of the gentleman who is to follow me, not as to whether he forges a chain of evidence, but if he connects one end of the chain to William E. Sturtevant and the other to the bodies of the murdered people.

"It is well to weigh with the utmost carefulness every detail of circumstantial evidence, if a person determined to throw suspicion on an innocent man, he would have left the stake just where it was found. How easily it might have been concealed or destroyed by the murderer! There is not a particle of evidence in the case that this stake was seen on that cart after the 3rd of January, no evidence that it was ever used or missed after that date. They assert the prisoner took the stake from the cart on Sunday night, February 15th, but they have not shown the stake was ever there after January 3rd. Any person could have taken it between those dates, any person may have taken it; there is no evidence that it was there, and it was not connected in any way with William Sturtevant. The room in which Simeon lay was seven-and-a-half-feet-high. How improbable that William Sturtevant would have used it there!"

Sturtevant beamed with confidence. He was pleased with Harris's argument.

"And now for the shoe track. Upon the jury I observe men who do not require to be told anything about the marks of a shoe. What were the means by which Officer Pratt might have known about the track? Mr. Thompson tells us he found a track leading from the house to the spot where Miss Buckley lay. That it was made as if by a person running; Mr. Pratt was with him. Why did not that officer take a measurement of that certain track in the soft ground made by the murderer, but on Wednesday afternoon he fitted the shoe to a single track made a quarter of a mile from the place, by nobody knows who, and which might have been made by anybody crossing lots?

"The government did not put into their case the track leading from the door to the body; it was only alluded to in the cross-examination of their witness by myself. When all those interested were around on Monday, is it not strange that not one of these citizens of Halifax looked for a moment at the track from the door, or compared it afterward with the print by the roadside, quarter of a mile away? And shall we not conclude that the only reason the government says nothing about it is that the two tracks did not correspond?

"Nor is the fact of the shoe print connected with any other part of the chain of evidence. It is not shown that William Sturtevant was at the Sturtevant house; the shoe print is not connected with the stake, the money, and the bloody clothes, so as to make a strong chain of evidence."

Harris took a deep breath and stepped back to the defense table to quench his thirst.

"As to the bloody clothes, there was blood upon the coat, there was no blood upon the pants and vests, nor upon the shoes; there was blood upon the hat and upon the collar."

Harris went to the evidence table and picked up the stake.

"Here is the stake, it is shown that over and above the bed where Simeon lay, the blood was spattered and thrown up 'like the rays of the sun,' as a witness stated. Even upon the wall next the foot of the bed the blood flew. Whoever did the deed spattered all the walls in all directions, and must have been completely spattered from head to foot.

"The undercoat is not produced," Harris continued as he returned the stake to the table, "but it is not pretended that there is any blood upon it, there is none on the vest, none on the pants, only two little drops on the collar, and one on the hat. Is it unusual that a man who habitually shaved should have a bloodstain upon his collar?

"In the room of Simeon nowhere is a drop of blood shown to have fallen, but that on the hat must have fallen there. There was blood on the mantel, on the table, on the chairs, on the paper, everywhere, but it had been thrown there, none had fallen. Where Thomas had lain was a pool of blood, but no evidence of spatters at all, and neither at this place or the spot where Mary Buckley was found, could this hat have received the stain. And if this applies to the hat, with blood upon it, the fact that there is blood upon the coat is no evidence to be received in this crime.

"We are dealing with things that no human being ever saw, with a question which involves life or death, and the probabilities must be overwhelming of the existence of fact before it can be received. Professor Wood tells us there are no stains on the coat which have been washed with water at any time, and that many stains that appear are not blood. There has been no attempt made by this poor boy to wash his coat, or in any way obliterate the stains and this is proved by the evidence.

"We have the evidence that on Sunday the prisoner goes to his sister-in-law's house to spend the day. He wears a suit of black and no overcoat. A great deal of stress is laid upon the fact that the overcoat could not be found, and the circumstances under which it was finally produced. It would have been a pretty theory, of course, that during its disappearance it had been washed and was drying. But Dr. Wood has testified that the stains were never washed at all. We have not been told that until they found the coat hanging in the entry they had ever looked there for it. There is not a particle of evidence that anyone had ever looked there for it until the moment when they found it.

"I approach the question of science with modesty, and yet with confidence. I knew the government would move heaven and earth in this direction, to prove the guilt of this prisoner, but unless they have proved conclusively that this is human blood, the stains might as well be bees wax or any other substance.

"At the best, where blood is in question, we can go only on probabilities, and no scientific man will say that with absolute certainty the question can be settled. A reasonable doubt remains, and, gentlemen, in this case the prisoner must have the benefit of it. If we had a bench of seven judges, and all of them gave a different opinion, you would say law was somewhat uncertain, so we say that science is somewhat uncertain where her votaries differ so widely in their conclusions. And if the government does not prove that the stains produced were human blood they are useless as evidence.

"And so, if the acts of the prisoner are consistent with any theory of innocence, the government has not proven its case."

Harris had grown weary but he plodded on.

"And as to the money. It has been already stated that the government started out with the theory that the prisoner was poor the day before the murder and had plenty of money the day after.

"The counsel examined and compared the testimony regarding the money, asserting that there was no evidence that the prisoner knew of the existence of money in the Sturtevant house, or that he ever had any that came from that place. The case depended entirely upon facts proved and not at all upon conjecture. The mere fact that the prisoner had money was no evidence of itself that it came from the Sturtevant house.

"If it is conjectured that the money found on the prisoner came from the Sturtevant house, so with equal certainty it may have been the proceeds of Joel White's gold, the theft of which he was urged by the arresting officer to confess. If he stole the gold from White, there was sufficient incentive to conceal it, and if conjecture is to be used in the case, let it be on the lightest side, and if conjecture only is used the case must fall to the ground.

"When the money, $208, was picked up at the barn, is it not conceivable that being conscious that if the roll was found upon him it would be evidence of the Joel White robbery, which the officer was pushing him to confess, and therefore he tried to get rid of it?

"In regard to the time when the murder was committed, all the circumstances are inconsistent with the theory that the murder was done at a late hour, probably not later than nine o'clock. Miss Buckley had not been in bed, neither had Thomas. The feed for the cattle was mixed in the pails, which would have been given to them certainly before ten o'clock. The prisoner would not run the risk of leaving his own house before the people in the other part of it had retired, and the two houses were four-and-a-half miles apart and, upon the theory of its early committal, he could not have been the murderer.

"Remember that the maxim of the law is that it is better that ten guilty men should escape than that one innocent should suffer," Harris closed. "You should take the responsibility individually, not forgetting that, after all is over and the verdict rendered, that as individuals you are to go away into the world with your own consciences in the future and with your God. You must settle the question of faithfulness to duty on this occasion."

Co-counsels Keith and Lord quietly congratulated Harris when he returned to the defense table and collapsed in his chair, his legs in severe pain. Sturtevant looked in his direction and acknowledged him with a smile "as bright as any person's among the audience."

Judges Ames and Wells conferred briefly at the bench and deemed it appropriate to recess. "Court is recessed until nine o'clock tomorrow morning," Ames declared and, after rapping his gavel, stepped with Wells from the bench and out of the courtroom.

Chapter Eighteen: The Trial

Day Five – Friday, July 3, 1874 – Afternoon Session

Closing Argument of the Prosecution

All rose when Judges Wells and Ames emerged from their lobby, entered the courtroom, and took their seats at the bench. Wells motioned to Attorney General Train after the jury filed in.

Train rose from the prosecution table and approached the jury box. He thanked the jurors for their attentiveness during trial and the manner in which they had approached their civic responsibilities.

"Hereafter," Train began, "it would never lay in the prisoner's mouth to say that he did not have a fair chance. No effort has been made by the officers engaged in this cause to hurry the proceedings; every safeguard known to the law has been thrown around the prisoner. No special proceedings prejudicial to his interests have been instituted. His is in no sense a peculiar case, so far as the trial is concerned. In no way to oppress the defendant is this trial brought at this particular hour. Counsel for his defense has been assigned him without expense to himself. The Treasury of the Commonwealth is opened to him to furnish funds for every necessary outlay. In no place in the world could or would so much have been done for him in these respects as in this part of America.

"The case is an important one in its effects upon society and its effects upon the defendant, and so it must be conducted with care. All have assumed responsibilities, knowing them to be what they are, and there is no need of special reminder that this is the case. The jury is to try the facts. The court is to render the law. All have respective responsibilities, which are peculiar to each, and it is of no consequence to one what is the responsibility of another.

"The indictment charges that this prisoner killed Simeon Sturtevant in February last. In fact, there were three murders. The law says that a person who kills another with premeditated malice aforethought is guilty of murder in the first-degree. Premeditation does not mean that he had thought of it for six months, or for six days, but that at the time he performed the deed he intended that death should result. If the crime was committed with the purpose of concealing the matter from all witnesses, then it was premeditated. If it was committed with a weapon carried some miles for the purpose, then it was premeditated murder. If *this* man has committed murder at all, it was with premeditated malice aforethought and so you must find.

"The crime committed on February 15 was never in the experience of the counsel equaled but once – in another part of this state," said the attorney general, referring to George Kimball and the triple tragedy in Charlestown the previous December.

Train outlined the details of the crime as presented by the government, its witnesses, and the evidence. He stated that there was no dispute either by the prosecution or the defense, that a murder had occurred and that robbery was the obvious motive.

"The [Sturtevant] family was a peculiar one; two old men and one old woman, peculiar in their habits. They hoarded their money and were not businessmen. Their money was placed in secret places about the house, and their accumulations were large, and this fact was well known to all acquainted with them. The inference from the confusion in which everything about the rooms was found is that robbery was an object, and we start with the theory that whoever committed one crime committed the other, and that if one is established the other also is.

"A track is found in the line of the scattered coin. Putting those two things together, we say the man who made that track and the man who dropped the coins is the same person. There is no difficulty of reconcilement. I assume that the man who made the track was the thief. We say that the man who made the track dropped the stake, and that there was but one person engaged in the transaction. The object now is to find the man who dropped the coin and the stake and made the track.

"In the house we find some peculiar scrip. They are peculiar because they have been so nicely preserved; they are rarely seen in the community now. They attracted natural attention from their peculiarity at the time of finding, and indicated the peculiarities of the Sturtevants. It is not impossible that the thief got some of this scrip, and if a person can be found with some upon him, and cannot otherwise account for it, the presumption is that he is responsible for the robbery and, also, for the homicide."

Train went to the evidence table and picked up the scrip found within the house and showed it to the jurors. He then showed them the scrip found in possession of the defendant and recalled the less than satisfactory explanation the defendant had given to investigating officers as to how he had come to possess it.

"When a man is found with unusual property upon him and lying about it, the presumption is that he is lying for a purpose. If a man upon being searched in the neighborhood where a homicide has been committed is found lying, he may be presumed to have a purpose, and likely to be connected with the homicide.

"At the barn door he [the defendant] drops $208. He not only has the money, but he is trying to conceal it. We know that at some time he had made a division of what money he had, dividing $333 into two parcels, for some particular purpose, which purpose must weigh against him. He is a very poor man. That may well be. He is not to blame for being poor, but as lawyers know, a man can be poor and honest."

Sheriff Bates thwacked his gavel and called for order when several spectators in the courtroom laughed at Train's remark.

"He is so poor that on Saturday night he could not pay twenty cents for a salt fish. He has not money enough to go to his grandmother's funeral within a month of the homicide."

Sturtevant shook his head. Train was mistaken. He had told Pratt that he had attended his grandmother's funeral.

"He is so poor," Train continued, "that he walks to his work and

197

says he never had so hard a time in his life. He was extremely poor. The scrip was all the money he had, or had had for some time, and that scrip is so remarkable that Drayton puts it away for further examination, and not many hours after he drops $208, and $125. If that is not accounted for, he got it at the Sturtevant house.

"How is it that this relative of the Sturtevants, who is so miserably poor, suddenly becomes rich, and that his track was found on the way to the Sturtevants? If the money found upon him was honestly earned, why lie about it? Counsel met the whole theory of the prisoner showing him to be a liar in every direction, who had lied to his counsel persistently from the beginning and to everybody else during most of his life.

"It is not true that the prisoner is not called upon to prove how he came into possession of this money. He is bound to do it, and if he cannot, he is to be looked upon as the thief and the murderer. All his explanations are falsehoods, and demonstrated to be so, and still he would like to have us believe that he stole Joel White's gold.

"Concealment of crime, fraud, and falsehood, we always regard, and rightly, as the strongest evidence of guilt. All the conversation of the prisoner regarding the overcoat is a tissue of lies, told for a purpose, and that purpose was concealment of crime which the possession of that coat would help establish. If he had been an innocent man, striving to aid the officers in their investigation, would he thus have concealed the $333 and the overcoat? Did he show by all those concealments desire to aid the officers? He did not know the $208 had been found by Officer Pratt. He thought the $125 was all he had to account for. The prisoner never told his counsel anything in regard to this $208, and the officers and interested persons on the part of the government had nothing to do with letting him know of it."

Train paused a moment and wiped his brow with a handkerchief.

"As to the track found by the roadside, of little importance in itself, it becomes of importance when the prisoner undertakes to lie about it. And this prisoner never would have lied about his congress boot, if the congress boot had not made the track. If he was not conscious of having worn them on that night's journey, he would have owned he wore them on Sunday and not have said that he had not put them on his feet for two months. The fact that it was necessary to lie about them proves how important the matter was to him.

"It is very remarkable that with all the diligence of the counsel for defense, since the crime was committed, not a particle of evidence has been found pointing to any other person as the perpetrator, and every grain of evidence found does point directly to William Sturtevant as the man who did the deed.

"Counsel did not regard the blood investigation as of particular consequence in this trial, but it was of some significance as indicating probabilities. Nobody disputes that they are blood stains. The defense only claims they are not human bloodstains. Why then conceal any bloody articles, if the prisoner was conscious that the stains were animal blood? The prisoner was conscious that the blood of Simeon Sturtevant stained his garments.

"The counsel submitted that the prisoner had been put upon his answer to the charge of theft and murder, which he had failed satisfactorily to meet, and that consequently the evidence presented of the prisoner's guilt ought to be conclusive."

Train now directed his attention to Sturtevant's alleged alibi and suggested that the prisoner's wife refused to testify on her husband's behalf because she knew that the prisoner was not at home the entire night of the murder.

"The prisoner tells his counsel to show an alibi, that he was in bed with his wife and child all that Sunday night, a matter perfectly susceptible of proof. Why is the wife of the prisoner not here to prove this fact? It is perfectly competent for her to do so. The court will allow all reasonable delay.

"She would be here could she help the prisoner in this case, even if she were brought here on a litter. She is the only person on the face of the earth, except the one who stands in the dock, who can absolutely prove this alibi. Why is she not brought here?" he demanded to know.

Sturtevant leaned forward and gripped the iron bar encircling the dock, fury in his eyes.

Train next discussed the legal aspects of circumstantial evidence. He retrieved a document from the prosecution table and cited an interpretation by the chief justice of the state of Maine.

"The probative force of circumstantial evidence depends upon the closeness of the connection between the inference and the fact. What is claimed in the evidence in this case is not that they are links in a chain, but that they are strands in a cable growing stronger as they are added, which finally has for its two ends the house of the Sturtevants and the house of this prisoner."

Train thanked the jurors for their attention and took his seat at the prosecution table. Judge Wells then announced a brief adjournment and the jury filed out. Spectators remained in their gallery seats and avidly discussed the merits and weaknesses of the arguments presented by the government and defense.

A deputy supplied Sturtevant with a glass of water and, as he sipped it, his attorneys huddled around him offering words of encouragement and advice. Harris informed his client that when court reconvened, Judge Wells would give him an opportunity to speak before delivering his charge to the jury. Harris pleaded with Sturtevant to respectfully decline.

"We have done everything possible to prove your innocence," Harris said. "If you try to explain yourself at this step of the proceedings, the jurors will certainly ask themselves why you didn't take the stand and testify on your own behalf."

Sturtevant shrugged his shoulders and nodded.

Chapter Nineteen: The Verdict

Judges Wells and Ames returned to the bench fifteen minutes later and
called for the jury. A hush settled over the courtroom. As soon as the
jurors had settled into their seats, Judge Wells directed his attention to
the defendant.

"Mr. Sturtevant, you now have the privilege of addressing the jury
if you so please."

Sturtevant rose from the bench inside the dock and with his usual
apathy, informed the court he had no desire to do so.

"Very well," Judge Wells said, "you may be seated."

Wells conferred briefly with Judge Ames then moved his chair to
the side of the bench nearest the jury box. Wells consulted his notes
from time to time as he reviewed the evidence and explained how the
law applied to the facts in question. In a clear, even tone he began his
charge by congratulating the jury for their attentiveness during the trial
and explaining the court's role in the process.

"The court…is to deal only with the law, in its application to the
facts and arguments which have been presented, and is not to deal with
the facts or the evidence except so far as to see that the law is rightly
applied to the evidence."

Wells emphasized the importance of deliberating with open minds.

"…And your duty, gentlemen, is to have listened carefully to the
testimony which has been produced before you; to have made that use
of your minds which it is the duty of every intelligent man to make of
that intellect and judgment with which he is endowed; to see that you
are free in your minds from every influence that shall warp your
judgment, which shall lead you to give undue weight to evidence, or to
reject evidence which ought to be considered; to free your minds from
every disturbing influence, whether of fear, of anxiety, of passion, or of

prejudice or bias or undue scruple as to the results, whether to the prisoner or to the community; to free your minds from all considerations of this sort, so that they will, like a magnet upon its pivot, answer to the influence which every fact presented to you shall have upon them, to attract them towards, or repel them from, their conclusions."

Reporters in the courtroom scribbled furiously in their notebooks, doing their utmost to capture every word of Wells's charge.

"It is the intent of the statute to make murder in the first-degree one of those cases where the murder is of such a character as to show a deliberate purpose," he said, "but deliberation does not require any considerable length of time. The mind deliberates rapidly, sometimes instantaneously, going from it premises to its conclusion in an instant of time; so that a deliberately premeditated murder aforethought may result from an intent to kill which the mind conceived the instant before the weapon was taken or the blow struck.

"The charge here," Wells continued, "is that this prisoner is guilty of the murder of Simeon Sturtevant. The indictment is a charge of murder, but upon an indictment for murder, where there has been a homicide, if the evidence warrants it, there may be a conviction either of murder or manslaughter. Manslaughter is a homicide, not excusable, not justifiable, but yet not intentional; a homicide which results from wrong conduct, but not from the cool intent to kill; from misbehavior, from misconduct which results differently from what the party had reason to expect from the act which was done."

The judge paused to let the jury absorb the full import and gravity of his remarks. Peering over his spectacles, he continued.

"Of course where a person kills another, the most direct evidence as to the perpetrator of the assault is, by the very act of killing, destroyed. Here the three persons who were the occupants of the house were killed. The direct evidence, therefore, is put beyond reach, and necessarily circumstantial evidence must be resorted to. It may be that the purpose of the killing was merely to put the evidence beyond reach;

it may be that it was merely as a means of reaching the object in view – to secure booty. Whatever it may be, the direct evidence has disappeared, and you are left, therefore, to circumstantial evidence. The closing remarks of the government attorney, which adopted language which had been used by the court in similar proceedings to this, so far as I could see, were not open to any exception. He has stated substantially what the nature of circumstantial evidence is. It is indicated by the very term itself.

"Circumstantial evidence is the evidence from facts which stand around the main fact to be proved. Direct evidence, as has been stated, is evidence from the sight, or some of the senses, of the very fact in controversy; but when such evidence is gone, we resort, in capital trials, as in all the business of life, to what is called circumstantial evidence; that is we resort to those inferences which the mind draws from surrounding circumstances, and it is stronger or weaker according to the nature of those circumstances – their nearness in relation to the fact to be established, and their concurrence with each other towards one and the same conclusion. If you find all the facts which are developed in regard to a transaction or in regard to a person to indicate one line of results, then you draw from those facts an inference as to other facts which are not brought to your vision, and not brought to your actual knowledge."

Sturtevant listened intently to the judge's remarks and cast his eyes intermittently on the judge, the jury box, and the defense table.

Wells cited several examples of circumstantial evidence presented at trial and explained how jurors might draw an inference from each as to the truth of the matter.

"I need not go into these matters in detail," the judge continued. "My purpose was not to touch upon the question of the force of them, but to call your attention to the relation which each circumstance has to the question you are investigating."

"The confessions of the prisoner, obtained in the mode these were obtained, the court thought were competent to be admitted here against him; but it is due to him to say, that confessions by one under arrest, or charged with an offense, or one who is subjected to scrutiny and surveillance, are always to be scrutinized carefully, lest he may be misunderstood in his statements, or the interrogator, from zeal, or preoccupation of mind as to the bearing of those statements, may either understand them incorrectly, or report them incorrectly. Here they are competent evidence, and you are to consider them under all the circumstances in which they were made, and seek how far they tend to show guilt, and how far they are to be explained by anything in the circumstances of the prisoner when he made them, which weakens or strengthens their force.

"The omission of the prisoner, as I have already suggested, to explain any facts which bear upon him personally, may be taken into consideration just so far as you think it is reasonable to expect that he would have explained them if he were innocent. It is often beyond the power of a man to explain a fact which bears against him. The mere omission to explain a fact which bears against him is not of itself evidence against him, because the burden is all the time upon the government to furnish you the evidence upon which to convict him, beyond a reasonable doubt. But when a fact which bears upon him personally is brought to his attention, and it is such a fact as you think he may reasonably be expected to explain, and would explain if he were innocent; that is, if it may reasonably be supposed that the explanation would be within his power, and he fails to produce it; then that is to be taken into consideration, and to bear against him just so far as you think that failure is inconsistent with innocence and indicative of guilt."

Wells then turned to the absence of the prisoner's wife as a witness in the case.

"And that consideration you are to apply to his omission to produce his wife as a witness. If you think, if he had been innocent, she would have been able to prove his innocence then the non-production of his wife is a ground of inference that her production would not establish any fact favorable to him. You have heard the suggestions of his counsel, and it is right for you to take into consideration all reasonable suggestions as to the reason of her absence. Of course, it would be a severe trial for her to come here on such an occasion as this, and if her evidence would have been merely negative, even though, so far as it went, it would be consistent with his innocence, the prisoner might well forbear to produce it. But you will consider upon all the circumstances how far his omission to produce her shows that her production here would not aid him, and, if it would not aid him, how far it is a ground for any inference to the contrary. As I said, you must take into consideration all the suggestions which are made in regard to her absence, and if suggestions have not been made, you will take into consideration those which occur to your own minds, including, also, the position in which both the prisoner and his wife are placed.

"All the circumstances which have been called to your attention are to be treated in their relation to each other, and you are to see, not whether each one may be explained away, not whether each one shows guilt, but whether all together point in such a direction as to indicate one result only, and that result the guilt of the prisoner. If it does so, beyond a reasonable doubt, to your minds, then it is your duty to find him guilty. If it fails to do so, if it points elsewhere, or if all which points toward him is not enough to remove from your minds serious doubts, all reasonable doubts, as to his being the person who committed the offense, then it is your duty to say that he is not guilty, because he is not guilty unless the government, by the evidence which they have produced here before you, have sustained the burden upon them, which is to satisfy in your minds, beyond a reasonable doubt, that this defendant committed this offense of robbing this house and murdering Simeon Sturtevant. If you are satisfied, from all the evidence, that he, and no one else, committed this offense, or that he committed it with someone else – for it is immaterial whether he committed it alone or with someone else, if he was engaged in it – if you are satisfied, beyond a reasonable doubt, that all the evidence points to him, that there is no reason to suppose that there is anyone else to whom the evidence would apply, then the government have sustained that burden, and our duty is fulfilled by simply declaring him guilty. If they have failed to sustain that burden in all respects, so as to remove from your minds all reasonable doubt, then it is your duty to find him not guilty. If as I before said, you find him guilty of murder, you will indicate, in your verdict, whether it is murder in the first-degree or in the second-degree."

Attorney Harris addressed the court and asked for further explanation as to the defendant's right to abstain from testifying on his own behalf.

"I desire, Your Honor, to qualify one remark which was made in the charge, which was this: That if the evidence points to the prisoner in such a manner that it seems to require of him an explanation, and he has not made it, then the jury may draw certain conclusions. What I desire is that Your Honor will say to the jury that in that remark you did not intend to imply that it devolved upon the prisoner, upon the stand, to explain it."

"Thank you," Judge Wells responded as Harris sat down. "I intended to say so, and I should say so, because the statute expressly requires it."

Wells turned to the jury and said, "In all these suggestions as to his failure to explain, you must carefully exclude all suggestions that would require him to go upon the stand; because, although he may go upon the stand, it is a privilege which a prisoner rarely takes, and which, under the advice of counsel, he may decline to take, without any inference against him on account of his not going upon the stand. There, when I said that if any fact against him is brought to your attention which you think might explain if he were innocent, and can reasonably be expected to explain, and he does not explain it, you may draw the inference that the fact exists unfavorably to him, I intended that you should exclude, in considering whether it is reasonable to expect him to explain it, any idea of his explaining it by his own personal testimony. If there are any facts which tell against him, and which can only be explained by himself – that is, which no one else could be brought to explain, or which he by his knowledge could not, unless he went upon the stand, explain – you will not draw any inference against him because he does not go upon the stand himself. But so far as he had attempted to explain any facts brought against him, you will consider how far the explanation is satisfactory; and if he has failed to give a satisfactory explanation, or given a false explanation, then you will consider that. You will be careful to exclude any inference against him, because he does not explain by going upon the stand here in the trial."

It was 5:30 p.m. when Wells concluded his charge, dismissed the jurors, and adjourned with a rap of his gavel. Deputies allowed Sturtevant an opportunity to speak briefly with his attorneys, then removed him from the dock, handcuffed him, and marched him back to the jail to await the jury's decision.

Many spectators remained in the courtroom in anticipation of a swift verdict. Others mingled in the courthouse corridors and outside in the courthouse square and animatedly discussed the trial and its possible outcome.

***

Inside the jury room, foreman Isaac Hathaway held an informal poll before deliberations began in earnest. Less than two hours later, Hathaway emerged from the room and informed the deputies posted outside that the panel had reached a unanimous verdict. One of the deputies notified Sheriff Bates, who in turn notified the clerk of court, the prosecutors, and the defense attorneys. Two other deputies removed Sturtevant from his cell, marched him to the courthouse and up the stairs to the second floor courtroom, removed his restraints, and placed him in the dock.

Attorney General Train and District Attorney French, as well as attorneys Keith, Harris, and Lord, were seated at their respective tables inside the bar. At 7:35 p.m., Judges Wells and Ames spiritedly stepped from their lobby through a door on the left side of the courtroom, ascended to the bench, and called for the jury.

When the jury was seated, Clerk of Court Whitman turned to the prisoner and instructed him to rise. Sturtevant slowly stood up inside the dock with a sullen look on his face.

Whitman then addressed Jury Foreman Isaac Hathaway.

"Mr. Foreman and gentlemen of the jury, have you agreed upon a verdict?"

"We have, sir," Hathaway replied as he stood.

"William E. Sturtevant, hold up your right hand," Whitman ordered.

"Prisoner, look upon the foreman; foreman, look upon the prisoner."

"What say you Mr. Foreman and gentlemen? Is William Sturtevant, the defendant at the bar, guilty or not guilty?"

"Guilty," Hathaway answered.

A collective gasp emitted from the gallery followed by the muted sobs of several Sturtevant family members in the audience. Sheriff Bates rapped his gavel to restore order. Sturtevant rocked back and forth, fiddling with his moustache.

"What say you as to the degree of murder?" asked the clerk.

"In the first-degree," Hathaway answered in a low but clear and distinct voice.

A smug smile crossed Sturtevant's lips as he took his seat in the dock, and "all his concern apparently vanished," according to a *Boston Globe* reporter. He looked out over the gallery with the stolid indifference he had displayed throughout his trial, refusing to betray his claim of innocence.

Attorney General Train moved immediately for sentencing. Judge Wells turned to Attorneys Keith and Harris and asked if they intended to file exceptions on behalf of the defendant. Keith rose and told the court that they would file exceptions without delay. Wells suspended sentencing and, after agreement between the prosecution and defense, ordered Keith to file his exceptions on July 11.

Judge Wells thanked the jurors, dismissed them, and adjourned. All in the courtroom rose as the judges and jury departed the courtroom. Deputies handcuffed Sturtevant as he spoke quietly with his attorneys, and when the conversation concluded, they removed him from the dock and took him back to the jail.

Despite his stoic demeanor in the courtroom, Sturtevant expressed his surprise and dismay at the verdict as the deputies removed his irons and placed him in his cell. He had fully expected an acquittal. His only hope now was that the court would overturn his conviction after hearing the arguments presented by his attorneys at the hearing on exceptions. Unable to withhold the emotional pressure of his predicament any longer, Sturtevant began to weep.

Chapter Twenty: The Sentence

On Monday morning, January 25, 1875, Sturtevant was brought before the Supreme Judicial Court for sentencing. DA French, Attorney General Train, Attorneys Keith, Harris, and Lord, and State Constable George Pratt were present when Judges Wells and Ames entered the courtroom. Reporters in the gallery sat poised with pencil and notebooks at the ready.

Judge Wells instructed Attorney General Train to proceed with the formalities.

"Thank you, Your Honor. At a term of the Superior Court holden on the eighth of May the Grand Jury of this county, after mature deliberation, found a true bill against William E. Sturtevant for the murder of Simeon Sturtevant. This indictment was duly certified to the Supreme Court, and the prisoner on being arraigned pleaded not guilty. Able and learned counsel were assigned the prisoner, and after a careful and laborious trial the jury found him guilty of murder in the first degree. Exceptions were taken to some of the rulings of the court, and these exceptions have been argued before the full bench and have been solemnly overruled. The prisoner is now at the bar, and as I know of no motion pending, or of any motion to be made by which judgment can be postponed, I now move for sentence."

"Thank you, Mr. Train."

Wells turned to Sturtevant in the dock and asked him if he had anything to say before sentence was passed. Sturtevant stood, his shackles still restraining him.

"There are a good many reasons why I do not want to be sentenced now, and one is that the officers have known of testimony in my favor and kept it back," he said, a flash of anger in his eyes. "When I was arrested I had five five-dollar counterfeit bills, three ten-dollar counterfeit bills, and a fifty-dollar bill in my possession. I will now state, if the court desires to hear it, how I came in possession of about seven hundred dollars."

"You have a right to say anything you desire," said Judge Wells.

"I got the money on the tenth of April, and the officers found I had it, yet they testified I did not have it. I did not come by that money honestly, and the officers did not prove that I got any gold. On the tenth of April I spent thirty or forty dollars at number three Dock Square, and also spent considerable money at Holbrook's, at South Abington.

"I will now state how I spent the money, and why I kept it a secret. On the tenth of April I went to Boston, having first taken the morning train to South Abington, where I went with Frank Osborn. After I got to Boston I obtained a pocket book containing about six hundred dollars, and among the money was five five-dollar and three ten-dollar counterfeit bills, a fifty-dollar bill, a season ticket on the Maine Central Railroad, with most of the numbers punched out, a letter from New York with a man's name signed to it, and a lot of postage stamps. When I got to Boston I spent thirty or forty dollars in Dock Square; spent a lot of money at a jewelry store opposite the Tremont House and at Holbrook's in South Abington; and at North Bridgewater spent about two hundred fifty dollars; then I went to Maine and spent forty or fifty dollars more. The pocket book and ticket I destroyed, and the reason why I kept it a secret was because I was told the officers would suspect me of stealing Joel White's pocket book.

"When the officers came to my house," Sturtevant continued, "I went to the box and took out one hundred and twenty-five dollars to get counsel with, and I intended to put the rest back, but when Pratt and Copeland came I might have put it in my pocket. I might have dropped the money, but did not put my hand in the hay-mow as officer Pratt testified. I wore congress boots on that Sunday, and I lied to Pratt when I told him I wore shoes. I didn't intend to secrete the money until after I found they were going to arrest me.

"I have yet to plead that I am not guilty of the crime, and was not

211

away from the house on Sunday. I wish the court would look further in the case so that evidence may be introduced which the officers kept back. Pratt had been to see me once before in relation to a shoe pattern and I had to lie to him then to avoid suffering the consequences."

Sturtevant glared at Pratt for a moment then continued.

"I will now say how I got the blood on my clothes. The coat I had on when arrested I had worn three or four years, and three or four weeks before my arrest I got kicked in the chest by a horse, and the wound bled very freely. The men in the shop and around knew it, but it was not possible for me to bring the witnesses here.

"There have been stories that I accused [Daniel] Blake, and the reason he went against me was because of hard feelings toward me. I told Pratt that Blake had nothing to do with it. I haven't got anything left but the stamps; the check and the pocket book I destroyed."

Reporters shook their heads at the absurdity of Sturtevant's pleas as they jotted down his every word.

"I knew that if I went on the stand to testify in my own behalf I should have to tell the truth, and I didn't want to say where I got the money. I wish the case [sentencing] to be put off in order that evidence in my favor may be offered. The counterfeit money taken from me by Mr. Pratt I have never seen, nor the fifty-dollar bill. This bill was a peculiar one, and I have never seen one like it. That is all I have to say."

Sturtevant moved to take his seat in the dock but a court officer sternly ordered him to remain standing. Judge Wells then addressed him.

"You, William Sturtevant, stand charged with the crime of murder. The grand jury indicted you, and you were brought before a jury selected in all fairness. Earnest and faithful counsel defended you, and the jury, after weighing the evidence, have [*sic*] declared that the charge against you is true. The court who presided were [*sic*] entirely satisfied, and concur in the verdict. The rulings excepted have been presented to the full [Supreme Judicial] court, and no error was found. You therefore stand convicted of murder in the first-degree, a crime for which the community demands the severest punishment.

"One who imbrues his hands in the blood of his fellow man is not entitled to ever again mingle in society, or to be in such position as to endanger the lives of others. Having had all the opportunity necessary to defend your case, there is nothing further to be allowed, and the statement you have made only goes to satisfy the court that the verdict of the jury was a just one. Therefore, there remains nothing for you but to meet the final result, and as the circumstances of the crime were such – the murder of three old and unoffending people, your own relatives – it offers you little hope for executive clemency.

"Nothing now remains for the court to do but to pass the sentence provided by law, which is, that you, William E. Sturtevant, be taken from this place and kept in close custody in the prison of this county until such day as the executive [governor] shall by warrant appoint, thence to be taken to the place of execution and there be hanged until you are dead. And may God in His infinite goodness have mercy on your soul."

His fate now sealed, the condemned man again concealed any emotion as deputies led him away. At the jail, however, he angrily expressed "no feeling other than a desire," according to a *Boston Daily Advertiser* reporter, "to seize a chair and smash the head of the officer [Pratt] who had been most active in securing the evidence against him."

***

Sturtevant had always maintained his innocence and considered a confession a display of weakness. He refused to admit his guilt for fear of passing on a legacy of shame to his children. In his mind, the circumstantial evidence used to convict him had left a significant shadow of doubt as to his involvement in the deaths of his uncles and their housekeeper.

"It was easier to convict me of murder on circumstantial evidence at the time of my trial than it would have been ten years before," Sturtevant remarked, "and it will be still easier if I add to the strength of such evidence by confessing, to convict in the future. It is too easy, anyhow."

Sturtevant professed not the slightest concern for what awaited him in the hereafter. The prison chaplain, Reverend Edward Hathaway, had visited him on numerous occasions, ministering to him and urging him to confess his past transgressions in hope of eternal salvation.

"How shall I walk to my death?" Sturtevant inquired of the chaplain. In answer to his own question, Sturtevant said, "Just as I walk this floor today." To Sheriff Bates, visiting his cell with the chaplain, Sturtevant declared, "I shall be on the scaffold, as I am in this cell; I have no fear nor care for death."

Chapter Twenty-One: The Execution

On Sunday, May 2, 1875, Warden Harmon stopped by Sturtevant's cell for a talk.

"I will never be the first man hung in Plymouth County," Sturtevant declared at the outset of their conversation. "I will cheat the gallows even if a guard is sitting on either side of me." (Sturtevant and his keepers were unaware that John Armung de la Forest was the first to be executed under the laws of Plymouth County after it was established by the General Court of Plymouth Colony. He was hanged in Plymouth on July 30, 1690, after a jury convicted him of murder. Only one other person had been executed in Plymouth County after Armung and before Sturtevant. Elizabeth Colson, a black woman convicted of murdering her out-of-wedlock child at Scituate, Massachusetts, was hanged on May 25, 1727.)

Sturtevant's avowal alarmed Harmon and he called on a guard to strip and search him and inspect the cell for potential hazards. When he was satisfied the cell was reasonably safe, Harmon ordered that two guards remain posted outside the cell around the clock. As an added precaution, Harmon had the empty cell next to Sturtevant's inspected on Wednesday morning, May 15th. When the inspection was complete, Sturtevant was stripped and searched once more, removed from his old cell, and transferred to the new one.

At two o'clock that same afternoon, Abbie Sturtevant visited her husband at the jail with one-year-old Edith. It was the first time Sturtevant had laid eyes on his daughter, who was born nearly two months after his arrest. His aunt and uncle, Joseph and Angeline Dow, and their two daughters, nine-year-old Minnie and five-year-old Francena, accompanied Abbie. Sturtevant's two-year-old son, George, was left in the care of Abbie's mother.

215

Warden Harmon escorted Abbie from his office to Sturtevant's cell and dismissed guards Jacob Howland and Merritt Shaw.

"Mrs. Sturtevant," Harmon said, "you are not to have any physical contact with your husband. You are to stay back at least four feet from the cell. Do you understand?"

Abbie nodded. Harmon retreated a respectable distance to allow husband and wife a measure of privacy. The distraught couple conversed in hushed tones, tears flowing freely, Abbie gently rocking Edith in her arms. Sturtevant desperately wanted to caress the child but Harmon would not permit it.

The prisoner assured his wife that he was innocent of the murders and expressed his bitterness towards those who had testified against him, particularly Daniel Blake and Constable George Pratt. Abbie could not respond. She was overcome with emotion.

"Don't cry, Abbie," Sturtevant pleaded with his wife.

Abbie continued to sob and, through her tears, asked if he had drawn any new pictures.

"I was very much pleased with the ones you recently sent me," Abbie said.

Ten days before he had arranged to have the warden deliver several framed renderings to his family. One was of a bust he had copied from a magazine; another, which he had drawn for his son, depicted a group of soldiers; a third, for his daughter, was of children blowing bubbles.

Abbie had agonized for months over the fate of her children. How would she support them? Her mother would help, but she didn't want to impose upon her; she had children of her own.

"What will I do with the children?" Abbie implored.

"I don't know, Abbie," he replied. "I only ask that you try to keep them together."

Sturtevant asked for several friends and family members, requesting that Abbie send them his regards. The couple paused for a moment, struggling for expressions of consolation, but none would come. Abbie broke down again and could no longer speak with her husband. Warden Harmon stepped forward and, with Joseph Dow, led the prostrated woman from the cell block. As she approached the corridor door she cried out, "Good-bye, Willie!" He responded in kind, "Good-bye, Abbie!" and for the first time the condemned man trembled with remorse and tears.

In a reflection of the amity of small-town Halifax, Charles Paine of Halifax, who had served as an inquest juror and had testified at Sturtevant's trial, accompanied Abbie Sturtevant and the Dows to the jail. After Abbie left the cellblock, she went to the warden's office where Angeline Dow helped her regain her composure. Meanwhile, Paine and Dow returned to the cellblock and had a brief conversation with Sturtevant who was in a sullen mood.

"Have you any word to leave for any of your friends or any message?" Dow asked the prisoner.

"Not a damned thing. I don't have a friend in the world that I care about," Sturtevant replied.

"None for your father, who lies sick at his home?"

"Not a damned word. I do not care to see or send to him!"

Sturtevant expressed concern about the disposition of his body after the execution.

"What will become of my body after I am dead?" Sturtevant asked Paine.

"I will see to a proper burial, unless you prefer otherwise," Paine assured him.

"I don't care a damn what becomes of it if you don't deliver it to Dan Blake!" Sturtevant railed.

He would never forgive his uncle for testifying against him.

Sheriff Bates granted access to an *Old Colony Memorial* newspaper correspondent after Sturtevant's family left the building. The reporter offered his reflections on the condemned man's inexorable suffering and anticipation of death in the paper's next edition:

"Haggard, pale, intensely anxious, his head leaning forward against a bar of his cell door, while either hand grasped another, his eyes deep set and roving about in a despairing manner, never finding a place to settle, the miserable man presented an appearance which would have carried a deeper lesson to the heart of a beholder, than any illustrated rehearsal or widely spread knowledge of the fact of his execution can ever do. The true lesson and the true terrors of his situation were contained rather in the terrible suspense of those waiting hours, than the short sharp agony of the last moment."

Outside Sturtevant's cell and within the brick walls of the gloomy jail-yard, Winslow Drew, a sixty-four-year-old Plymouth carpenter, was busy building the gallows on which Sturtevant would be hanged. Inmates with a view of the yard watched with interest through the bars of their cell windows. The simple scaffold consisted of two upright posts, eighteen feet high, connected by a crossbeam. It was unlike the gallows used to execute murderer George Hersey in Norfolk County twelve years before in that it lacked a "drop," or trap door, through which the prisoner plunged. Instead, a half-inch-thick Manila hemp rope ran over a wheel in the center of the crossbeam. A noose on one end dangled above a platform several inches high; on the other end was a heavy counterweight. The contraption was secured with a mechanism that, when triggered, caused the weight to plummet and propel the condemned five to six feet into the air.

Developed in New York in 1831, it became New York City's standard gallows by 1845. The contraption became known as the "upright jerker" and was intended to improve on the inefficient and, therefore, cruel results of the drop by fracturing the condemned prisoner's neck in a painless, instant death. It was not infallible however; miscalculation of the prisoner's height and weight, the amount of counterweight, the heft and stretch of the rope, or other factors could result in failure to snap the neck, bringing about a prolonged and excruciating death by strangulation.

Sturtevant would be the first in the history of legal executions in Massachusetts to die by this inventive, if barbaric, method.

***

Sturtevant's trial and sentencing had generated widespread publicity. As soon as the court had scheduled an execution date and the information had become public, Sheriff Bates's office was deluged with telegrams, letters, and personal visits from individuals seeking admission to the morbid spectacle. Among them were many of the state's county sheriffs, all anxious to witness the effectiveness of the new method of execution.

Bates was forced to issue a limited number of passes to those who were not required in an official capacity. Two hundred and fifty heavy cardboard tickets, bordered in black, were printed and addressed to those who had requested them.

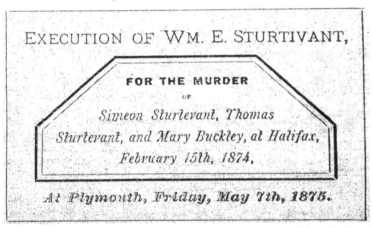

219

The vast majority of the general population had no doubt that the jury in Sturtevant's case had reached the appropriate verdict and that his sentence of death by hanging was both fitting and proper. There were others, however, who protested Sturtevant's execution, arguing that capital punishment was neither a deterrent to crime, nor "the best protection for society." They believed that the death penalty "diminished the 'natural sensibility of man for the sufferings of his fellow man,' and generally promoted 'cruelty and a disregard for life.'" On Thursday morning, May 6, William T. Davis and other prominent citizens of Plymouth County appeared before Governor William Gaston's Executive Council and filed a petition urging that Sturtevant be spared and his sentence commuted. The council rejected their pleas and denied Sturtevant's last hope for clemency.

Nine members of the state's Legislative Committee on Prisons arrived in Plymouth by train from Boston at 6:45 p.m. and registered at the Plymouth Rock House for an overnight stay. Other dignitaries found accommodations at the Samoset House a block from the courthouse. County sheriffs from throughout Massachusetts also converged on the town to witness the first test of the rope and pulley system in the state.

***

At 8:00 p.m., Deputy Sheriff James Collingwood and turnkey Persis Harmon (brother of the warden) relieved watchmen Jacob Howland and A. Merritt Shaw of their duties. As Howland prepared to leave the cell block, Sturtevant handed him a folded half-sheet of paper and asked Howland to deliver it to Sheriff Bates.

Dated April 17, 1875, the letter appeared in Plymouth's *Old Colony Memorial* newspaper a month later and read (verbatim):

> *My faithful Friends:*
> *My Brotherly friends. I am grately Oblidge for your Godlike kindness and trubles, Witch you have been two for me, In getting up this Potison (petition) Witch has ben more ore les truble and expence two*

you. You hav proven your selves A Worthy friend two me, And meny of you are strangers two me. You have done more for me than my Father ever did. You have ben more like A Father then hee. You are intitled two my thanks for what you hav done for me. I shal never alow myself two be hung for my Children sake let alone the dis grase of this county, Witch has been so clear of for years. My name shall not bee the first So all I can do is two give my thanks two you for your kindness Witch I have received from thes men – Mr. T. D. Shumway; Mr. C. H. Paine; Mr. E. Y. Perry; Mr. J. Howlon; Mr. A.(Alpheus) K. Harmond; Mr. (Persis) Harmond; Mr. James Bates.

(signed) *Mr. William Sturtevant*

***

A chilly northeast rain continued throughout the night and into the morning of Friday, May 7. Sturtevant slept fitfully. When he rose at seven, he had a light breakfast of fruit and pastry and a cup of coffee. According to his guards, Shaw and Howland, the prisoner's demeanor was calm and indifferent.

At eight o'clock, Warden Harmon appeared at Sturtevant's cell. Sturtevant presented him with a six-inch piece of wire bent at one end and sharpened on the other.

"Sturtevant smiled at me as if to say he could have committed suicide if he had wished, but had concluded not to, despite his threats," Harmon later told reporters. "I have no idea how he came into possession of this contraband, nor where he might have hidden it. He was searched thoroughly the day before and had been kept under the watchful eyes of two guards, but Sturtevant is a sly bird."

Outside the jail, additional safety was provided by sheriffs from nearby counties assisting Sheriff Bates's staff with crowd control and security along the perimeter of the jail. Bates assigned Deputy Sheriff Josiah Cushman of Abington to guard the jail's main (east) gate and prohibited access through this entrance due to the proximity of the gallows. All visitors were directed to enter the jail through the South Russell Street gate where Deputy Sheriff Charles Spring of Hingham stood by to verify credentials and inspect tickets.

When Sturtevant finished his breakfast, Jacob Howland assisted him in trimming his beard and moustache and had him change into a shiny, black three-piece suit provided the day before by Joseph Dow. Sturtevant donned a collarless white shirt, pants, vest, and jacket, and a pair of black brogan shoes, then combed his hair and laced his shoes. Sheriff Bates, armed with a holstered revolver, and Warden Harmon escorted him from the cell out into the corridor where the chaplain of the jail and twenty witnesses were waiting. Inmates in the cells facing the corridor gawked as Sturtevant nonchalantly shuffled by with his guards. Sturtevant seated himself, tipped back in his chair, stroked his beard, and casually looked upon those in attendance. District Attorney Asa French, State Detectives Philbrick and Pinkham, Constable Pratt, prison committee members, state senators and representatives, and reporters were among those who lined the corridor.

A *Boston Globe* correspondent present in the corridor later described Sturtevant as "a small and slightly built man of some one-hundred twenty-five pounds weight. His profile, at first view, seemed almost good looking; the features were regular, the forehead of good height, the nose very slightly retroussé. His black beard and moustache were closely trimmed and his hair neatly combed. His hands were white and delicate looking. When his full face was seen, however, his physiognomy was decidedly repulsive; it was then seen that his eyes were sunken and treacherous, and there was a brute expression impossible to define about his small mouth."

Chaplain (Rev.) Edward Hathaway, facing Sturtevant, took his hand, and after all present removed their hats, he began his prayer.

"He who sits there," Hathaway said, his voice strained with emotion, "is far more eloquent in his silence than I could be with my speech. Here we see one, with all the blessings of life before him, who chose a course God could not and did not approve. O, my God, teach us to realize the lesson of the hour – that only they who dwell in the shadow of the Almighty are safe, secure, and prosperous. Our own dear native town is so shocked that we scarcely know what to make of it, and this terrible event has unfitted us for the scene on which we now look. How sad it all is, and yet it is soon all over. May God impress upon us the lesson. May God Almighty help you."

Sturtevant remained stoic and unemotional during the proceedings. At the conclusion, Deputy Sheriffs James Collingwood and George Wheeler escorted him back to his cell. There the officers pinioned his arms close to his sides with a leather strap.

Sturtevant thanked both men for the kindnesses they had extended to him during his incarceration. Before Wheeler passed from the cell, Sturtevant turned and asked him to convey his regards to Daniel Blanchard and his family in East Bridgewater.

Collingwood remained on guard while Wheeler notified the sheriff that the prisoner was ready to proceed. Sturtevant gestured to Collingwood to come near. Collingwood approached and waited several moments for him to speak, but Sturtevant remained mute. Finally, Collingwood, hoping Sturtevant would finally confess his crime, asked him if he had anything to say in confidence now that his death was at hand. Sturtevant hesitated, then said, "I don't know that I do."

"Under your circumstances," Collingwood advised, "if you have anything to communicate, you should be careful to state only truth, otherwise, silence should govern all thoughts of utterance on the subject which might be uppermost in your mind."

"I am innocent of the crime," Sturtevant replied.

At 9:55 a.m., Wheeler returned with Deputy Sheriff Torrey and Sheriff Bates. Wheeler and Torrey each took one of Sturtevant's arms and marched him outside the jail to the yard with Bates leading the procession. Warden Harmon, Deputy Collingwood, and Chaplain Hathaway trailed close behind. The rain had stopped, skies had started

223

to clear, and the temperature had risen to fifty degrees.

One hundred spectators had assembled inside the quadrangle and watched as the deputies led Sturtevant to the deadly noose. Late arrivals continued to trickle in throughout the proceedings. A separate crowd of those unable to get tickets gathered at the summit of Burial Hill, the final resting place of the Pilgrim Fathers and their descendants. They strained to witness the execution but their view was restricted by the height of the jail wall, rendering visible only the crossbeam of the gallows. Sheriff Bates went to some lengths to prevent prying eyes from witnessing the event from other angles by erecting canvas screens at strategic points atop the ten-foot high brick wall.

Sturtevant stepped to the platform and positioned himself beneath the rope. According to a *Boston Globe* reporter covering the execution, "[Sturtevant] scanned the throng before him with great sangfroid, letting his eyes rest here and there on some familiar face; no muscle twitched, and not the slightest tremor agitated his frame. He was to all appearances the most unconcerned person in the yard."

Deputy Wheeler placed a black cap atop Sturtevant's head while Torrey and Collingwood tightly fastened heavy leather straps around his knees and ankles. Sturtevant scanned the sky "as if he would once more see the sun, whose beams were even then struggling breaking through the clouds, and which he was to look no more upon forever."

Sheriff Bates, Harmon, Wheeler, Torrey, and Collingwood shook the condemned man's hand before Wheeler lowered the cap over his face and tightened the noose around his neck. Bates's booming voice pierced the air with his sudden pronouncement of Governor William Gaston's death warrant.

"By virtue of my office," Bates concluded as he faced Sturtevant, "it now becomes my duty, however painful, to proceed to the execution of this warrant, and my prayer is that you may hear the voice of that Savior, who said to him who was crucified by His side, this day shalt thou be with me in Paradise."

The sheriff triggered the release at 10:07 a.m.

"There was no sound other than the dull thud of the weight as it fell," the *Globe* reporter later wrote, "and Sturtevant's body glided rather than bounded to a height of five feet, and there hung almost motionless. After ten seconds there was a convulsive contraction of the whole body, the legs being drawn up and then relaxed. This was repeated four times all within the space of a minute, and after that there was no further motion. The corpse hung perfectly still, and the extreme penalty of the law was fulfilled."

A *Hartford Courant* correspondent in attendance described the execution in the following day's edition:

"The body was jerked up five feet and as it settled back to the natural tension the rope suggested a ball attached to a rubber string."

A *Boston Post* reporter, who had previously witnessed a legal hanging by means of the drop or trap door method, added still another version writing "…the body of William Sturtevant shot into the air. The movement was so easy that there was not the involuntary exclamation from the spectators that generally occurred under the old system of hanging, and the dreaded scene was ended almost before it could be realized. Sturtevant was drawn up about five feet, and death must have been nearly instantaneous. There was hardly the usual twitching of the muscles that takes place in such cases. The body swung around twice, after which it remained perfectly still with the exception of an occasional contraction of the muscles."

To the dismay of those inside the walls, the side entrance to the yard was opened and scores of people, including young children, both boys and girls, raced to the scaffold and gaped at the dangling body. Bates immediately ordered Deputy Sheriff Spring to close the gate.

The body remained suspended for twenty minutes before Bates ordered his officers to lower it for a cursory examination by two physicians. Both men declared Sturtevant dead, but nonetheless recommended that he hang for ten additional minutes. Bates ordered his officers to raise the body once more and lower it at the designated interval. A stretcher was laid alongside the platform and Wheeler,

225

Torrey, and several other deputies loosened the noose, placed the corpse on the stretcher, and carried it inside the jail where the physicians waited to perform a more extensive examination in a private room on the upper floor.

In the opinion of the *Old Colony Memorial*, the upright jerker "had performed its work with singular accuracy and completeness, and was entirely successful in accomplishing the purpose for which it was employed," but the fact was that the jerker had failed. Doctors determined that Sturtevant's neck had been elongated but not broken. He had met a slow, agonizing death by strangulation.

Sheriff Bates authorized general admission to the prison yard after the body was removed. A *Boston Advertiser* correspondent commented on the carnival atmosphere that prevailed.

"During the afternoon the prison yard opened and a large number of people inspected the gallows. Pieces of rope were in great demand and a considerable portion of it was cut off in small bits to be preserved as relics. Ladies, even children, were among the most interested visitors and inspectors. There was no solemnity about the occasion whatever. Men talked and joked and laughed, and, in fact, one was reminded of a town meeting gathering."

At 5:40 p.m., when the physicians completed their examination, Sturtevant's body was placed in a stained pine coffin and released to Charles Paine and Joseph Dow. The two men transported the body in a hired wagon to the Plymouth depot and placed it on a train bound for Halifax.

Winslow Drew dismantled the gallows in the late afternoon and stacked the components in the old jail building. Drew would be called upon less than seven weeks later to assemble another scaffold, this time in the yard of the Norfolk County Jail at Dedham, Massachusetts, for the execution of James Costley, the smug visitor who had mocked Sturtevant the year before.

In a curious side note to the execution, *The Daily Argus* of Rock Island, Illinois, praised Sturtevant's deportment at the scaffold and held him up as a model example to others waiting to meet their maker at the end of a noose:

"The attention of murderers about to be hanged ought to be called to the behavior of Sturtevant, who was hanged at Plymouth, Mass., last week Friday. It is true that in the freedom of private conversation before his execution Sturtevant permitted himself some profane expressions of disregard for his surviving kindred, but nothing of that sort can be alleged against his demeanor in public when he actually came to be hanged. He did not assume that to commit a murder and be hanged for it entitled a man to put on airs of moral superiority on the scaffold, and talk the talk of Brooklyn to people who had not committed murder nor been condemned to be hanged. Neither, on the other hand, did Sturtevant insult the chaplain, but met his death in a very decent manner. It is to be hoped that all men who are capable as he was of murdering three people for the sake of plundering them may make as fair an ending as speedily as possible."

Deputy Sheriff George Wheeler reflected years after the execution about Sturtevant's transformation while a prisoner at the jail.

"When William Sturtevant was arrested and charged with the murder of Simeon Sturtevant we carried to Plymouth jail as undesirable a person as could have been found in any county. When I helped lead him to the gallows, I helped lead a good citizen of Massachusetts. So far as I know he had not 'experienced religion,' as the saying is, but he responded to humane treatment while a prisoner at the jail and I believe would have been an entirely different man if allowed to live. I have no excuses to make for William Sturtevant. I merely tell you my convictions after observing the change which came over him."

***

The *Boston Globe* of November 11, 1879 reported that two boys setting snares in a wooded area in the town of Pembroke, near South Hanson, happened upon two weathered suitcases. In one of the suitcases they found clothing covered with what they believed to be blood. They took the suitcases and clothes, including a suit, to

Pembroke Selectman W. H. H. Bryant who immediately notified the town constable, state police, and the district attorney. Residents were alerted and the clothing was put on public display in an effort to identify its origin. A local seamstress recognized the garments as those she had sewn years before for a man named Joseph Dow of South Hanson.

Pembroke officials recalled that Dow was an uncle of William Sturtevant and that he had testified during the condemned man's trial. Rumors spread quickly suggesting that Dow was somehow involved in the Halifax murders five years prior. According to the *Globe*, "The discovery of the bloody suit, and subsequent events, coupled with Sturtevant's protestations that he had not murdered Mary Buckley [or the Sturtevant brothers], point strongly to Dow as having been the author of the deed."

Pembroke and Hanson town constables sought out Dow and learned he had deserted his wife and children, allegedly fleeing to Colorado with another woman. It was said that Dow's wife, Angeline, had placed her children with friends and relatives to search for her husband.

In a follow-up to this sensational story, the *Globe*'s afternoon edition downplayed the significance of the bloody clothes, reporting that State Detective Wade, contacted by the newspaper for comment, denied he was investigating the case. Wade said the state had overwhelmingly proved Sturtevant's guilt as the lone murderer. He suggested that any allegation that Dow or any other person was an accomplice to the crime was pure folly. Pembroke Selectman Bryant also told the *Globe* that a chemical analysis of the stains on the clothing had ruled out the presence of blood.

The *Old Colony Memorial* commented on the "cock and bull story" in a November 13th edition. The *Memorial* refuted Dow's flight to Colorado, but confirmed he had left his wife and children for parts unknown. Apparently, as they reported, Dow had not taken up with another woman but his wife, Angeline, had absconded with "a miserable fiddler" from Hanson.

The *Memorial* concurred with Detective Wade's assertion of Dow's innocence in the Sturtevant murders. Police had thoroughly investigated Dow's whereabouts at the time of the murder and had eliminated him as a suspect. Besides, argued the *Memorial*, "The man who was hanged for that crime was not the kind of fellow to have let an accomplice go 'scot free' while he alone suffered, especially when that accomplice appeared again and again before his eyes, as an important witness in the case ending so disastrously for himself."

***

Plymouth County did not witness another legal execution until 1887, when Samuel Besse was hanged at Plymouth Jail after a jury found him guilty of murdering a Westport egg dealer in Wareham, Massachusetts. Upon Besse was bestowed the honor of being the last man executed in the county.

Eight more men would swing from the gallows in other counties before sweeping legislative changes altered the course of capital punishment in the Commonwealth of Massachusetts. In 1898, Governor Roger Wolcott signed a bill that replaced the noose with the electric chair, prohibited capital punishment in the county of conviction, and ordered that all legal executions take place at the state prison in Charlestown.

The bill also eliminated public executions. Only certain officials – necessary physicians, the surgeon general of the governor's staff, the sheriff of the county where the crime was committed, and not more than three others – were authorized to attend as witnesses.

Chapter Twenty-Two: The Aftermath

Edward Hathaway, the county prison's chaplain, officiated at funeral services for William Sturtevant in the Universalist Church of Halifax on the afternoon of Saturday, May 9, 1875. Sturtevant's wife, Abbie, and her two children, George and Edith, were present, as were Dan and Margaret Blake, Joseph and Angeline Dow, and other family and friends.

During the service, Margaret Blake, wracked with sorrow and shame, fainted in her pew. The proceedings also proved too much for Abbie, who wept uncontrollably as friends assisted her from the church at the service's conclusion.

Dan Blake, Joe Dow, and others conveyed Sturtevant's body in a wagon to Tomson Cemetery and there, on a line just a few feet from the final resting places of his two murdered granduncles, he was interred in an unmarked grave.

The *Old Colony Memorial* in a postscript to the sordid affair commented, "Life for life has been rendered; all that human retribution can accomplish on the head of the criminal has been brought to pass, and murderer and victims now repose together, beyond the reach of the rewards or punishments of men."

***

Abbie Sturtevant sought refuge with her mother, Lucy Parris, on the Friday after her husband's arrest. She placed George and Edith in Lucy's care in East Bridgewater and found employment as a live-in domestic in the home of Cephas Washburn on Pond Street in Halifax.

In 1893, Abbie's daughter, Edith, married Alton Richards, a box factory foreman, in East Bridgewater.

Abbie married Cephas Washburn, twenty-two years her senior, in 1897. She and her son, George, remained at Washburn's farm in Halifax until Cephas sold the property and moved his family to a house on School Street in Whitman, Massachusetts. Cephas died there in 1907.

By 1910, Abbie's daughter, Edith, and Edith's husband, Alton Richards, had moved into her School Street home. Edith and Alton later divorced, and Edith never remarried.

Abbie's son, George, was never married. He died in Whitman in 1905 and is buried in Northville Cemetery in East Bridgewater.

Abbie Standish Sturtevant Washburn married Charles Rollins in Brockton, Massachusetts, on April 30, 1917. The couple lived with Abbie's daughter, Edith, who was then living at Karl Place in Brockton. Abbie later purchased a home at 719 Belmont Street in Brockton and lived there until her death in 1935. She is buried in Brockton's Melrose Cemetery.

Edith Sturtevant Richards died on July 12, 1948, and is buried beside her mother in Melrose Cemetery.

On the afternoon of November 7, 1881, a fire broke out in the upper floors of the Plymouth County Courthouse, causing extensive damage. Court officials had stored the gallows used to hang both William Sturtevant and James Costley in the attic. It was completely destroyed.

Notes

Chapter 1

1 picked up his spectacles: University, Hay Library, Curtis B. Norris and Lowell Ames Norris Papers; Box 135, Lowell Ames Norris - The Sturtevant Case (No. 31), manuscripts and story material; Accession No. A89-74 – reference to Lull's use of glasses.

1 onto the glowing embers: "Halifax Murder," *Old Colony Memorial* [Plymouth, MA], July 2, 1874, Stephen Lull testimony.

1 born in the nearby town of Kingston: Massachusetts Bureau of Vital Records and Statistics, Boston, MA; Deaths, Halifax, 1908, volume 45, page 280.

1 died in 1850: Massachusetts Bureau of Vital Records and Statistics, Boston MA; Deaths, Kingston, 1850, volume 49, page 159. Simon Lull died on June 23, 1850.

1 at the Kingston and Carver almshouses: 1850 United States Census, Kingston, Plymouth, Massachusetts; roll M432-333, page 97A. Lucy was enumerated in Kingston.

1 at the Kingston and Carver almshouses: 1850 United States Census, Kingston, Plymouth, Massachusetts; roll M432-333, page 184A. Mary was enumerated in Carver.

1 in neighboring Plympton: 1850 United States Census, Plympton, Plymouth, Massachusetts; roll M432-333; page 52A.

1 after he married Mary: Massachusetts Bureau of Vital Records and Statistics, Boston, MA; Deaths, Kingston, 1857, volume 112, page 296. Lucy Lull died on December 6, 1857, of consumption.

2 after the wedding: Massachusetts Bureau of Vital Records and Statistics, Boston, MA; Marriages, Halifax, 1857, volume 109, page 321. The couple married on December 5, 1857.

2 carried off by dysentery in 1859: Massachusetts Bureau of Vital Records and Statistics, Boston, MA; Deaths, Halifax, 1859, volume 130, page 207. Charles died on September 26, 1859.

2 in memory of Stephen's mother: Massachusetts Bureau of Vital Records and Statistics, Boston, MA; Births, Halifax, 1860, volume 133, page 374. Lucy was born on September 14, 1860.

2 second son in November 1869: Massachusetts Bureau of Vital Records and Statistics, Boston, MA; Births, Halifax, 1869, volume 215, page 364. They named him Charles after his deceased brother. He was born on November 6, 1869.

2 took him twenty-four days later: Massachusetts Bureau of Vital Records and Statistics, Boston, MA; Deaths, Halifax, 1869, volume 221, page 309. Charles died on December 1 of "canker," known today as scarlet fever.

2 parents passed away: Massachusetts Bureau of Vital Records and Statistics, Boston, MA; Deaths, Halifax, 1861, volume 148, page 315. Albert Morton died of consumption on March 27, 1861.

2 parents passed away: Massachusetts Bureau of Vital Records and Statistics, Boston, MA; Deaths, Halifax, 1871, volume 239, page 332. Rachel Morton died on February 27, 1871.

2 "…near the deep pond: Lincoln Newton Kinnicut, *Indian Names of Places in Plymouth, Middleboro, Lakeville and Carver, Plymouth County* (Worcester, MA: Commonwealth Press, 1909), 48.

2 woodlands, and cedar swamp: Guy S. Baker, *History of Halifax, Massachusetts* (Halifax, MA: by the author, 1976), 15.

2 were related to each other: 1870 United States Federal Census, Halifax, Plymouth, Massachusetts; see also, Baker, *History of Halifax.*

3 had accumulated overnight: *Surface Weather Observations* (Boston: Signal Service, U.S. Army, Division of Telegrams and Reports for the Benefit of Commerce, 1874), 11; Boston Public Library call number QC984.M4S97x. Light snow began to fall at 3:20 a.m. and continued now and then interrupted until 2:00 p.m.

4 Cold Harbor, and Petersburg: Adjutant General, *Massachusetts Soldiers, Sailors and Marines in the Civil War* (Norwood, MA, The Adjutant General, 1932), 57.

4 physically unscathed: National Archives and Records Administration, Washington, DC; Pension File of Stephen P. Lull, Application #1136514, Certificate #947278, October 31, 1892; file in possession of William C. Morton.

4 blood obscured her features beyond recognition: "Horrible Tragedy in

Halifax, Mass.; Three Aged Persons Murdered; Money Evidently the Object; The Murderers Unknown," *Boston Evening Transcript*, February 17, 1874; see also, "Halifax Murder," *Old Colony Memorial* [Plymouth, MA], July 2, 1874, Stephen Lull testimony.

8   and state representative: Dean Dudley, *Historical Sketches of Towns in Plymouth and Barnstable Counties, Massachusetts* (Boston: D. Dudley & Co., 1873), 110.

10 to recover Mary Buckley's body: *Surface Weather Observations* (Boston: Signal Service, U.S. Army, Division of Telegrams and Reports for the Benefit of Commerce, 1874), 11; Boston Public Library call number QC984.M4S97x. Light snow began to fall at 3:20 a.m. and continued now and then interrupted until 2:00 p.m.

10 Buckley's body and the apparent murder weapon: "Halifax Murder," *Old Colony Memorial* [Plymouth, MA), July 2, 1874, testimony of Stephen Lull on June 29, 1874; see also, statement of Ephraim Thompson at coroner's inquest - Plymouth County Coroner's Records, 1874, Judicial Archives, Massachusetts State Archives, Boston, MA.

11 undertaker Judah Keene: "The Halifax Murders; What Was Found on the Premises; What the Murderer Probably Obtained; Arrest of a Nephew of the Deceased Brothers," *Boston Evening Transcript*, February 18, 1874.

12 paid three dollars a day plus expenses. Faculty of Political Science of Columbia University, eds., *Studies in History, Economics and Public Law*, Volume VIII (New York: Columbia University, 1896-1898); Robert Harvey Whitten, Ph.D., *Public Administration in Massachusetts: The Relation of Central to Local Activity* (New York: Columbia University, 1898), 464-468; 80-84. See also, "Massachusetts Legislature," *Boston Post*, May 11, 1865.

12 reinstated the office of chief constable. Mitchell P. Roth, *Crime and Punishment: A History of the Criminal Justice System*, 2nd ed. (Belmont, CA: Wadsworth Publishing, 2011), 150.

12 state force in 1866: D. Hamilton Hurd, *History of Plymouth County, Massachusetts, with Biographical Sketches of Many of its Pioneers and Prominent Men*, Part 1; (Philadelphia: J.W. Lewis & Co., 1884), 482.

12 "...Commonwealth," with great pride: "The State Constable," *Cambridge Chronicle*, July 29, 1865. See also, Massachusetts State Police Museum and Learning Center Facebook post, August 3, 2016.

12 the skies had cleared: *Surface Weather Observations* (Boston: Signal Service, U.S. Army, Division of Telegrams and Reports for the Benefit of Commerce, 1874), 11; Boston Public Library call number QC984.M4S97x.

13 Thomas Sturtevant, seventy-four years of age: Massachusetts Vital Records to 1850, Halifax, volume 1, page 25. Thomas was born on July 11, 1799.

13 Simeon Sturtevant, Jr., age seventy: Ibid. Simeon was born on July 26, 1803.

13 Mary Buckley, sixty-eight-years-old: Gravestone inscription, Plympton Cemetery.

13 Thomas had been widowed: Massachusetts Bureau of Vital Records and Statistics, Boston, MA; Marriages, Halifax, volume 46, page 233 (They were married on November 14, 1850).

13 by the death of his wife, Mary: Massachusetts Bureau of Vital Records and Statistics, Boston, MA; Deaths, Halifax, volume 184, page 279 (she died on July 27, 1865).

13 twenty years at the state prison in Charlestown: Charles G. Davis, *Report of the Trial of Samuel M. Andrews, Indicted for the Murder of Cornelius Holmes before the Supreme Judicial Court of Massachusetts, December 11, 1868* (New York: Hurd and Houghton, 1869).

14 with a straight razor: "Murder and Suicide; A Triple Tragedy in Charlestown; A Man Murders his Wife and Step-Daughter, and then Completes the Horrible Affair by Cutting his Own Throat; Jealousy the Supposed Cause of the Deed; The Scene of the Appalling Occurrence; Full Particulars," *Boston Post*, December 12, 1873.

14 and sister-in-law on Smutty Nose Island: "The Smutty Nose Murders," *Boston Daily Globe*, June 14, 1873.

14 their one-year-old daughter in Thorndike: "The Thorndike Tragedy," *Boston Post*, June 18, 1873.

14 built it in 1715: Massachusetts Historical Commission: MHC Reconnaissance Survey; Town Report; Halifax, 1981.

14 as a wedding gift for his wife: Susan Basile, Halifax Historical Commission, Halifax, MA.

14 cedar shingle siding: Massachusetts Historical Commission: MHC Reconnaissance Survey; Town Report- Halifax, 1981.

14 when the sun is high: Jonathan F. Scott, *The Early Colonial Houses of Martha's Vineyard*, (Minneapolis, MN: University of Minnesota, 1985; revised and updated in 2013).

15 of the house in the rear: Massachusetts Historical Commission: MHC Reconnaissance Survey; Town Report; Halifax, 1981.

15 unbroken to the day of the murders: Massachusetts, Plymouth County, Probate Estate Files, Estate of Amasa Tomson, 1807, File 20512.

17 East Abington depot with the unusual coins. "North Abington; Robbery," *Boston Post*, August 3, 1870.

17 since the time of the murders: *Old Colony Memorial* Office, *Trial of William E. Sturtivant for the Murder of Simeon Sturtevant, in Halifax, Mass., on Sunday, February 15, 1874* (Plymouth: Avery & Doten, 1874), 29-30.

18 "...then retired for the night," said Blake: "The Triple Tragedy," *Middleboro Gazette*, February 28, 1874.

Chapter 2

20 Martin Howland, and Charles Lyon: Plymouth County Coroner's Records, 1874, Judicial Archives, Massachusetts State Archives, Boston, MA.

21 the duty of holding an inquest: Paul F. Mellon, M.D. and Elizabeth C. Bouvier, "Nineteenth-Century Massachusetts Coroner Inquests." *The American Journal of Forensic Medicine and Pathology*, 17, no. 3, (1996): 207-209. See also, Massachusetts General Laws, Chapter 200 (1877).

21 with his sons, James and Joseph: Langworthy, G. H., ed. "Another Atherton Store," *The Furniture World*, (New York, NY: Towse Publishing) October 2, 1919, 45. www.books.google.com

21 named "Captain Kidd" by Mary: Oral statement of Walter Alonzo Keene as dictated to his son, Walter H. Keene, in 1920. Written account in possession of Allan Clemons, Hanson, MA.

21 and apparently untouched: "Halifax Murder," *Old Colony Memorial* [Plymouth, MA] July 2, 1874; Lull testimony.

23 bullet at the siege of Petersburg: The Adjutant General, *Massachusetts Soldiers, Sailors, and Marines in the Civil War* (Norwood, MA, The Adjutant General, 1932), 55; also, Guy S. Baker, *History of Halifax, Massachusetts* (Halifax, MA: by the author, 1976), 138-140. Blake convalesced in a Washington hospital for six months before he mustered out in December 1864.

26 sufficient to warrant an arrest: "The Halifax Tragedy; Trial of William E. Sturtevant; Fourth Day," *Boston Journal*, July 3, 1874.

26 naval and marine service for the same period: William Schouler, Adjutant General, Annual Report of the Adjutant General of the Commonwealth of Massachusetts for the year ending December 31, 1865 (Boston: Wright & Potter, State Printers, 1866), 23.

26 deserted two months after he enlisted: "United States Naval Enlistment Rendezvous,1855-1891," William E. Sturtevant, Feb 1864; citing p. 87, volume 31, place of enlistment Boston, NARA microfilm publication M1953 (Washington, DC: National Archives and Records Administration, n.d.), roll 23; FHL microfilm 2,381,764. (Records indicate Sturtevant enlisted for three years on February 10, 1864, as a second class boy on the receiving ship *Ohio*.); see also, Adjutant General, *Massachusetts Soldiers, Sailors and Marines in the Civil War* (Norwood, MA, The Adjutant General, 1932), 57.

27 "...a year in the Plymouth House of Correction: "Arrest of a Horse Thief," *Boston Post*, September 13, 1866. See also, Plymouth County [Massachusetts] Sheriff's Department Archives, Ledger Book #96, Entry #103, September 11, 1866.

27 "...and paid his respects: Massachusetts Bureau of Vital Records and Statistics, Boston, MA; Deaths, Halifax, 1874, volume 266, page 314. Sturtevant's paternal grandmother, Lucinda (Christian) Sturtevant, died of consumption on January 30, 1874.

27 "...children already, Mary and George: Massachusetts Bureau of Vital Records and Statistics, Boston, MA; Deaths, Plymouth, 1875, Volume 275, Page 324. William's birth record was calculated by his age at death on May 7, 1875. According to the town record, he was twenty-six years, ten months, and eighteen days old when he died (born Jun 19, 1848).

27 "...Willie's brother, James: *Massachusetts Vital Records to the Year 1850*, Halifax, October 17, 1849, 150-151.

27 "...Margaret and I live in now: 1850 United States Federal Census, Halifax, Plymouth, Massachusetts, roll: M432-333; page: 36A.

27 "...Benjamin was born in 1851, I think: Massachusetts Bureau of Vital Records and Statistics, Boston, MA, Births, Halifax, 1851, volume 52, page 251.

27 "...died of dysentery: Massachusetts Bureau of Vital Records and

Statistics, Boston, MA; Deaths, Halifax, 1852, volume 67, page 247.

27 "…they named him James as well: Massachusetts Bureau of Vital Records and Statistics, Births, Halifax, 1853, volume 73, page 277.

27 "…She was only twenty-nine-years of age: Massachusetts Bureau of Vital Records and Statistics, Boston, MA; Deaths, East Bridgewater, 1854, volume 85, page 200 (she died on October 1, 1854).

28 "…East Bridgewater with his five children: Massachusetts State Census, 1855, East Bridgewater, September 21, 1855, volume 30, page 69, household 696.

28 "…Mary, died: Massachusetts Bureau of Vital Records and Statistics, Deaths, Boston, MA; Plympton, 1856, volume 103, page 221 (she died on May 29, 1856 of "inflammation").

28 "…in Lewiston, Maine: "Record of Crime; Latest Developments in Relation to the Halifax Tragedy," *Boston Daily Globe*, February 19, 1974.

28 "…Willie's brother, George: 1860 United States Census, Halifax, Plymouth, Massachusetts, roll: M653-518; page 562.

28 "…Joseph and Angeline in East Bridgewater: 1860 United States Census, East Bridgewater, Plymouth, Massachusetts, roll: M653-518; page: 787.

28 "…placed with friends: "Record of Crime; Latest Developments in Relation to the Halifax Tragedy," *Boston Daily Globe*, February 19, 1974.

28 Willie was gone: "Record of Crime; Latest Developments in Relation to the Halifax Tragedy," *Boston Daily Globe*, Thursday, 19 Feb 1874.

28 "…to the nautical school: Massachusetts State Archives, Boston, MA; HS8.06/series 849X, Nautical School, Case Histories of Boys, 1861-1870, William E. Sturtevant, Commitment Date: October 4, 1862.

29 "…the honor of our national flag": "The State Nautical School; History of the Undertaking; Description of the School Ship," *Boston Post*, March 17, 1860; see also, *Eleventh Annual Report of the Trustees of the State Reform School, at Westborough, Together with the Annual Reports of the Officers of the Institution* (Boston: William White, Printer to the State, 1857), 74.

29 a few months later, Willie deserted: "United States Naval Enlistment Rendezvous, 1855-1891," William E Sturtevant, Feb 1864; citing p. 87, volume 31, place of enlistment Boston, NARA microfilm publication M1953 (Washington, DC: National Archives and Records Administration, n.d.), roll 23; FHL microfilm 2,381,764. (Records indicate Sturtevant enlisted for three years on February 10, 1864, as a second class boy on the

receiving ship *Ohio*.)

29 fighting guerillas: "Halifax Murder," *Old Colony Memorial* [Plymouth, MA], July 2, 1874.

29 "...He married her in the fall of 1871: Massachusetts Bureau of Vital Records and Statistics, Boston, MA; Marriages, Hanson, 1871, volume 236, page 391 (They were married on October 3, 1871).

29 "...their first child, George: Massachusetts Bureau of Vital Records and Statistics, Boston, MA; Births, Hanson, 1872, volume 242, page 412 (he was born on October 9, 1872).

29 "...That's where they live now: "Halifax Murder," *Old Colony Memorial* [Plymouth, MA), July 2, 1874, testimony of Frank Osborne on June 30, 1874

30 folding, shoemaker's size-stick: John Bedford Leno, *The Art of Boot and Shoemaking; A Practical Handbook* (London: Crosby Lockwood and Company, 1885), 31.

30 footwear that left it to be a size seven: "The Halifax Murders; Trial of W. E. Sturtevant; Third Day," *Boston Journal*, July 2, 1874; Pratt testimony; Pinkham testimony.

30 "...not at all appear sociable: "Sturtevant's Crime; Circumstances and Discovery of the Murder; Arrest of the Murderer; Strong Circumstantial Evidence; The Trial and Conviction; Subsequent Prison Life of Sturtevant," *Boston Daily Globe*, 7 May 1875; also, Hearn, 253.

30 "...in the old Sturtevant homestead: "The Triple Tragedy," *Middleboro Gazette*, February 28, 1874.

31 "...'stern logic of events'": "Halifax," *Old Colony Memorial* [Plymouth, MA], April 16, 1874.

32 home of a prominent physician: "Crime; A Young Man Swindled Out of $1000 by Boston Sharpers; Another Gambling Raid but No Gamblers Found; Arrested on Suspicion of House Robbery; Other Criminal Matters," *Boston Post*, February 14, 1874.

32 Battle of Fredericksburg, Virginia: National Archives and Records Center, Washington, DC, Compiled service records of volunteer Union soldiers who served in organizations from the State of Massachusetts. Roll: RG94-CMSR-MA-15INF-Bx1645.

32 appointed him to the state constabulary: H.A. Wadsworth, compiler, *History of Lawrence, Massachusetts, with Portraits and Biographical*

Sketches (Lawrence, MA: Lawrence Eagle Steam Job Printing Officer, 1880), 161-162.

32 Second Cavalry Regiment: National Archives and Records Center, Washington, DC, Compiled service records of volunteer Union soldiers who served in organizations from the State of Massachusetts. Roll: RG94-CMSR-MA-1CAV- Bx0081_MISC

32 to the state constabulary in 1872: *Biographical Review, Volume XXV, Containing Life Sketches of Leading Citizens of Norfolk County* (Boston: Biographical Review Publishing Co., 1898) 48.

33 "...unable or unwilling to pay: Brown University, Hay Library, Providence, RI, Curtis B. Norris and Lowell Ames Norris Papers, Box 135, Lowell Ames Norris – The Sturtevant Case (No. 31), manuscripts and story material; Accession No. A89-74 (Manuscript: "Doom House on Sodom Road," by Lowell Ames Norris).

34 "...robbery and murders: Dean Dudley, *Historical Sketches of Towns in Plymouth and Barnstable Counties, Massachusetts* (Boston: D. Dudley & Co., 1873), 110.

35 "...call on Drayton today: "Halifax Murder; Tuesday, June 30," *Old Colony Memorial* [Plymouth, MA], July 2, 1874.

36 entering the state constabulary: "George C. Pratt Dead; Member of State Police Force for Many Years, and Had Served in the Old Constabulary," *Boston Daily Globe*, April 15, 1904.

Chapter 3

37 the rest of the house overnight: US Army, Signal Corps, *Annual Report of the Chief Signal-Officer to the Secretary of War for the Year 1874* (Washington, DC: Government Printing Office, 1874), 138 (High temperature, 33 degrees; low temperature, 18 degrees).

37 an ice house at nearby Silver Lake: Susan Basile, Halifax Historical Commission, notes.

37 covered each with a sheet: Norman L. 3Cantor, *After We Die: The Life and Times of the Human Cadaver* (Washington, DC: Georgetown University Press, 2010), 83.

37 in a game of "Indians": J[osiah]. B. Millet, *Recollections: A Biographical Essay about Asa Millet* (Smithsonian Institution, Archives of American Art, Francis David Millet and Millet Family Papers, Writings about F. D. Millet, Reel 5906, Frame 863..

38 under General George McLellan: George B. Shattuck, M.D., and Algernon Coolidge, Jr., M.D., eds., *The Boston Medical and Surgical Journal*, Volume CXXVIII, Obituary: Asa Millet, M.D., (Boston: Damrell and Upham, 1893), 611.

38 severe head injury: Christine Quigley, *The Corpse: A History* (Jefferson, NC and London: McFarland & Company, Inc., 1996), 124.

38 at ten o'clock in the sitting room: "The Halifax Murders; What Was Found on the Premises; What the Murderer Probably Obtained; Arrest of a Nephew of the Deceased Brothers," *Boston Evening Transcript*, Wednesday, 18 Feb 1874.

38 "...so help you, God?: William A. Richardson and George P. Sanger, eds., *The General Statutes of the Commonwealth of Massachusetts: Enacted December 28, 1859, to Take Effect June 1, 1860: with the Constitutions of the State and the United States, a Glossary, List of Acts Previously Repealed, and Index* (Boston: Published by the Commonwealth, 1873), 848-849.

40 from one to nine days: Francis Delafield , *A Handbook of Post-Mortem Examinations and of Morbid Anatomy*, (New York: William Wood & Co., 1872), 6.

41 House of Correction in 1869: Thomas L. Stedman, M.D., ed., *Medical Record, A Weekly Journal of Medicine and Surgery*, Volume 86 (Boston: William Wood and Co., 1914), 887. Francis Russell Stoddard, Jr., *The Stoddard Family, Being an Account of Some of the Descendants of John Stodder of Hingham, Massachusetts Colony* (New York: The Trow Press, 1912), 98-99.

41 practiced in Hanson: *History of the Town of Hanson* (Hanson, MA: Hanson Historical Commission), 958.

41 February 23, at nine o'clock: "The Halifax Murders; What Was Found on the Premises; What the Murderer Probably Obtained; Arrest of a Nephew of the Deceased Brothers," *Boston Evening Transcript*, February 18, 1874.

41 fractured the top of the skull: Plymouth County Coroner's Records, 1874, Judicial Archives, Massachusetts State Archives, Boston, MA; Testimony of Dr. Asa Millet at inquest.

42 and burial arrangements: "Criminal; The Recent Triple Murder at Halifax; Close of the Coroner's Inquest and Rendition of the Verdict; William E. Sturtevant, the Nephew of the Murdered Brothers, Charged with the

Crime; Resume of the Testimony," *Boston Daily Globe*, 24 Feb 1874.

42 accounted for all but $650: "The Triple Tragedy," *The Middleboro Gazette*, February 28, 1874.

Chapter 4

44 arriving at about ten-thirty: *Directory of Brockton, Bridgewater, East and West Bridgewater, and Abington for 1874-1875* (Boston: Greenough, Jones & Co., 1874), 257.

45 at his office desk: Benjamin Hobart, *History of the Town of Abington, Plymouth County, Massachusetts, from its First Settlement* (Boston: T. H. Carter & Son, 1866), 350.

49 "...blood or not," Pratt suggested: "The Halifax Murders; Trial of W. E. Sturtevant; Third Day," *Boston Journal*, July 2, 1874; Pratt testimony.

49 during the war: D. Hamilton Hurd, *History of Plymouth County, Massachusetts, with Biographical Sketches of Many of Its Pioneers and Prominent Men* (Philadelphia: J.W. Lewis & Co., 1884), 521.

50 Pratt went inside: "The Halifax Murders; Trial of W. E. Sturtevant; Third Day," *Boston Journal*, July 2, 1874; Pratt testimony.

50 Keene's Corner in South Hanson: "Halifax Murder," *Old Colony Memorial* [Plymouth, MA], July 2, 1874, Lydia Reed testimony.

51 and the team lurched forward: "The Halifax Murders; Trial of W. E. Sturtevant; Third Day," *Boston Journal*, July 2, 1874; Pratt testimony.

52 "...capable of such a thing": "The Halifax Murders; Trial of W. E. Sturtevant; Third Day," *Boston Journal*, July 2, 1874.

52 on Oak Street in Bridgewater: *Greenough's Directory of Brockton, Bridgewater, East and West Bridgewater, for 1876-1877* (Boston: Greenough & Co., 1878), 208.

53 toddler began to cry: "Tried for His Life; Third Day of Sturtevant's Trial at Plymouth; Testimony of Experts on the Blood Stains on Sturtevant's Clothing; The Usual Diversity of Opinion; Evidence of the Officers Who Arrested the Prisoner; Interesting Details; The Excitement Increasing, Etc., Etc.," *Boston Daily Globe*, July 2, 1874.

55 "...at Inglee's later this evening: Ibid.

55 they reached South Hanson: "Trial for Murder; The Triple Tragedy at Halifax; Opening Day of the Trial of William E. Sturtevant for the Murder of His Two Uncles and Their Housekeeper; Large Attendance and Deep Interest; Yesterday's Evidence," *Boston Daily Globe*, June 30, 1874.

57 left for Sturtevant's house: "The Halifax Tragedy; Trial of William E. Sturtevant; Fourth Day," *Boston Journal*, July 3, 1874.

Chapter 5

58 inhabited the other: Ibid. Newspapers erroneously reported Daland's name as Dolan.

59 "...until a late hour: "Suburban Matters; Halifax; The Triple Tragedy," *Boston Post*, February 19, 1874.

59 inadmissible as hearsay evidence: Massachusetts General Laws, Chapter 393, Section 1 (1870) "No person of sufficient understanding shall be excluded from giving evidence as a witness in any proceeding, civil or criminal, in court or before a person having authority to receive evidence, except in the following cases: First: Neither husband nor wife shall be allowed to testify as to private conversations with each other. Second: Neither husband nor wife shall be compelled to be a witness on any trial upon an indictment, complaint or other criminal proceeding, against the other."

60 in East Bridgewater in June 1852: Massachusetts Bureau of Vital Records and Statistics, Boston, MA; Deaths, East Bridgewater, 1852, volume 67, page 245 (He died on June 16, 1852).

60 her mother, Lucy, widowed and destitute: Massachusetts Bureau of Vital Records and Statistics, Boston, MA; Deaths, Braintree, 1852, volume 67, page 185 (He died on November 30, 1852).

60 nearly forty years her mother's senior: Massachusetts Bureau of Vital Records and Statistics, Boston, MA; Marriages, Halifax, 1854, volume 79, page 252 (They were married on May 2, 1854).

60 Lydia, was born the next year: Massachusetts Bureau of Vital Records and Statistics, Boston, MA; Births, East Bridgewater, 1855, volume 91, page 278. (Lydia was born on August 28, 1855).

60 followed by Emma, in 1858: Massachusetts Bureau of Vital Records and Statistics, Boston, MA; Deaths, East Bridgewater, 1859, volume 130, page 205. (No birth record was found for Emma. However, the death record indicated she was one-year-old when she died on July 8, 1859).

60 Edith, in 1860: Massachusetts Bureau of Vital Records and Statistics, Boston, MA; Births, East Bridgewater, 1860, volume 133, page 372. (Edith was born on September 11, 1860).

60 in the summer of 1859: Massachusetts Bureau of Vital Records and

Statistics, Boston, MA; Deaths, East Bridgewater, 1859, volume 130, page 205.

60 croup in the winter of 1862: Massachusetts Bureau of Vital Records and Statistics, Boston, MA; Deaths, East Bridgewater, 1862, volume 157, page 339.

60 Abbie met Willie Sturtevant there: 1870 United States Federal Census, Hanson, Plymouth, Massachusetts; roll: M593-638; page: 280B.

60 over the Hanson town line in East Bridgewater: 1870 United States Federal Census, East Bridgewater, Plymouth, Massachusetts; roll: *M593-638*; page: *242A.*

60 South Hanson Baptist Church three years prior: Massachusetts Bureau of Vital Records and Statistics, Boston, MA; Marriages, Hanson, 1871, volume 236, page 391 (they were married on October 3, 1871).

60 gave birth to George: Massachusetts Bureau of Vital Records and Statistics, Boston, MA; Births, Hanson, 1872, volume 242, page 412 (he was born on October 9, 1872).

61 stowed it in his carriage: "Halifax Murder," *Old Colony Memorial* [Plymouth, MA], July 2, 1874; Pinkham testimony.

62 "...never heard them up so early": "Halifax Murder," *Old Colony Memorial* [Plymouth, MA], July 2, 1874; testimony of Lydia Reed.

62 "...to clean out his stove: Ibid.; testimony of Hollis Pinkham

63 "...came into its possession: Ibid.; "Halifax Murder," testimony of John Drayton.

63 moved into his grandfather's house: 1860 United States Census, East Bridgewater, Plymouth, Massachusetts, page 181, household 1163; "Halifax; The Triple Tragedy," *Boston Post*, February 19, 1874.

64 but he found nothing: "The Halifax Murders; Trial of W. E. Sturtevant; Third Day," *Boston Journal*, July 2, 1874

65 tossed it in his carriage: "Halifax Murder," *Old Colony Memorial* [Plymouth, MA], July 2, 1874.

67 two holes in one of the pockets: "Tried for His Life; Third Day of Sturtevant's Trial at Plymouth," *Boston Daily Globe*, July 2, 1874.

68 all bid each other good-night: "The Halifax Massacre; Ferreting Out the Assassin of the Brothers Sturtevant and Miss Buckley; A Nephew Arrested for the Crime; Strong Evidence Obtained," *The New York Herald*, February 19, 1874.

Chapter 6

69 steered him toward the carriage: "The Halifax Massacre; Ferreting Out the Assassin of the Brothers Sturtevant and Miss Buckley; A Nephew Arrested for the Crime; Strong Evidence Obtained," *The New York Herald*, February 19, 1874.

69 by re-lapping the boot: "The Report in Detail; Testimony of Detective Pinkham at the Morning Session," *Boston Daily Globe*, 3 Jul 1874.

70 old jail into a storehouse: Massachusetts House of Representatives, Documents Printed by Order of the House of Representatives of the Commonwealth of Massachusetts during the Session of the General Court, 1872; *First Annual Report of the Commissioners of Prisons* (Boston: Wright and Potter, 1872), 17.

70 description into the jail ledger: Plymouth County [Massachusetts] Sheriff's Department Archives, Ledger Book #96, Entry #463, February 18, 1874.

70 well acquainted with Sturtevant: "Death Near; Pensive, Silent and Sad in His Cell; Besse Suffers Mental Agony." *Boston Daily Globe*, March 10, 1887

70 for horse stealing in 1866: Plymouth County [Massachusetts] Sheriff's Department Archives, Ledger Book #96, Entry #103, September 11, 1866.

70 to escape if given the chance: "Escape Frustrated," *Old Colony Memorial* [Plymouth, MA], April 23, 1874.

71 murder and received a life sentence: The Stoughton Murder; Second Day of Trial; Additional Testimony; the Case Given to the Jury," *Boston Post*, May 25, 1871; "The Stoughton Murder Case; A Verdict of Murder in the Second-Degree," *Boston Post*, May 26, 1871; "Moran, the Murderer, Sentenced," *Boston Post*, July 6, 1871.

71 district attorney for Norfolk and Plymouth counties in 1870: Duane Hamilton Hurd, *History of Norfolk County, Massachusetts with Biographical Sketches of Many of Its Pioneers and Prominent Men* (Philadelphia: J. W. Lewis and Company, 1884), 25.

71 brief march to the courthouse: US Army Signal Corps, *Annual Report of the Chief Signal-Officer to the Secretary of War for the Year 1874*, (Washington, DC, Government Printing Office, 1874), 138 (a high of 37 degrees and a low of 12 degrees was recorded).

72 furnaces that provided heat: William S. Russell, *Pilgrim Memorials, and Guide to Plymouth with a Lithographic Map and Eight Copperplate*

Engravings (Boston: Crosby and Nichols, 1864), 219-220.

72 behind the judge's bench: Plymouth Redevelopment Authority, *Historic Structure Report; 1820 Courthouse-Corridor Project – Phase 1 Study*, September 2011. See also, "To Report Murder Trial; Sheriff Porter Makes Arrangements for Newspaper Men at Trial of Mrs. Eaton," *Old Colony Memorial* [Plymouth, MA], October 10, 1913.

72 Civil War Battle of Malvern Hill: Edwin Monroe Bacon, ed., *Men of Progress; One Thousand Biographical Sketches and Portraits of Leaders in Business and Professional Life in the Commonwealth of Massachusetts* (Boston: New England Magazine, 1896), 165-166.

73 "Not guilty," the prisoner declared: "Halifax Murder," *Old Colony Memorial* [Plymouth, MA], July 2, 1874.

73 "Yes," Sturtevant replied. "I am": "The Plymouth County Crime; The Implement of Murder Identified; Continued Belief in Sturtevant's Guilt," *Boston Journal*, February 19, 1874.

73 "…free himself from the accusation: The Halifax Horror; Further Facts," *Boston Daily Globe*, February 20, 1874.

74 "…one of the heirs to his property": Ibid.

74 "…pursuing the investigation unhindered": Ibid.

74 until the June term of the Supreme Judicial Court: Ibid.

75 outside of the front door: Gary Laderman, *The Sacred Remains: American Attitudes Toward Death, 1799-1883* (New Haven and London: Yale University Press, 1996), 30, 31.

75 fastened to the coffin lids: "The Triple Tragedy," *Middleboro Gazette*, February 28, 1874.

75 grossly distorted his features: "The Halifax Horror; Further Facts," *Boston Daily Globe*, February 20, 1874.

75 white vests, and neckcloths: "The Triple Tragedy," *Middleboro Gazette*, February 28, 1874.

76 to his now deceased sons, Simeon, Jr. and Thomas: Plymouth County, Massachusetts, Probate Estate Files, Estate File 1979, Simeon Sturtevant, Halifax, 1851.

77 she and her mother had amassed: *Plymouth County, MA: Probate File Papers, 1686-1881, Case #3230, Administration of Deborah Buckley Estate*. Online database. *AmericanAncestors.org*. New England Historic Genealogical Society, 2015. (From records supplied by the Massachusetts

Supreme Judicial Court Archives.)

77 "...won't go on right": "The Triple Tragedy," *The Middleboro Gazette*, February 28, 1874.

77 attended each of the coffins: Ibid.

78 sounds of a reedy seraphine organ: Rev. Joseph A. C. Wadsworth, III, *The History of the Halifax Congregational Church*, Volume 1 (Halifax, MA: by the church, 2008), 234.

79 "...her longing to benefit and bless": "The Halifax Victims; Thousands of Spectators at the Scene of the Triple Assassination; Touching Funeral Address; The Nephew, William Sturtevant, Committed for Trial," *Boston Journal*, February 20, 1874.

80 church to the hearses: "Bridgewater," *North Bridgewater Gazette*, February 26, 1874.

80 and her sister, Angeline: Ibid.

Chapter 7

81 "...he did after that: "Halifax Murder," *Old Colony Memorial* [Plymouth, MA], July 2, 1874, Daniel Blake testimony.

82 "...never put it together: "Halifax Murder," *Old Colony Memorial* [Plymouth, MA], July 2, 1874; Osborne testimony, June 30, 1874.

82 "...loaned the money to him: Ibid., Hill testimony, June 30, 1874.

83 found in that area to seven: "Halifax Murder," *Old Colony Memorial* [Plymouth, MA], July 2, 1874; Pratt testimony, July 1, 1874.

83 to Wood two days later: Ibid.; Wood testimony, July 1, 1874.

87 1854 and converted to government service: Guy S. Baker, *History of Halifax, Massachusetts* (Halifax, MA: by the author, 1976), 29-30.

87 had heard about the murders: US Army Signal Corps, *Annual Report of the Chief Signal-Officer to the Secretary of War for the Year 1874*, (Washington, DC, Government Printing Office, 1874), 138 (a high of 52 degrees and a low of 35 degrees was recorded).

88 "I stayed for about seven hours: Plymouth County Coroner's Records, 1874, Judicial Archives, Massachusetts State Archives, Boston, MA.

90 "...where the stake was taken from: Ibid.

91 midnight on Sunday, February 15: Ibid.

91 in the hands of William E. Sturtevant, of Hanson: Ibid.

92 the other, "1830": "Bridgewater," *North Bridgewater Gazette*, February 26, 1874.

92 had stolen assorted jewelry and timepieces: "East Bridgewater," *North Bridgewater Gazette*, January 8, 1874.

92 taken from his shop: *Boston Traveler*, February 24, 1874.

92 one-half-foot cell: Prison Commissioners of Massachusetts, *Annual Report of the Board of Prison Commissioners of Massachusetts*, Volume 1 (Boston: Wright and Potter Printing Co., 1902), 135.

94 "...exemplified in their experience: "The Halifax Murderer; His Escape from Plymouth Jail Frustrated by the Vigilance of the Warden," *Boston Daily Globe*, 24 Apr 1874, page 5; also, "Escape Frustrated," *Old Colony Memorial* [Plymouth, MA], April 23, 1874.

Chapter 8

95 Monday, June 29, was scheduled: "Massachusetts," *Boston Daily Globe*, May 18, 1874.

95 told Chandler of his call on Sturtevant: John F. Gallagher, *A History of Homicide in Hanover: Murder on Broadway* (Whitman, MA: Riverhaven Books, 2015).

96 and Costley smiled: Charles Devens Notebook, call number mss. N-1114, box number 8, folder F61-V58, Norfolk County Special Term for Trial of J. H. Costley, December 1874, Massachusetts Historical Society, Boston, MA, page 18.

97 he had rented from Reidell's: Gallagher, *A History of Homicide in Hanover*.

97 Six months later, he was hanged: "The End! Execution of Costley," *Dedham Transcript*, June 26, 1875.

100 "...Let's reconvene with him tomorrow: "Halifax Murder," *Old Colony Memorial* [Plymouth, MA], July 2, 1874.

101 "...to himself of his own acts: "Execution of William E. Sturtevant, The Halifax Murderer," Old Colony Memorial [Plymouth, MA], May 13, 1875.

Chapter 9

102 "...the trial of William Edward [*sic*] Sturtevant: "Trial for Murder; The Triple Tragedy at Halifax; Opening Day of the Trial of William E. Sturtevant for the Murder of His Two Uncles and Their Housekeeper; Large Attendance and Deep Interest, Yesterday's Evidence," *Boston Daily Globe*, 30 Jun 1874.

103 "...cheerful and unembarrassed: "Halifax Murder," *Old Colony*

Memorial [Plymouth, MA], July 2, 1874.

103 "…indifferent and unmoved: "Suburban Matters," *Boston Post*, June 30, 1874.

103 soared to ninety-seven degrees: *Annual Report of the Chief Signal-Officer to the Secretary of War for the Year 1874* (Washington, DC: Government Printing Office, 1874), 138.

103 on a table in the back of the room: "Halifax Murder," *Old Colony Memorial* [Plymouth, MA], July 2, 1874.

103 "…devoid of sentiment," a *Boston Journal* reporter noted: "The Halifax Murder; Trial of W. E. Sturtevant; Second Day," *Boston Journal*, July 1, 1874.

106 "…one of the safest of crimes: (No headline), *Old Colony Memorial* [Plymouth, MA], February 26, 1874.

106 a verdict of manslaughter: Alan Rogers, *Murder and the Death Penalty in Massachusetts* (Amherst and Boston: University of Massachusetts Press, 2008), 112-113.

107 attorney general had exclusive jurisdiction: Ibid., 301.

107 Suffolk County bar in 1841: William Thomas Davis, *History of the Judiciary of Massachusetts* (Boston: Boston Book Company, 1900), 289.

107 ended in an acquittal: Franklin Fiske Heard, *Report of the Trial of Leavitt Alley: Indictment for the Murder of Abijah Ellis* (Boston: Little, Brown & Co., 1875).

107 "…when a conviction was warranted: Rogers, 302.

108 opposes capital punishment: "Halifax Murder," *Old Colony Memorial* [Plymouth, MA], July 2, 1874.

108 ordered a recess until 2:30 p.m.: Ibid.

Chapter 10

110 "…used in the murder, if established: Ibid.

111 "…of his inability to pay: Ibid.

119 "…in the habit of frequent altercations: "Trial for Murder; The Triple Tragedy at Halifax; Opening Day of the Trial of William E. Sturtevant for the Murder of His Two Uncles and Their Housekeeper; Large Attendance and Deep Interest; Yesterday's Evidence," *Boston Daily Globe*, 30 Jun 1874; see also, *Old Colony Memorial* Office, *Trial of William E. Sturtivant for the Murder of Simeon Sturtevant, in Halifax, Mass., on Sunday, February 15, 1874* (Plymouth: Avery & Doten, 1874), 10.

120 "...that morning in some places: "Halifax Murder," *Old Colony Memorial* [Plymouth, MA], July 2, 1874.

Chapter 11

121 under fair skies: *Surface Weather Observations* (Boston: Signal Service, U.S. Army, Division of Telegrams and Reports for the Benefit of Commerce, 1874), 52; Boston Public Library call number QC984.M4S97x.

129 "...and of quick motion": "Halifax Murder," *Old Colony Memorial* [Plymouth, MA], July 2, 1874.

Chapter 12

142 "...he had not money to ride": Ibid.

Chapter 13

143 "...of good spirits and unconcern: "The Halifax Murders; Trial of W. E. Sturtevant; Third Day," *Boston Journal*, July 2, 1874.

145 "...by Sturtevant's on the way back": Ibid.

147 after receiving his medical degree: Howard A. Kelly, M.D., *A Cyclopedia of American Medical Biography, Comprising the Lives of Eminent Living and Deceased Physicians and Surgeons from 1610 to 1910*, Volume II (Philadelphia and London: W. B. Saunders Company, 1912), 523.

148 "...or any other branch of science: Commonwealth v. Sturtevant, 117 Mass. 122.

149 "...can judge as well as he can: Ibid.

150 "...if it is anything else, we do: Ibid.

150 "...not upon the coat," Wood answered: Ibid.

152 belonged to the murdered brothers and their housekeeper. Suzanne Bell, *Crime and Circumstance: Investigating the History of Forensic Science*, (Westport, CT and London: Greenwood/Pragear:, 2008), 137.

153 confirm the presence of blood: L. Landois, M.D., *A Manual of Human Physiology*, Volume 1 (Philadelphia: P. Blakiston, Son, and Company, 1885), 34.

154 if the blood was human or animal: Charles G. Davis, *Report of the Trial of Samuel M. Andrews, Indicted for the Murder of Cornelius Holmes, Before the Supreme Judicial Court of Massachusetts, December 11, 1868, Including the Rulings of the Court Upon Many Questions of Law, and a Full Statement of Authorities Upon the Subject of Transitory Insanity* (New

York: Hurd and Houghton, 1869) 66-67.

155 originating from a human source: George F. Shrady, Editor, *Medical Record – A Weekly Journal of Medicine and Surgery* (New York: William Wood and Co., 1895), 685.

155 established the same year: Colin Evans, *Criminal Investigations: Crime Scene Investigation* (New York: Infobase Publishing, 2009), 11.

155 to confirm human origin: Ibid.

156 "...four tickets in all on Saturday and Monday": "Halifax Murder," *Old Colony Memorial* [Plymouth, MA], July 2, 1874.

Chapter 14

162 "...to Plymouth and committed him": Ibid.

163 "...continue your direct examination of the witness": Commonwealth v. Sturtevant, 117 Mass. 122.

165 "...talked with Miss Reed on two occasions": "Halifax Murder," *Old Colony Memorial* [Plymouth, MA], July 2, 1874.

168 seemed his usual self: Ibid.

Chapter 15

169 responded with a bright smile: "The Halifax Tragedy; Trial of William E. Sturtevant; Fourth Day," *Boston Journal*, July 3, 1874.

174 "...came from Simeon's room": "Halifax Murder," *Old Colony Memorial* [Plymouth, MA], July 2, 1874.

175 "'...at the funeral of my grandmother: Ibid.

176 to corroborate the detective's statements: "The Halifax Tragedy; Trial of William E. Sturtevant; Fourth Day," *Boston Journal*, July 3, 1874.

176 "...the government rests its case: "Halifax Murder," *Old Colony Memorial* [Plymouth, MA], July 2, 1874.

Chapter 16

178 "...to the prisoner and the Commonwealth: Ibid.

178 twice before in capital trials: Richard Herndon and Edwin Monroe Bacon, *Boston of Today: A Glance at Its History and Characteristics*, (Boston: Post Publishing Company, 1892), 178.

180 "...one fifty-four-hundredths of an inch," the physician replied: "Halifax Murder," *Old Colony Memorial* [Plymouth, MA], July 2, 1874.

180 "...be of the same class": "The Halifax Tragedy; Trial of William E. Sturtevant; Fourth Day," *Boston Journal*, July 3, 1874.

180 "...if I was making the test": "Halifax Murder," *Old Colony Memorial* [Plymouth, MA], July 2, 1874.

181 "...consider the result unsatisfactory": Ibid.

181 The court sustained his objection: Commonwealth v. Sturtevant, 117 Mass. 122 (1875).

181 "...Nothing could be predicted upon it: "The Halifax Tragedy; Trial of William E. Sturtevant; Fourth Day," *Boston Journal*, July 3, 1874.

182 the type of shoes he wore: "Halifax Murder," *Old Colony Memorial* [Plymouth, MA], July 2, 1874.

183 "...testify on the subject," Judge Wells ruled: Commonwealth v. Sturtevant, 117 Mass. 122 (1875).

186 "It is the same proposition...: Ibid.

186 "...his getting up in the night: "The Halifax Tragedy; Trial of William E. Sturtevant; Fourth Day," *Boston Journal*, July 3, 1874.

187 "...rest our case": "Halifax Murder," *Old Colony Memorial* [Plymouth, MA], July 2, 1874.

187 "...dismissed for deliberation: Ibid.

Chapter 17

188 a renal condition that had weakened him: Massachusetts Bureau of Vital Records and Statistics, Boston, MA; Deaths, Boston, 1875, volume 276, page 34 (Harris died of kidney disease and uremic poisoning in his Boston hotel room).

188 "...the theories are improbable: "Halifax Murder," *Old Colony Memorial* [Plymouth, MA], July 2, 1874.

194 "...faithfulness to duty on this occasion: Ibid.

194 "...as bright as any person's among the audience: "The Trial Ended; Sturtevant Found Guilty in the First-Degree," *Boston Daily Globe*, July 4, 1874.

Chapter 18

195 "...as in this part of America: "Halifax Murder," *Old Colony Memorial* [Plymouth, MA], July 2, 1874.

197 courtroom laughed at Train's remark: "The Halifax Murders; Trial of William E. Sturtevant; Fifth Day," *Boston Journal*, July 4, 1874.

197 "...within a month of the homicide: "Halifax Murder," *Old Colony Memorial* [Plymouth, MA], July 2, 1874.

200 "…the house of this prisoner: Ibid.

Chapter 19

201 "…rightly applied to the evidence: Francis Wharton, LL.D., *A Treatise on the Law of Homicide in the United States to Which is Appended a Series of Leading Cases* (Philadelphia: Kay and Brother, 1875), 742-753.

202 "…from the act which was done: Ibid.

204 "…with innocence and indicative of guilt: Ibid.

206 "…in the first-degree or in the second-degree: Ibid.

207 "…upon the stand here in the trial": Ibid.

208 "In the first-degree," Hathaway answered: "Halifax Murder," *Old Colony Memorial* [Plymouth, MA], July 2, 1874.

208 to betray his claim of innocence: "Sturtevant's Crime; Circumstances and Discovery of the Murder; Arrest of the Murderer; Strong Circumstantial Evidence; The Trial and Conviction; Subsequent Prison Life of Sturtevant," *Boston Daily Globe*, May 7, 1875.

209 Sturtevant began to weep: "The Halifax Tragedy; Trial of Wm. E. Sturtevant; Verdict – 'Guilty of Murder in the First-Degree;' Exceptions Filed," *Boston Journal*, July 6, 1874.

Chapter 20

210 "…I now move for sentence: "The Triple Murder at Halifax; Sentence of Wm. E. Sturtevant; The Death Penalty Imposed," *Boston Journal*, January 26, 1875.

212 "…all I have to say": "The Gallows; Execution of Sturtevant, the Triple Murderer," *Chicago Daily Tribune*, May 12, 1875.

213 "…have mercy on your soul": Ibid.

213 "…securing the evidence against him: "Execution of William E. Sturtevant at Plymouth; The Last Hours of the Condemned Man; Strangers, Friends, Clergyman and the Face of Death Itself Do Not Move Him; A Reckless Bravado," *Boston Daily Advertiser*, May 8, 1875.

214 "…I have no fear nor care for death": "The Gallows; Execution of Sturtevant, the Triple Murderer," *Chicago Daily Tribune*, May 12, 1875.

Chapter 21

215 "…on either side of me: "Preparing for the Execution; The Murderer to be Hung by the New York Method; He Maintains His Ugly and Blasphemous Bravado; Precautions Against Suicide; The Legislative

253

Committee on Prisons on the Ground," *Boston Daily Globe*, 7 May 1875.

215 jury convicted him of murder: Daniel Allen Hearn, *Legal Executions in New England: A Comprehensive Reference, 1623-1960* (Jefferson, NC: McFarland & Co., 1999), 61.

215 hanged on May 25, 1727: Ibid., 122.

215 transferred to the new one: "Preparing for the Execution," *Boston Daily Globe*, May 7, 1875.

217 with remorse and tears: "The Scaffold; Hanging of Sturtevant, the Halifax Murderer; Details of the Tragedy; An Unrepentant, Blaspheming Criminal," *The New York Herald*, May 8, 1875.

217 "...that I care about, Sturtevant replied: "Execution of William E. Sturtevant at Plymouth; The Last Hours of the Condemned Man; Strangers, Friends, Clergyman and the Face of Death Itself Do Not Move Him; A Reckless Bravado," *Boston Daily Advertiser*, May 8, 1875.

217 "...I do not care to see or send to him": Ibid., also, "Execution of William E. Sturtevant, the Halifax Murderer," *Old Colony Memorial* [Plymouth, MA], May 13, 1875.

217 for testifying against him: "Suburban Matters; Plymouth; The Execution of Sturtevant," *Boston Post*, May 8, 1875.

218 "...agony of the last moment: "Execution of Wm. E. Sturtevant, the Halifax Murderer," *Old Colony Memorial* [Plymouth, MA], May 13, 1875.

218 condemned six feet into the air: "The End; Execution of Costley," *Dedham Transcript*, June 26, 1875.

218 excruciating death by strangulation: Stuart Banner, *The Death Penalty: An American History* (Cambridge, MA and London, England: Harvard University Press, 2002), 170-172.

218 to die by this inventive, if barbaric, method: "Preparing for the Execution," *Boston Daily Globe*, May 7, 1875.

219 to those who had requested them: "Execution of William E. Sturtevant, the Halifax Murderer, *Old Colony Memorial* [Plymouth, MA], May 13, 1875.

220 "...cruelty and a disregard for life": Alan Rogers, *Murder and the Death Penalty in Massachusetts* (Amherst and Boston: The University of Massachusetts Press, 2008), 81-82.

220 last hope for clemency: "The Gallows; Sturtevant, the Halifax Murderer, Dies, Today; History of the Shocking Triple Crime; The Arrest, Trial,

Conviction, and Prison Life of William Everett Sturtevant; Preparations for the Execution," *Boston Daily Globe*, 7 May 1875.

220 a block from the courthouse: Ibid.

221 (signed) *Mr. William Sturtevant*: "Execution of Wm. E. Sturtivant [*sic*], the Halifax Murderer," *Old Colony Memorial* [Plymouth, MA], May 13, 1875.

221 and a cup of coffee: "Execution of William E. Sturtevant at Plymouth; The Last Hours of the Condemned Man; Strangers, Friends, Clergyman and the Face of Death Itself Do Not Move Him; A Reckless Bravado," *Boston Daily Advertiser*, May 8, 1875.

221 demeanor was calm and indifferent: "Notes of Preparation; Rainy Weather; The Crowd in the Town; The Last Hours of the Doomed Man; He Concludes Not to Commit Suicide," *Boston Daily Globe*, 8 May 1875.

221 "...is a sly bird: Ibid.

222 and inspect tickets: "Execution of William E. Sturtivant [*sic*], the Halifax Murderer," *Old Colony Memorial* [Plymouth, MA], May 13, 1875.

222 "...about his small mouth": Ibid.

223 his family in East Bridgewater: "Notes of Preparation; Rainy Weather; The Crowd in the Town; The Last Hours of the Doomed Man; He Concludes Not to Commit Suicide," *Boston Daily Globe*, 8 May 1875.

223 "I am innocent of the crime," Sturtevant replied: Ibid.

224 had risen to fifty degrees: *Annual Report of the Chief Signal-Officer to the Secretary of War for the Year 1874* (Washington, DC: Government Printing Office, 1874), 138.

224 ten-foot high brick wall: "Execution of William E. Sturtivant [*sic*], the Halifax Murderer," *Old Colony Memorial* [Plymouth, MA], May 13, 1875.

224 "...no more upon forever: Ibid.

225 "...penalty of the law was fulfilled": "The Death Scene; A Quick and Merciful Execution; Sturtevant Sent to His Last Home," *Boston Daily Globe*, 8 May 1875.

225 "...attached to a rubber string": "The Hanging of Sturtevant at Plymouth," *Hartford Daily Courant*, May 8, 1875.

225 "...contraction of the muscles": "Suburban Matters; Plymouth; The Execution of Sturtevant," *Boston Post*, May 8, 1875.

225 gaped at the dangling body: *The Christian Union* [New York, NY], August 11, 1875.

226 agonizing death by strangulation: "Execution of William E. Sturtivant [*sic*], the Halifax Murderer," *Old Colony Memorial* [Plymouth, MA], May 13, 1875.

226 "...a town meeting gathering: "An Enjoyable Affair," *St. Louis Post-Dispatch*, May 14, 1875.

226 a train bound for Halifax: Ibid.

226 mocked Sturtevant the year before: "The Hanging of James H. Costley for the Murder of Julia Hawkes," *The Sun* [New York, NY], June 26, 1875.

227 "...as speedily as possible: No headline, *The Daily Argus* [Rock Island, Ill.], May 12, 1875.

227 "...which came over him": Elroy Sherman Thompson, *History of Plymouth, Norfolk, and Bristol Counties, Massachusetts, Volume I* (New York, NY: Lewis Historical Publishing Co., 1928), 571.

228 to search for her husband: "Tell-Tale Garments; Discovery of an Important Clew [*sic*] in the Sturtevant Murder Case; Evidence that a Guilty Man Has Escaped," *Boston Weekly Globe*, morning edition, November 11, 1879.

228 ruled out the presence of blood: "Those Blood-Stained Clothes; They Didn't Tell Much of a Story, After All; Evidence that the Clothes Found at Pembroke Had No Connection with the Halifax Murder," *Boston Daily Globe*, November 11, 1879.

229 "...so disastrously for himself": "Halifax Murder," *Old Colony Memorial* [Plymouth, MA], November 13, 1879.

229 the last man executed in the county: "Besse Executed," *Fitchburg Sentinel*, March 10, 1887.

229 at the state prison in Charlestown: Rogers, 10.

229 authorized to attend as witnesses: Frank Moore Colby and Harry Thurston Peck, eds., *The International Year Book, 1898* (New York: Dodd, Mead and Company, 1899), 504.

Chapter 22

230 assisted her from the church at the service's conclusion: "The Funeral of Sturtevant," *New Hampshire Patriot and State Gazette*, May 12, 1875, 2.

230 "...rewards or punishments of men": "Execution of William E. Sturtevant [*sic*], the Halifax Murderer," *Old Colony Memorial* [Plymouth, MA], May 13, 1875.

230 after her husband's arrest: "Halifax Murder," *Old Colony Memorial*

[Plymouth, MA], July 2, 1874; Lydia Reed testimony.

230 Cephus Washburn on Pond Street in Halifax: 1880 United States Federal Census: Halifax, Plymouth, Massachusetts; roll: *549*; page: *487A*; Enumeration District: *538*.

230 box factory foreman, in East Bridgewater: Massachusetts Bureau of Vital Records and Statistics, Boston, MA; Marriages, East Bridgewater, 1893, volume 434, page 555.

230 twenty-two years her senior, in 1897: Massachusetts Bureau of Vital Records and Statistics, Boston, MA; Marriages, Halifax, 1897, volume 470, page 577.

231 Cephas died there in 1907: Massachusetts Bureau of Vital Records and Statistics, Boston, MA; Deaths, Whitman, 1907, volume 105, page 245.

231 into her School Street home: 1910 United States Federal Census: Whitman, Plymouth, Massachusetts; roll: T624-613; page: 4A; Enumeration District: 1251.

231 Northville Cemetery in East Bridgewater: Massachusetts Bureau of Vital Records and Statistics, Boston, MA; Deaths, Whitman, 1905, volume 96, page 103.

231 on April 30, 1917: Massachusetts Bureau of Vital Records and Statistics, Boston, MA; Marriages, Brockton, 1917, volume 191, page 83.

231 in Brockton's Melrose Cemetery: Massachusetts Bureau of Vital Records and Statistics, Boston, MA; Deaths, Brockton, volume 28, page 521; Abbie died on November 7, 1935.

231 beside her mother in Melrose Cemetery: Massachusetts Bureau of Vital Records and Statistics, Boston, MA; Deaths, Brockton, 1948, volume 29, page 343.

231 It was completely destroyed: "Fire Record; The Plymouth County Court House Partially Destroyed," *Boston Daily Globe*, November 8, 1881.

Bibliography

Adjutant General of Massachusetts. *Massachusetts Soldiers, Sailors, and Marines in the Civil War*. Norwood, MA: The Adjutant General, 1932.

Andrews, George F. *Official Gazette, State Government 1886; Biography of Members, Councillor, House, and Senate Committees, State House Directory, Department Commission and Clerical Register*. Boston: Alfred Mudge & Son, Printers, 1886.

Bacon, Edwin Monroe, ed. *Men of Progress; One Thousand Biographical Sketches and Portraits of Leaders in Business and Professional Life in the Commonwealth of Massachusetts*. Boston: New England Magazine, 1896.

Baker, Guy S. *History of Halifax, Massachusetts*. Halifax, MA: by the author, 1976.

Bakker, Gordon Morris, ed. *Invitation to an Execution: A History of the Death Penalty in the United States*. Albuquerque: University of New Mexico Press, 2010.

Banner, Stuart. *The Death Penalty: An American History*. Cambridge, MA and London: Harvard University Press, 2002.

Bell, Suzanne. *Crime and Circumstance: Investigating the History of Forensic Science*. Westport, CT and London: Greenwood/Pragear, 2008.

Biographical Review Publishing Co. *Biographical Review, Volume XXV, Containing Life Sketches of Leading Citizens of Norfolk County*. Boston: Biographical Review Publishing Co., 1898.

Cantor, Norman L. *After We Die: The Life and Times of the Human Cadaver*. Washington, DC: Georgetown University Press, 2010.

Chief Signal Officer, U.S. Army. *Annual Report of the Chief Signal-Officer to the Secretary of War for the Year 1874*. Washington, DC: Government Printing Office, 1874.

Colby Frank Moore, and Peck, Harry Thurston, eds. *The International Year Book, 1898*. New York: Dodd, Mead and Company, 1899.

Cook, Louis A., ed. *History of Norfolk County, Massachusetts*. New York: S.

J. Clarke Publishing Co., 1918.

Davis, Charles G. *Report of the Trial of Samuel M. Andrews, Indicted for the Murder of Cornelius Holmes, Before the Supreme Judicial Court of Massachusetts, December 11, 1868, Including the Rulings of the Court Upon Many Questions of Law, and a Full Statement of Authorities Upon the Subject of Transitory Insanity.* New York: Hurd and Houghton, 1869.

Davis, William T. *Bench and Bar of the Commonwealth of Massachusetts,* Volume I. Boston: The Boston History Company, 1895.

Davis, William Thomas. *History of the Judiciary of Massachusetts.* Boston: Boston Book Company, 1900.

Delafield, Francis. *A Handbook of Post-Mortem Examinations and of Morbid Anatomy.* New York: William Wood & Co., 1872.

Dudley, Dean. *Historical Sketches of Towns in Plymouth and Barnstable Counties, Massachusetts.* Boston: D. Dudley & Co., 1873.

Evans, Colin. *Criminal Investigations: Crime Scene Investigation.* New York: Infobase Publishing, 2009.

Faculty of Political Science of Columbia University, eds. *Studies in History, Economics and Public Law,* Volume VIII. New York: Columbia University, 1896-1898.

Gallagher, John F. *A History of Homicide in Hanover: Murder on Broadway.* Whitman, MA: Riverhaven Books, 2015.

Harrington, Thomas Francis. *The Harvard Medical School: A History, Narrative and Documentary,* Vol. II. New York, Chicago: Lewis Publishing Company, 1905.

Heard, Franklin Fiske. *Report of the Trial of Leavitt Alley: Indictment for the Murder of Abijah Ellis.* Boston: Little, Brown & Co., 1875.

Hearn, Daniel Allen. *Legal Executions in New England: A Comprehensive Reference, 1623-1960.* Jefferson, NC: McFarland & Co., 1999.

Herndon, Richard, and Bacon, Edwin Monroe. *Boston of Today: A Glance at Its History and Characteristics.* Boston: Post Publishing Company, 1892.

Hobart, Benjamin. *History of the Town of Abington, Plymouth County, Massachusetts, from its First Settlement.* Boston: T. H. Carter & Son, 1866.

Hurd, D. Hamilton. *History of Plymouth County, Massachusetts, with Biographical Sketches of Many of Its Pioneers and Prominent Men.*

Philadelphia: J.W. Lewis & Co., 1884.

Hurd, Duane Hamilton. *History of Norfolk County, Massachusetts with Biographical Sketches of Many of Its Pioneers and Prominent Men.* Philadelphia: J. W. Lewis and Company, 1884.

Kelley, Howard A., M.D. *A Cyclopedia of American Medical Biography, Comprising the Lives of Eminent Living and Deceased Physicians and Surgeons from 1610 to 1910,* Volume II. Philadelphia and London: W. B. Saunders Company, 1912.

Kinnicut, Lincoln Newton. *Indian Names of Places in Plymouth, Middleboro, Lakeville and Carver, Plymouth County, Massachusetts.* Worcester, MA: Commonwealth Press, 1909.

Kimball, George. *A Corporal's Story: Civil War Recollections of the Twelfth Massachusetts.* Norman, OK, University of Oklahoma Press, 2014.

Laderman, Gary. *The Sacred Remains: American Attitudes Toward Death, 1799-1883.* New Haven and London: Yale University Press, 1996.

Leno, John Bedford. *The Art of Boot and Shoemaking; A Practical Handbook.* London: Crosby Lockwood and Company, 1885.

Mellen, Paul, and Bouvier, Elizabeth. *The American Journal of Forensic Medicine and Pathology,* "Nineteenth-Century Massachusetts Coroner Inquests," Volume 17, September 1996, Issue 3.

Nason, Rev. Elias, M.A. *A Gazetteer of the State of Massachusetts with Numerous Illustrations in Wood and Steel.* Boston: B. B. Russell, 1876.

Old Colony Memorial Newspaper. *Trial of William E. Sturtivant for the Murder of Simeon Sturtevant, in Halifax, Mass., on Sunday, February 15, 1874.* Plymouth: Avery & Doten, 1874.

Picken, Mary Brooks. *A Dictionary of Costume and Fashion, Historic and Modern.* Mineola, NY: Dover Publications, Inc., 1985.

Prison Commissioners of Massachusetts. *Annual Report of the Board of Prison Commissioners of Massachusetts,* Volume 1. Boston: Wright and Potter Printing Co., 1902.

Quigley, Christine. *The Corpse: A History.* Jefferson, NC and London: McFarland & Co., Inc., 1996.

Richardson, William A., and Sanger, George P., eds. *The General Statutes of the Commonwealth of Massachusetts: Enacted December 28, 1859, to Take*

Effect June 1, 1860: with the Constitutions of the State and the United States, a Glossary, List of Acts Previously Repealed, and Index. Boston: Published by the Commonwealth, 1873.

Rogers, Alan. *Murder and the Death Penalty in Massachusetts*. Amherst and Boston: The University of Massachusetts Press, 2008.

Roth, Mitchell P. *Crime and Punishment: A History of the Criminal Justice System*, 2 ed. Belmont, CA: Wadsworth Publishing, 2011.

Russell, William S. *Pilgrim Memorials and Guide to Plymouth with a Lithographic Map and Eight Copperplate Engravings*. Boston: Crosby, Nichols and Company, 1855.

Russell, William S. *Pilgrim Memorials, and Guide to Plymouth with a Lithographic Map and Eight Copperplate Engravings*. Boston: Crosby and Nichols, 1864.

Sargent, Lucius M. *Dealings with the Dead*. Boston: Dutton and Wentworth, 1856.

Scott, Jonathan F. *The Early Colonial Houses of Martha's Vineyard*. Minneapolis, MN: University of Minnesota, 1985; revised and updated in 2013.

Shattuck, George B. M.D., and Coolidge, Algernon Jr., M.D., eds. *The Boston Medical and Surgical Journal*, Volume CXXVIII, Obituary: Asa Millet, M.D. Boston: Damrell and Upham, 1893.

Shrady, George F., ed. *Medical Record – A Weekly Journal of Medicine and Surgery*. New York: William Wood and Co., 1895.

Signal Service, U.S. Army. *Surface Weather Observations*. Boston: Division of Telegrams and Reports for the Benefit of Commerce, 1874.

Stedman, Thomas L., M.D., ed. *Medical Record, A Weekly Journal of Medicine and Surgery*, Volume 86. Boston: William Wood and Co., 1914.

Stoddard, Francis Russell Jr. *The Stoddard Family, Being an Account of Some of the Descendants of John Stodder of Hingham, Massachusetts Colony*. New York: The Trow Press, 1912.

Taylor, Alfred Swaine M. D., F. R. S. *The Principles and Practice of Medical Jurisprudence*. Philadelphia: Henry C. Lea, 1873.

Thompson, Elroy Sherman. *History of Plymouth, Norfolk and Barnstable Counties*, Volume I. New York: Lewis Historical Publishing Company, 1928.

Thompson, Elroy Sherman. *History of Plymouth, Norfolk, and Bristol Counties, Massachusetts,* Volume I. New York: Lewis Historical Publishing Co., 1928.

Trustees of the State Reform School. *Eleventh Annual Report of the, at Westborough, Together with the Annual Reports of the Officers of the Institution.* Boston: William White, Printer to the State, 1857.

Wadsworth, H. A., compiler. *History of Lawrence, Massachusetts, with Portraits and Biographical Sketches.* Lawrence, MA: Lawrence Eagle Steam Job Printing Officer, 1880.

Wadsworth, Joseph A. C., III. *The History of the Halifax Congregational Church,* Vol. 1. Halifax, MA: by the Church, 2008.

Wharton, Francis, LL.D. *A Treatise on the Law of Homicide in the United States to Which is Appended a Series of Leading Cases.* Philadelphia: Kay and Brother, 1875.

Wheeler, Jr., Albert Gallatin. *The Genealogical and Encyclopedic History of the Wheeler Family in America.* Boston: American College of Genealogy, 1914.

Wright, Carroll D. *The Census of the Commonwealth of Massachusetts*: 1875, prepared under the direction of the Chief of the Bureau of Statistics of Labor, Volume I, Population and Social Statistics Boston: Albert J. Wright, State Printer, 1876.

Made in the USA
Lexington, KY
01 February 2017